Ringing the Children In

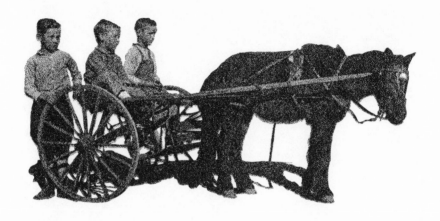

Ringing the Children In

Texas Country Schools

by Thad Sitton and Milam C. Rowold

Texas A&M University Press
College Station

Library of Congress Cataloging-in-Publication Data
Sitton, Thad, 1941–
  Ringing the children in.

  Bibliography: p.
  Includes index.
  1. Rural schools – Texas – History. I. Rowold,
Milam C. II. Title.
LB1567.S54 1987   370.19′346′09764   86-14444
ISBN 0-89096-290-1

Manufactured in the United States of America
FIRST EDITION

FRONTIS: Adapted from three brothers and their mode
of transportation to Adkins School, 1934–35.
Courtesy East Central Historical Group, East Central
ISD, Bexar County.

To the teachers of the Texas
common school districts

"Gladly did they learn,
and gladly teach"

Contents

Illustrations

🕮

ILLUSTRATIONS

Preface

🔔

OUR RESEARCH about the Texas country schools began in Caldwell County in 1979. Later we extended the research to other parts of the state. Caldwell is a sparsely populated county thirty miles southeast of Austin. In Caldwell County, as in other rural counties across Texas, the common schools had lasted rather late, not succumbing to the bureaucratic forces of "standardization and consolidation" until the early 1950s. Documentary sources for the common school districts were rare to nonexistent, and we decided to use oral history to record the details of daily life in the rural schools before it was too late. Our sources were personal – the students, teachers, and district trustees from the country schools. We drove the county's muddy roads to seek out one-room schools lost in the trees and underbrush of half a century. Later, we talked to the persons who had attended and taught in those schools, and the importance of what they had to tell us compelled us to travel far beyond Caldwell County.

Since 1979 we have interviewed scores of former teachers and students about their experiences and have searched out first-person descriptions from many written sources. County histories, personal memoirs, informal local histories of education, personal accounts gathered by the Texas Association of Retired Teachers and the Texas PTA, letters written over the years to the Common Schools Oral History Project at the University of Texas (as well as the taped interviews from that project) all have been grist for our mill.

Our research has been greatly aided by the unanimous conviction among former rural teachers that their story, and the story of the country schools and the lost communities they served, strongly deserved telling. Very early on, each of us emerged from interviews with certain extraordinary teachers, such as Lula Byars and Emma Shirley, with the definite impression that he had been given a compulsory assignment! Not only were such teachers willing to describe their experiences in great detail, but they responded to requests for personal accounts with extensive written memoirs and "self-interviews" on hours of audio tape. We discovered that the local historians of Texas rural education had been at work for decades in the many county histories published since World War II, and these proved a rich mine for primary accounts about the country schools. We also discovered that the nation's bicentennial in 1976 had produced a valuable legacy of personal accounts in the Texas Association of Retired Teachers' *As We Remember* and the Texas PTA's *Journey from Ignorant Ridge*, as well as in such remarkable local efforts as the *History of Bell County Public Schools*, published by the Temple-Belton Retired Teachers Association. In fact, from time to time we were overcome with an almost uncanny sense that we were not so much the lonely researchers of Texas' lost schools as the chosen agents of a collective historical enterprise impelled from both sides of the grave.

Without the detailed personal accounts of hundreds of former teachers and students, living and dead, this book would not have been possible. We particularly want to thank the Stilwell Memorial Residence, the Texas Association of Retired Teachers, the Temple-Belton Retired Teachers Association, the East Central Historical Group of Bexar County (with its remarkable photographic archive), the Institute of Texan Cultures, and Dr. O. L. Davis, Jr.'s oral history projects at the University of Texas at Austin, where it all began. Finally, sincere gratitude is expressed to our wives, Sarah Sitton and Linda Rowold, who were helpful and supportive through obsessions and dissertations.

All taped interviews, interviewer notes, written and oral memoirs, letters, and other documents accumulated in this research have been placed in a special Texas Common Schools Collection at Barker Texas History Center, the University of Texas at Austin. Former teachers and students from the rural schools wishing to contribute their personal remembrances to this developing collection are cordially invited to do so.

Ringing the Children In

If we work upon marble, it will perish; if we work upon brass, time will efface it; if we rear temples, they will crumble into dust; but if we work upon immortal minds, if we imbue them with principles, with just fear of God and love of our fellowmen, we engrave on those tablets something which will brighten to all eternity.

— *Daniel Webster*

1. *Introduction*

FOR THE BETTER PART of a century the common school district, with its one-, two-, and three-room ungraded schools, was the basic pattern of public education in rural Texas. For many persons the experience of attending the common schools was an important part of growing up Texan. Every crossroads community and rural district had its own school, and in this decentralized system the school and the community were one. There were no barriers between them, and the school served many local purposes beyond that of educating schoolchildren. With minor regional variation, what was true for Texas was true for the rest of the United States.

In many ways the testimony of the teachers, students, and trustees we interviewed seemed to come from a world much more remote than the time lapse a mere half-century would suggest. In Caldwell County today the only independent school districts are Lockhart, Luling, and Prairie Lea, but as late as 1940 there were more than twenty common school districts scattered across the county, each with several one-, two-, and three-room schools. On the older ordinance maps these ran like a roll call of county place names. In 1934 there were schools like Central Academy and Carl Wiegand; Harmony Grove, Elm Grove, and High Point; Rock Waterhole and St. John's Colony. Other common schools districts such as Bismarck, Black Ankle, Prinz Wilhelm, Bug Shuttle, and Shook had vanished by that time but were well remembered.

3

It was a totally decentralized system of education, a system of anomalies that was hardly a system at all. Each tiny community had its own school and resolutely defended its autonomy and continued existence. Within each common school district a three-member board of trustees administered the community schools, sometimes with a certain disregard for the county school superintendent and the state bureaucracy being served. They built and abolished schools, moved the school buildings around the district, hired and fired teachers, and tailored the official curriculum and school terms to meet local purposes and preferences. Weldon Hutcheson, a teacher, told us that the local schools "actually had full autonomy. You didn't have anybody from the state department interfering with them. Since you're sitting here and recording this, I'm not going to use that expression, but they'd have told them where they could go and what they could do about it right quick!"

The ethnic and economic diversity of Caldwell County was reflected in the diversity of its common schools. There were Polish districts, such as Polonia, where the trustees sometimes had to use an interpreter to tell English-speaking teachers how they wanted things done, and German districts, such as Prinz Wilhelm and Rogers Ranch, where instruction (up to World War I) was bilingual, in English and German. In other districts the children of Mexican tenants attended the Anglo landowners' abbreviated "plantation schools," which taught students (as one teacher told us) "to write their name and add and subtract a little bit, and baseball. From the earliest time they got there to the end of the day, nothing but baseball!" In general only Anglos were represented on the boards of education of the common school districts in Caldwell County, but there were exceptions even to that. Some districts followed the practice of appointing black "subtrustees" to advise the Anglo trustees about policy decisions affecting the black school. In the northern part of the county was the independent black settlement of St. John's Colony, which had been founded by a wagon train of freed slaves in the 1870s and which elected its own black trustees.

Between 1920 and 1960 all across the rural South the common school districts gradually were replaced by the larger bureaucratic structures of the independent school district and the rural consolidated school. Historians have chronicled the rise and dissemination of this "one best system," as the professional school administrators called it.[1] The bureaucratic school was explicitly modeled upon the factory system, striving for large-scale productive efficiency and standardization of products. The twin war cries of the proponents of the bureaucratic school were "standardization" and "consolidation," the first being a partial remedy on the way to the second, ultimate, resolution of the "rural school problem." These reformers dominated the colleges of education, the state bureaucracies, and professional associations such as the National Education Association, but for fifty years they often faced bitter grassroots opposition at the community level. Only when Texas rural society evolved into something very different did they finally succeed. In the remainder of this chapter we sketch the development of Texas public education from earliest times to the passage of the Gilmer-Akin Act, setting the stage for a detailed examination of the day-to-day functioning of the Texas common schools in chapters 2–10.

Beginnings of the Texas School System

The earliest attempt at formal education in Texas began with the Spanish mission schools near the end of the seventeenth century. The first such mission was built in Nacogdoches sometime around 1690, and the concept spread to other centers of population. The purposes of these institutions were primarily religious and political. Missions were designed to initiate the Texas Indians into the Catholic faith and to train the native populations to become loyal and productive Spanish citizens. The efficacy of the mission schools has been questioned by some educational historians, but the predominance of the Catholic religion among descendants of the Indian tribes of Texas and the Southwest, their universal usage of the Spanish language, and the bicultural nature of Texas is living testimony to the effectiveness of the mission schools.

After the Mexican Revolution in 1810 the influence of the mission schools declined, as did significant progress in developing a system for schooling the young. The small population, the great size of Texas, the geographical distance from cultural centers, and the more pressing concerns of survival in a frontier environment delayed the rise of education as a public priority. During the early decades of Anglo settlement in Texas the wealthy class sent their children to boarding schools in the United States and most of the general populace taught their children at home. Frederick Eby, the major chronicler of the development of Texas schools, commented on the effectiveness of home schooling during the era: "The fact that illiteracy in 1850 was only 12.2 percent of the population of white men over twenty years of age, and only 20.8 percent of the women of the same class, is evidence of considerable family instruction."[2] In sum, during the first half of the nineteenth century, public education in Texas was informal and private.

Shaping of the Community School System

Two years after the Texas Revolution, public education became at least a symbolic priority of the administration of Mirabeau B. Lamar, the second president of the Republic of Texas. In his inaugural speech of 1838, Lamar listed public education as the highest priority of government. The land grants of 1839 and 1840 were swiftly legislated for the purpose of financing a national educational system. However, no system of general education was implemented until after Texas had been admitted to the Union in 1845. The Permanent School Fund was established in 1854 from the ten-million-dollar indemnity paid to Texas by the United States government to settle the dispute over the boundaries of the state. Interest from the fund was used to establish a state school fund and to initiate a statewide school system.

Two types of educational organization evolved in Texas during the last half of the nineteenth century: the "community school" and the common school. The community schools were part of a larger social and political movement, a volatile reaction by Texas citizens against the Radical Reconstruction government of the post–Civil War period. When the state constitution of 1876 returned Texas to full statehood and restored all rights of citizenship to the voting public, sweeping political changes occurred. One of the first casualties of the outgoing regime was the highly centralized state school system headed by State Superintendent for

Public Instruction Herbert De Grees. As Eby observed, "The new constitution abolished the office of state superintendent for public instruction, together with all supervisory functions . . . eliminated compulsory [school] attendance . . . all provisions for districting counties . . . and local taxation for establishing and maintaining schools was rendered impossible."[3] This angry legislative response swept away the support structure for public schooling in the state and returned education to a status resembling that of the 1840s. Once again schooling became the total responsibility of parents. Many reform provisions of the Radical Reconstruction era would return to Texas public education only in the middle of the twentieth century.

As stated in Section 29 of the School Law of 1876, a community school could be initiated by "parents or guardians, or next friend of any minor resident of any county in the state." A petition of intent to open a community school, including the names of children expected to attend, was filed with the county judge. In granting the petition, the county judge appointed three members of the community as school trustees for the school term, and the school thus formed was eligible for a prorated share of the school fund. The community school had no district boundary lines, could not levy a local school tax, and was authorized for only one school year.

Monies received from the state school fund were used to pay the teacher's salary. A building, furniture and equipment, maintenance and upkeep of the facilities, instructional materials, and general school supplies were the responsibility of the parents of children in attendance. As can be seen, the local community assumed a large share of the financial responsibility for schooling. Because local school taxation was prohibited, much of the support for schools was by voluntary subscription and the contribution of various support services. Interestingly, the early school legislation does not use the word "free" to describe public education.

Although the community school organization allowed a maximum of local control, school reformers almost immediately began to complain about its shortcomings. For one thing the community school was impermanent. One-year charters for a three- to six-month school term discouraged the construction of permanent facilities and serious attempts at long-range educational planning.

Nor did the absence of school boundary lines contribute to a strong sense of parental affiliation. "It [the community school] offered a means by which petty jealousies, prejudice, and sectarian bitterness rather than community cooperation [could disrupt the process of schooling]."[4] Almost at once reformers began a movement to reinstate some elements for centralized control of schools, a movement that culminated in the School Law of 1884, which gave birth to the Texas common schools.

The law of 1884 revived many of the bureaucratic supports for schooling initiated by the Radical Reconstruction government.[5] For one thing the 1884 statute reestablished the office of State Superintendent of Public Instruction and began the movement toward supervision of public schools. Allowing counties once again to establish permanent school districts within their boundaries, the law returned to individual school districts the right to elect trustees. However, significant reform of the state's schools hinged on one final provision of the 1884 law: the right of local districts to levy taxes to support local schools. The reform goal of stability and permanence in the system of public schooling required a dependable source of money, and a local taxing authority provided ready access to additional funds. Because the mechanism to reform Texas public schools seemed to be in place, advocates such as Eby would remark almost gleefully, "From 1884 the development of Texas Education has been a steady growth without any of those cataclysmical disturbances which had formerly annihilated the various attempts to establish a state school system."[6] However, while some accomplishments of the School Law of 1884, particularly the establishment of independent school districts in urban areas, met the expectations of reformers, the rural common school did not differ greatly from its predecessor, the community school.

Characteristics of Rural Common Schools

A quick examination of the system of rural education established by the law of 1884 could be misleading. Beneath the surface the new organization retained the same qualities of indeterminacy and local control that characterized the community system it had replaced. For example, although the School Law of 1884 au-

8

thorized counties to form independent districts with permanent
boundaries, the former arrangement of establishing schools by parental petition remained in place. Independent rural school districts
were quite rare. School charters for common school districts now
were granted on a permanent basis, but as before, new districts
were formed regularly by means of the political pressure parents
exerted upon county commissioners and (at a later date) county
school boards. Instead of stabilizing the number of school districts
as reformers had hoped, the School Law of 1884 proliferated the
number of communities seeking to establish local schools and draw
from the state school fund. The biennial report of the state superintendent showed that in the school year 1904–1905 there were
10,169 rural common schools operating in the state, as compared
with 868 independent districts.[7] That number reached an all-time
high in 1909–1910, when 11,682 rural charters were in existence
with only 1,001 independent districts.[8]

A major stabilizing factor in school reform was the construction of permanent school facilities; but the rush to erect buildings
as predicted by Eby did not occur.[9] Rural children often attended
a district school with the same name at several different locations
during their school years, frequently in buildings temporarily re-
cycled from other purposes. District stability was still dependent
upon the whims of nature, the rural economy, and most of all upon
personal relationships among adult citizens of the community.
Breakdown of consensus could move the location of the school or
cause the creation of a new district, just as in the community school
system. In fact the rural common school may be seen as simply
a more permanent form of the community school. In 1923 Eby pin-
pointed the cause of the educational laissez-faire that would remain a thorn in the side of school reformers for at least another
quarter-century. Common school districts had the legal authority
to levy local school taxes to support the local rural school, but at
least in the early days "few districts voted a local tax."[10] As will
be shown, rural school patrons did not withhold support from the
local school; they simply refused to provide that support in the
form demanded by the reformers. The rural schools maintained
their own identity and thwarted reform aims by the simple expedi-
ency of refusing to exercise many of their lawful rights. In retro-

spect, and from the perspective of the school reformers, the School Law of 1884 had created a Frankenstein's monster – a legalized and highly popular version of the old community school chaos.

School communities, of course, viewed the matter very differently. The school reformers' characterization of rural common schools as utterly dependent on the state school fund and controlled by groups of ignorant, selfish citizens does not square with the perspective of those who lived and worked in those schools. The evidence makes it clear that local patrons contributed much in the way of time and money to the local rural schools. The establishment and maintenance of a common school required the participation and contributions of the entire rural community. From a historical perspective the longevity of the rural school may best be explained by the extreme personal commitment of rural people to the education of the young, a commitment that considerably exceeded the simple payment of taxes.

Once a rural school charter was issued, the community responsibility began in earnest. A suitable building had to be found and refurbished or constructed from scratch. When the school became operative the community was responsible for maintenance, which included cutting and stacking firewood, providing a well or other source of drinking water on the premises, constructing toilet facilities, and taking care of ongoing repairs to the building. Contrary to conventional wisdom, the major day-to-day duties of the early rural school trustees were not administrative but were these menial chores of school maintenance.

When the building was prepared, a certified teacher had to be selected (sometimes enticed) to work in the isolated rural district for a three- to six-month school term. Once a contract was made, the community had to locate a place for the instructor to room and board during the school session. Most often this was the home of a trustee or other community member. In the rural schools the teacher was likely to be an inexperienced young woman, often away from home for the first time, and possibly younger than some of the pupils. More often than not the community was required to socialize the teacher into the adult world, and to repeat the experiment time and again as the teachers moved on to marriage or to higher-paying urban schools.

During the school year the new teacher had to endure the prevailing drabness associated with rural living, homemade furnishings, a varied assortment of teaching materials collected by families over the years and handed down from child to child, an absence of equipment and supplies for teaching, and a lack of stimulation from the world outside the community. But however unstable and vulnerable the common school organization appeared, the system proved to be highly resilient. Resisting every effort to change the structure for schooling the rural young in the state, the Texas common schools continued to exist as a viable educational institution for nearly half of the twentieth century.

Forces for Change

As the twentieth century dawned, three powerful agents of change emerged to exert pressure on the loosely knit system of Texas education. These forces of change were urbanism, progressivism, and the school-reform movement, and the character of these early rural schools can best be understood by their resistance to the powers aligned against them. Perhaps the evolution and ultimate demise of Texas country schools may illuminate the general nature of real and lasting change in the schooling of the young. While the three elements that impinged upon the rural school system are identifiable as separate factors, all were interrelated, and each was itself a product of change.

Urbanism, the first of these operatives of change, was a world-wide phenomenon and would prove by far the most powerful of the three. Within the first two decades of the century, America emerged from the Great War as a politically dominant force in world affairs. World power alignments shifted dramatically. Technology and industry radically altered life-styles. The era was marked by monolithic business combinations: corporations, trusts, holding companies, and cartels. Disparities in wealth highlighted the inequalities of social conditions and gave rise to the labor movement. David Tyack observed that "as village patterns merged into urbanism as a way of life, factories and counting houses split the place of work from the home."[11] Urbanization of the workplace also would affect the structure of schooling. Not even their dis-

11

tance from these momentous events could long shelter Texas country schools from sweeping modifications.

A second element acting to alter the course of schooling came from within the educational profession, which, at the turn of the century, was marked by an influx of new and powerful ideas. During the early years of the century two opposing educational theories emerged. One was the thesis of Edward L. Thorndike, who proposed a psychologically oriented model for the education of twentieth-century children. According to Thorndike educators should begin to consider the results of learning as observable and quantifiable phenomena. A second important educational hypothesis, which came from John Dewey's application of philosophy and logic to the field of education, asserted that education and experience were inextricably joined. Thorndike's contributions would surface as behaviorism and be implemented as educational policy under the label of the "efficiency movement." Dewey's ideas would come to fruition as humanism and be implemented in the schools through the Progressive Education Movement. These eminent and in part opposing educational currents created an ideological conflict that would surface at the time of a major attempt to alter the Texas rural school system.

A third agent for change in the Texas rural schools was the School Reform Movement. Under the leadership of Elwood P. Cubberly, William Torrey Harris, and Charles W. Eliot a coalition of university presidents and big-city superintendents launched a nationwide campaign to remodel the structure and purposes of schooling. The principal goal of school reform was to transform schools into a prototype of industry – organizations based on the factory model. Such a model regarded pupils as raw materials and schools as the appropriate place for processing them. As verification of the effectiveness of schooling, this system required a tangible product, and both Thorndike's notion of learning as observable behaviors and his development of standarized tests provided convenient means of measuring school production.

School reformers also believed that the superintendent of schools and the board of trustees should function as corporate manager and corporate board of directors respectively. A great concern of school reform was the cost-effectiveness of schooling. The reformers' overarching preoccupation with relating cost to product has been labeled "the cult of efficiency" by R. E. Callahan.[12] If big business was the model that school reformers sought to emulate, and efficiency their primary goal, their natural enemy was the allegedly inefficient and unproductive rural common school system that operated throughout the country. As noted by Tyack, "Beginning in the 1890's and gaining momentum in the early twentieth century, reformers mounted an attack on the Rural School Problem." Cubberly in 1901 set the tone of the campaign against the rural schools and their supporters: "The rural school is . . . lacking in effective supervision, controlled by rural people, who, too often, do not realize their own needs . . . taught by teachers who, generally speaking, have little comprehension of rural life."[13] A specific plan to proceed against the rural Texas schools was not, however, immediately forthcoming. Not until 1914 was a blueprint for action against the Texas country schools unveiled by F. M. Bralley, state superintendent for public instruction, and described with characteristic certitude: "The consolidation of smaller schools into larger ones is an essential factor in the adjustment of our school system to the needs of expanding life. Our small, short-termed, poorly housed, inadequately equipped, and ineffectively taught schools must give place to larger schools."[14]

From Cubberly to Bralley and for decades thereafter school reformers were convinced of the correctness of their position. Rural school consolidation was the vehicle that would resolve the problem, but the implicit end of school reform was political power – to wrest control of community schools from community hands and place it in the hands of education professionals. The hidden reform agenda had been stated in 1907 by S. M. N. Marrs: "I am a democrat, but I believe there must be more centralization of power [in the Texas school system]."[15] From a reform perspective, there was altogether too much public control of the public schools. Seventeen years later, as state superintendent for public instruction, Marrs would remain true to his conviction despite evidence that rural school consolidation was being pursued for all the wrong reasons.

In their attempts to force school consolidation, school reformers were unable to influence the rural citizenry. Despite what would become nearly half a century of united professional opinion and repeated public attacks, with and without relevant data, the common school system would continue to function. There was not a misunderstanding between reformers and the rural adult population; there simply was no understanding. Each group spoke a completely different language.

From a business point of view, reform notions of schooling were quantitative; goodness of schooling, like profit, could be counted. The basic elements of the reform description of good schools represented an expanded agenda of Cubberly's call to action. What were needed were better school facilities and equipment; longer school terms, professional school supervision; and mandatory teacher certification, pay, and training. Since the turn of the century Texas rural schools could be shown to be grossly inferior on each of these counts when compared with their urban counterparts.

On the other hand, the view of good schooling held by the rural population was holistic, intangible, qualitative, and difficult to quantify. The transmission of beliefs, attitudes, and values, rather than observable behavior, formed the foundation of a rural community school. From the rural teachers' and parents' points of view, professional success in the rural schools depended more on interpersonal relationships than on scholarly credentials. At the heart of the matter was the sense of partnership between rural teachers and rural parents in the training and education of the young. Given the constraints of multiple grades in one room and a three- to six-month school year, the total learning process was not expected to be completed in school. The rural school was the place where learning was introduced and competence demonstrated. Drill, trial-and-error attempts, practice, and clarification was largely outside activities for which parents assumed significant responsibility. In addition, parental reinforcement of school discipline was generally swift and emphatic; rural students were well aware of the social norm that "a whipping at school meant a whipping at home."

An important requisite of good schooling in rural areas was the participation of the teacher in the life of the community. The teacher was expected to be an exemplar of adult culture, as much a disseminator of community morals and values as a distributor of academic knowledge. According to the testimony of many rural

14

teachers who taught early in this century, personal interaction was significantly more important to professional survival than pedagogical technique.[16]

The entire philosophy of the rural schools was an antithesis of the school-reform program. In a country school children were socialized to become participating members of a steady-state rural community. Basic academic skills were an important part of this growth, but they were more a vehicle for socialization than the be-all and end-all of schooling. School reformers, on the other hand, viewed schooling as a preparation for adult life in an increasingly urbanized America. Basic academic skills were seen as a means to a definite end; school was a place to learn competencies for production.

In the school-reform view, academic knowledge and skill acquisition could and should be measured against a standard. Meaning was prescribed, meaning was production, and in order to inject school-reform ideals into the day-to-day operation of the rural schools, standards had to be imposed. However, after a quarter-century of effort to standardize the instructional facilities and curricula of rural schools, reform gains had been negligible. As Eby noted, "After twenty years of effort . . . the movement has largely proved a failure."[17] The Texas legislature, sensitive to rural constituencies and their desire to retain control of rural education, had been slow to enact many laws needed to institutionalize school reform. To infuse new life into the school-reform movement reformers employed recently developed research technologies to dramatize the urgent need to redesign Texas rural education.

The Great Texas Educational Survey of 1924

Educational surveys had long been a favored tactic of school reformers in their attempts to bring public attention to weaknesses in the prevailing system of schooling. However, as can be seen in the studies of W. S. Sutton[18] and of E. V. White and E. E. Davis,[19] the research technologies of earlier times usually produced only nominal data. Because their findings could be dismissed as subjective, they failed to convince legislators and the general public. The work of Thorndike in standardizing test instruments, however, supplied a new procedure that suggested surveys could be more tangible, more quantified, and presumably more capable of influencing public opinion. Sutton, acknowledged leader of school reform in the state and dean of the School of Pedagogy at the University of Texas, had long advocated a comprehensive study of Texas schools.[20] In the gubernatorial campaign of 1922, incumbent Pat M. Neff listed as one of his educational platform planks, "Let the state make a thorough, scientific, and impartial survey of our entire educational life."[21] The proposal to adopt the Sutton Plan is not surprising: Sutton was the key educational advisor to Governor Neff during both his terms of office. A year after Neff's election, in March, 1923, the Thirty-eighth Legislature approved a comprehensive study of Texas schools and appropriated fifty thousand dollars for the project.[22] This long-anticipated research study would prove one of our few objective evaluations of rural-school function, as well as one of the great school-reform disappointments of the century.

To direct the survey of rural schools, Orville Brim, professor of elementary education at Ohio State University, was employed. In the spring of 1923 the survey data were gathered in line with the school reform agenda from visitations to Texas country schools. The data were quantitative, and they focused on such factors as school facilities, length of term, supervision, and teacher certification, experience, and pay. The initial survey data appeared to support every reform allegation against the rural schools. In the matter of buildings and grounds, the director of the study reported that "the inviting homelike atmosphere was rarely found. The schoolrooms were usually drab and cheerless."[23] Rural teachers were found to be less adequately prepared, less experienced, younger, and less well paid than their nonrural counterparts. Also confirmed was the fact that country schools had terms significantly shorter than those of the nonrural schools. An early comment on the data stated, "The country child is placed at a distinct disadvantage [by a shortened school year]."[24] Further, the survey team reported that supervisory activity was concerned "with an agenda other than improving the quality of teaching."[25] A cursory examination of the data validated most of the school-reform condemnations of rural schooling. If the commission had not analyzed the data further, school reformers along with a sympathetic governor and legislature might well have moved to abolish the rural common schools in Texas decades earlier. However, the survey commission made one more critical comparison, a measure of student achievement, expressed as "educational efficiency."

Nowhere was the conflict of opposing educational theories more apparent than between the survey committee members who evaluated the general setting of rural schooling and those who assessed the educational achievement of pupils. The former group was progressive and child centered and advocated "schooling as life" as described by Dewey. The team that measured academic outcomes was behavioristic and viewed schooling as "preparation for life," manifest by the production of observable behaviors. These behaviorists, who said, "The product of the school is a changed pupil," were disciples of Thorndike.[26]

Given the earlier survey returns, Texas school reformers had every right to anticipate that the test results would support their position. However, a surprise was in store. The conclusions, reached by behaviorist evaluators, would directly contradict the reform rhetoric of two decades. Even the "efficiency movement," then in full swing, would be turned back upon the Texas school reformers.[27]

The learning outcomes of schooling were described by the survey committee in the popular language of the day as "efficiency achievement quotients," or AQs. An AQ was a combination of an IQ estimate of innate ability and a measure of mastery of subject matter. In effect it "controlled for IQ," measuring the direct effects of education upon learning. The results were a grave setback for school reform in Texas. In reporting the three major subjects taught in public schools of the day, the commission stated that in reading, "smaller schools have a higher efficiency achievement quotient in nearly every case."[28] After stating that "arithmetic is probably a better measure of effectiveness of schooling than is reading," the commission reported, "Here again the small schools, rather than showing inferior effectiveness, are slightly superior to the larger schools."[29] In spelling, "The smaller school shows efficiency slightly beyond all other types of schools."[30] Such findings dealt a cruel blow to the reform contention that inexperienced teachers, low pay, poor facilities, and inadequate supervision adversely affected learning. Either these presumed negative factors had little or no actual effect upon the efficiency of learning, or else positive forces outweighed them in the face-to-face world of the country school. But the data were incontrovertible: the rural schools really worked.

Equally destructive to the reform platform were the commission findings about the effects of length of school term: "There is little evidence of a relationship between the length of school year and the efficiency of pupil learning."[31] Finally, the summary statement of the commission seemed a ringing indictment of the entire school-reform attack upon the rural schools: "It would appear from our data that the conclusions commonly reached regarding the ineffectiveness of the small school as compared with larger schools are unwarranted. Small schools rather than showing ineffectiveness, are slightly superior."[32] The school reformers had employed real empiricists who were committed to following the data wherever they led. The reformers, it seemed, had suffered a severe setback in their campaign for rural school consolidation.

In actual fact the school survey of 1924 had little impact on Texas education. The school-reform agenda for consolidation did not collapse beneath the weight of the empirical evidence, because the survey was suppressed by the school-reform leadership in the state's educational machinery. Although the final report of the survey was delivered ahead of schedule to state authorities, in December, 1924, S. M. N. Marrs noted in the Biennial Report of the State Superintendent, 1922–24, that "the educational survey commission report has not been printed in time to include any comment."[33] Nor was the survey mentioned in the official reports of subsequent years.

The losses incurred by the concealment of the report are incalculable. None of the survey findings have ever been used to expand the dialogue related to the recurring and unresolved questions of schooling. A striking example that lay buried for sixty years may be found in the final summation of the survey commission: "The finding that rural schools are not inefficient leaves open the possibility that the small school has compensating advantages which enable it, with the very obvious handicap of poorly trained teachers and less adequate facilities, to compete with the larger

18

schools in the final product."[34] What were these mysterious "compensating advantages" at work in the country schools of sixty years ago? Could open discussion of that question help us resolve our current problems with the teaching of basic skills? Today, long after the school reformers' fondest dreams were realized, there is great dissatisfaction with public education. That simple yet basic question still remains unanswered: What makes a school good?

The Demise of the Rural Schools

Following the debacle of the Texas Educational Survey, school reformers employed more subtle techniques in dealing with rural schools. Now both carrot and stick were employed. Lawrence D. Haskew, professor emeritus in the Department of Educational Administration at the University of Texas at Austin, observed: "The State Department of Education (and the legislature) has traditionally employed a permissive approach to the consolidation of schools. They coerced – made it costly to remain a common school – and they bribed – contributed extra monies to schools that did consolidate."[35] Nevertheless, as shown in the *Report of the Adequacy of Texas Schools* in 1937, the new reform campaign had only a marginal effect. In 1924, the year of the survey, 6,888 rural common schools operated in Texas, as compared with 868 independent nonrural districts. In 1936, 5,984 rural schools were in service, alongside 1,015 independent districts. Thus, eleven years after the Texas Educational Survey, 84 percent of the state's public school system was still rural.[36]

In the view of J. W. Edgar, Texas commissioner of education for twenty-five years (1950–74), the reluctance of rural schools to consolidate was based upon two primary attitudes: "The local people resisted consolidation mainly because they believed their community would disappear without a school to bind it together. In a number of cases, the community had already disappeared. Second, there was a prevailing attitude or philosophy of local control which permeated the legislature. Texas lawmakers always have insisted that it [consolidation] must come from the people."[37] Even as school reformers were experiencing great frustration in their attempts to alter the course of Texas schooling, other significant events were occurring that ultimately would transform the public schools. Texas was becoming industrialized. In 1923 there were 3,693 manufacturing establishments registered in the state. By 1939 the number had grown to 5,376; by 1958 it had reached 10,505.[38] More significant was the 300 percent increase in workers who earned a living in nonagricultural occupations.

The general growth of population in the state also affected schools. In 1920 the census showed that Texas was the home of 4,663,228 people. That number had grown to 5,824,715 by 1930, and to 6,414,824 by 1940.[39] Even so, although rapid growth in industry and population elsewhere had tended to usher in school consolidation, Texas rural schools resisted the change. Then, in the 1930s and 1940s, two overlapping world disasters not only intensified social changes in the state but also diverted resources from the public schools and accelerated the trend toward consolidation. During the Great Depression many resources were unavailable; afterward, funds and energy were channeled into World War II. By the time the war came to an end, in 1945, Texas schools had not been a priority of its citizenry for more than a decade.

Clearly the conditions for schooling in postwar Texas were strikingly different from those even a scant decade earlier. Wartime industry had created urban centers. The growing population had bought up the cheap land. Technological advances reduced the need for farm labor, and improved roads sped the former country dwellers on their way to town. Both cotton agriculture and the labor-intensive tenant system associated with it suffered swift decline. Rural decline eroded the ability to remain rural. In a significantly more interdependent society, the rural schools gave way both to massive demographic changes and to increased demands on the institution of public education. Reading, writing, and ciphering were no longer the only outcomes expected of schooling.

Education of the masses required a new structure for schooling the young. Edgar noted, "The depression and then the war had left the Texas schools in pretty sad shape. Schools became a major concern again after the war. In 1947, Governor [Beauford] Jester and, for once, the power structure of the state decided to get the schools on a firm financial basis. In 1949, the legislature passed the Gilmer-Akin Law . . . which gave public schools a stability they never had before."⁴⁰ Gilmer-Akin drastically revised the structure for financing public schooling. A Minimum Foundation Program was established for all school districts in the state, and state monies were no longer equally distributed to school districts. To support a statewide educational minimum foundation, monies were allocated on the basis of county wealth. Some school districts received no state support. A minimum teachers' salary was established. Accredited school districts were required to offer a specified curriculum, and a minimum class size and length of school year were required by law. Teacher certification became a responsibility of the state's Department of Education. The school-reform hope for greater centralization of power, expressed by Marrs forty years earlier, was realized in the passage of Gilmer-Akin. J. W. Edgar noted the results: "The year before I became State Commissioner [1949], there were about 4,000 school districts in Texas. By 1950, approximately 2,000 of those districts had consolidated. When I left office [1974], there were about 1,100 school districts in Texas. Today, there are still 1,100 districts."⁴¹

The Gilmer-Akin Act unquestionably institutionalized the old school-reform agenda for Texas schools, but clearly the passing of the rural schools did not result from the efforts of the school reformers. The demise of the rural schools was the result of social, economic, political, and cultural change. The old platitude that "the school reflects society" was never more evident than in the evolution of the rural common schools in Texas. Threats, bribes, and clever political tactics failed to accomplish the consolidation of rural schools while they still served social needs. But when rural society itself changed and Texans came to perceive schooling in the light of a different set of more urban needs, the rural schools passed away in a decade.

Lost in the general rush to consolidate was the sporadic resistance of those rural citizens and communities who still believed in the old country dictum, "When the school dies, the community dies." In Caldwell County the citizens of the little Lytton Springs community built at great cost a modern six-room brick school only a year or so before they were forced to consolidate with Lockhart. Farther north in the county, supporters of the black St. John's Colony School desperately filled school desks with nonstudents and posted lookouts to give advance warning of the arrival of the state administrators of Gilmer-Akin—all to no avail.

On Researching a Lost World

Except for a handful of survivors, such as Divide CSD, in Kerr County, the old rural common schools have passed away, leaving many questions unanswered. For example, what was it really like to attend and to teach in the country schools? How did teachers adapt their teaching to the presence of several grades in a single classroom? What relationships existed between school and community, teacher and trustees?

We might also ask if there were advantages, as well as the obvious disadvantages, to teaching and learning in the small-scale, face-to-face world of the country school. In the Texas Educational Survey of 1924, researchers suggested "the possibility that the small school has compensating advantages which enable it, with the very obvious handicap of poorly trained teachers and less adequate facilities, to compete with the larger schools in the final product."[42] What were these "compensating advantages," what perspective can they offer on our current problems with the teaching of basic skills, and what can all this suggest for the reawakening debate on the most effective "economy of scale" for American public education?[43] We will return to these important matters in our final chapter.

The most basic reason for researching the lost world of the common schools is simple historical justice. The common school district was the basic organizational invention of American education and the primary source of public schooling for American citizens for almost a century, yet it has never been adequately studied by historians. Perhaps we have been too willing to accept the consolidationists' view of rural education, too certain that we already knew what went on in the ungraded country schools of a few decades ago. In any case, the common schools merit a fresh look, one for which we have waited almost too long.

C. L. Sonnichsen once observed, "The grassroots historian must do his work before the night cometh, in which no man can work."[44] In Texas, as elsewhere, thousands of former teachers and students from the country schools are still among us, but "the night cometh." In the social history that follows we draw upon many first-hand accounts of former teachers and students to present a fresh view of the intimate workings of the common school districts, told as much as possible in the words of the "natives" themselves. In this book we reenter the lost world of the Texas country schools to tell their story from the inside out, rather than the outside in.

2. *Riding Shank's Mare*

Ⓐ

SOMETIME AROUND 1918, students who lived long miles from the one-room Reeves School, near Deadwood, gathered in the cold and dark of the winter morning to prepare for their daily trek to school through the deep woods. They met at a neighborhood farm, and there the older children lighted pine-knot torches and led the younger ones several miles to their school. In the depth of winter, the trip began and ended in this dark procession led by a pine-knot torch.[1]

Many thousands of living Texans attended the country schools and remember going to school by light of pine torch or coal oil lantern. Rural transportation in Texas during the first three decades of the twentieth century was extremely primitive – often more resembling that of the Middle Ages than that of today. Roads were usually just raw tracks across the land, unimproved by gravel or asphalt, and in certain seasons so deep in mud that travelers had to take to the nearby fields or fencerows. Often, as well, these country roads failed to run in the directions children needed to go to get to school, or were too roundabout. So, very commonly, students who lived great distances from their schools were forced to choose shorter and more direct routes cross-country, as these two accounts describe.

> We lived so far from school, it was at least five miles, and in cold weather, going home, we faced that north wind. Now, if it poured down

24

rain, Daddy would come and get us in the wagon, or we'd ride the horses. We had plenty of old horses. We'd ride the horses to school the days it was rainy and so muddy, and we had a creek that we called Pin Oak that would cut us off right at the school. Then we'd follow that stream so far till we could get down to a place where we'd jump across on the other side and then come back to the school. One man, Mr. Sam Harris, now, his children didn't have to cross this little creek, but he felled a tree and cut notches in that log and kind of leveled it off so we could cross. I'll always remember him for that.[2]

We moved to what was called the Banks Place. It was a house up there right in the middle of the Big Woods. There was not another house in a mile on either side. The Peach School, a one-room school, was about two and a half miles away right straight through the woods. Like a cow would make a trail through the woods, that's the way we went to school. We lived in that house about a year, then we moved across the creek in another house, and we had to walk a log across a creek to get to school. In the winter time, Daddy had to nail a plank on top of that log so we wouldn't fall off when it got slick with ice. That must have been about three miles to school. Going to school we'd pick huckleberries in the fall and pick up hickory nuts and things. We had a lot of fun walking to school. We just sort of meandered along down the trail.[3]

For students who rode "shank's mare" across the countryside, like the two above, parents often tried to smooth the way. Fathers felled trees across streams, nailing boards to the trunks or putting up handrails or handlines to give support. Others built stiles over barbed-wire fences so their little girls would not snag their school dresses. When there was a chance that children might get lost on the way to school, fathers would plow a furrow to the school (sometimes several miles distant) and tell their children to "walk the furrow" or would mark the route in other ways. From the time of the Texas Republic well into the present century, some students followed ax blazes on trees.[4] Teachers were often new to the rural communities in which they taught, and some had the same problems in finding their way as did their students. As this story attests, community fathers sometimes provided for them as well: "My teaching career began in 1929 in a one-teacher school called Cottonwood in Brown County. My first day of school began at 7:30 A.M., as I left my boarding place for a three-mile hike through a densely wooded area. I followed a trail that had been marked with yellow rag strings so that I would not lose my way. I came into a clearing, and there was my school in the midst of cottonwood trees."[5]

Sometimes the difficulties of their children's cross-country treks forced fathers into more serious engineering projects, as this former student described.

> In times of heavy rains we could not cross Owl Creek. Our father put footlogs across the creek for us to walk, but the first rain would wash them away. Finally he located two tall trees near the creek. He cut them down and fastened them together with boards like a ladder. He then fastened them to another tree with a log chain. When the creek flooded, the footlog, as we called the ladder, would float to the bank of the creek nearest our house and as soon as the waters subsided our father could throw it back across the creek and we could go home. If the creek remained flooded, we had to stay with a friend or a relative who lived on the same side of the creek as the school.
>
> It was a scary sight to look down and see the angry muddy water raging beneath one as he crossed the creek. My brothers and sister walked the ladder, but I was afraid, so I always crawled across, usually crying as I went. It was a terrible experience for me.[6]

Rivers and streams were impediments to travel to a degree only dimly comprehended by modern students. In the period just before World War I the Baker family lived across the Lampasas River from Cedar Knob School, in Bell County. The children could walk across the river on gravel bars and other shallow places under normal circumstances, but when the river rose, their father had to come for them with a rowboat. Some of the Baker children remembered how frightened they had been trying to find their way down rainslick banks to where their father could pick them up.[7]

The trip to and from school was a lark or an ordeal, depending on a variety of factors: the students' mode of transportation, the distance to school, the weather, the condition of the roads or footpaths, and the adequacy of the children's clothing. William Owens's mother, determined that her children would get an education, selected the family's tenant-farm assignments with an eye to accessibility of local schools, but bad weather, a lack of winter clothing, and the need for older children to labor for the family's survival often kept her children out of school. One particularly bad farming year in the Pin Hook community they did not make enough money to buy shoes for the older boys, who had to go to school barefooted. This had consequences for their school attendance. "In December and January they would have to miss some days when blue northers swept down and left ice on the ruts in the road, but they were pushed to get as much learning as they could while they could."[8]

The personal accounts gathered by the students of Bill O'Neal in northeast Texas contain many similar stories.[9] In some cases we hear of children kept out of school an extra year or so when they were judged not yet strong enough to walk to school, sometimes seven and even ten miles distant.[10] At the Africa School for black children, in Shelby County, all the students dressed alike in clothing inadequate for the really bad weather. Boys wore overalls, and girls wore homemade flour-sack dresses. It was normal to be issued one pair of shoes a school year, "after the first frost fell."[11] Some children had no shoes. Some came to school comically draped in adult clothing of every conceivable description, often wearing parents' long coats that came to their ankles and had sleeves rolled up.[12] As one former student observed, "Once cold weather set in we came to school bundled in everything we had to wear that mother wasn't washing at the time. . . . My mother got me a pair of Union suits, and I had to wear those long-legged things to school. Oh, I was so ashamed!"[13] The necessities of cold weather survival often conflicted with social sensitivity. About 1905 in Ochiltree County, in West Texas, the Ellis family lived in a dugout close to the school. One day when it snowed even Carl Ellis's leathery feet could no longer stand the cold. Because he had no shoes of his own to wear to school, he had to wear a pair of his mother's and one girl at the school made fun of him – something he never forgot.[14]

Even when parents could afford shoes, students were often made to go without them for the longest possible time in the fall so they would last longer. One black family had a rule that children could not wear their shoes in the rain, only when it was dry and very cold.[15] In another poor black community in East Texas people walked nearly everywhere they went, and when going to school, church, or some other social occasion they often carried shoes, stockings, and a towel along with them. Just before they arrived at their destination, they wiped the mud off their feet with the towel and put on the stockings and shoes.[16]

Some teachers ministered to their pedestrian students' foot problems, using regular programs of first aid. The teacher at Reeves School, near Deadwood, soaked weather-damaged and nail-injured feet in kerosene. A former student at China Grove School, in King County, remembered that the teacher, J. H. Doss, was very kindly and considerate of the children who walked to the school barefooted through the ice and snow. He daily examined the children's feet, rubbed their frostbitten heels, and applied medication to make them feel better.[17]

If distance, water crossings, and cold weather were three common afflictions of the rural school traveler, a fourth was mud. In rainy weather attendance was always poor, especially in counties that had particularly forbidding varieties of this "fifth element," with which many moderns have all but lost touch. In Bell County, for example, "during extremely rainy seasons, mud and slush would be up to the horses' bellies. A common sight was to see a father with one, two, or three children riding the same horse, escorting another horse load of two or three children to school." Every resident of the area remembered "Schneider's Mudhole," the muddiest and most impassable place on any road in Bell County.[18]

Children in Bell County and elsewhere sometimes were kept out of school a year or so later than normal because they "could not pull the mud." In the String Community, the U.S. Post Office just up the road from Dyess Grove School was closed after three years because of problems with the mud, and it is easy to imagine the difficulties experienced by area schoolchildren. "The smaller children, too small to pull the mud, would drop out of school. If the rainy season lasted too long for them to catch up, they would wait until the next year and start over."[19] A former student from Little Elm School in Bell County remembered that about 1916 the children from her part of the district often joined forces in mud time. They walked in a single column, the big boys going first. The smaller children stepped in the path, the larger scholars in effect "breaking trail" for the smaller and weaker.[20] Families living in more isolated parts of the school district could not take advantage of this sort of strength in numbers. In the 1920s, Cobb Whitley, who lived east of the Bell Plains School, often carried his little girl to school on his back because of the deep, black mud.[21] Other counties had their own epic varieties of mud – black, gray, or red – and their named mudholes, like Schneider's Mudhole, which were regarded as permanent features of the landscape. In Caldwell County Black Ankle School was even named for the mud.

Although the majority of Texas rural schoolchildren rode their own two good feet to school, no other possible means of transportation was neglected. Many children used horses, mules, or burros or drove or were driven in buggies, surreys, wagons, carts, and every other conceivable sort of animal-powered vehicle. A boy attending Enterprise School, near Center, trained a bull to answer commands, made a special bridle, and rode him to school every day, much to the amazement of his classmates. He left his bull untied to graze during the day, except during recess, when the other boys lined up to try to ride it. At the end of each school day, he whistled the bull up and rode off for home.[22] Schools that had many riders sometimes had special facilities, such as hitching racks or stables, to accommodate students' animals.[23]

At the Matador School, in Motley County, "The teacher and pupils at the Jeffries' home came down the creek in a two-wheeled cart. The Cammack kids (about seven in number) went up the river on a bunch of broom-tailed mustangs like a band of Sioux Indians. Jake and Nora Cooper waded the waters of Teepee Creek. . . . We had a regular rodeo show every evening after school, but nobody was killed."[24]

When Charles Higgins was a student in Deaf Smith County, in the 1920s, his family used an old car until it literally fell apart, at which time their father salvaged certain of its parts to rig up a four-wheel, rubber-tired, horse-drawn trailer. A fresh team was used every day because "Papa was particular with his horses." The horses were unhitched when they got to school, and one was tied on each side of the trailer, where feed was placed for them. Sometimes a gentle horse was teamed with a bronc they wanted to break, and this could pose problems. Once, going downhill approaching a playa lake, the trailer went so fast it bumped the team and the bronc began kicking. The team was brought under control only when it reached the upgrade on the far side of the playa. The

Three brothers and their mode of transportation to Adkins School, 1934–35. Courtesy East Central Historical Group, East Central ISD, Bexar County.

Higginses' wagon picked up a whole series of other children from the west end of the school district. Riders would bundle up with quilts and blankets in the trailer. When they got too cold, they would jump out and run alongside for a while, holding on to the trailer so the driver could not run off and leave them.[25] A teacher in Motley County drove a similar school transport in 1910, gathering up most of the children in a covered wagon at designated stops. Children ran in front of and behind the wagon to rest the team and just for fun. A former rider reported that "kids were strung out half a mile in either direction from that wagon — some running behind throwing sticks and stones — some running ahead to wait for the wagon to catch up."[26]

In Ochiltree County the Murphy children went nine miles to the Ochiltree School, at first in a two-horse buggy and later in a Model T Ford. The Murphy children were models of decorum until out of sight of home, but then "devilish things began to happen: the girls rolled their cotton stockings down, and their long bulky underwear up, and Mike often became a speed demon at the wheel!"

30

A neighbor turned them in for driving twenty miles an hour cross-country chasing coyotes.[27]

In the 1930s and 1940s, the first school buses began to run rural routes, but, as Donald Shires tells, these buses were very unlike the modern versions – were, in effect, as irregular and jury-rigged as the other varieties of rural school transportation:

> The first school bus I rode was from Rockhill to Beckville. Back then they were homemade from a truck frame. Wooden and painted different colors, [they] had windows like a house. We sat on benches that ran lengthwise inside. The school didn't own them but contracted individual people who had built them to pick up kids. Mr. Davis owned and drove our bus. Back then all the roads weren't paved, and this long hill going by Aunt Ellen Briggs's, which is from Rockhill to Beckville, was red clay. One morning the road was wet and slick. The bus just wouldn't go up the hill, so Mr. Davis told all the boys to get out and push. Well, we weren't all that excited about going to school anyway and sure didn't want to get in that red clay. So instead of pushing forward we pushed sideways, and the bus slid into the ditch. No school that day! Far as I know, Mr. Davis never did know what we did. He just figured the bus slid in the ditch by itself.[28]

As we have seen, teachers often helped their students get to school, but their first task was to get themselves to the school building in time to have it ready when the students arrived. Noel Thomas Curb painted a charming word picture of one teacher of his acquaintance on her way to work: "Look back sixty-nine years down a dusty, white wagon rut that serves as a road and see seventeen-year-old Sadie Oliver walking to school – the schoolmarm – younger than some of her pupils, followed by a large, yellow lion-like dog, property of the R. L. Birdwell family, with whom Miss Sadie boards."[29]

Sadie Oliver's yellow dog was not just for companionship, but for protection. Many students also were accompanied by dogs, to guard against rattlesnakes and rabid animals. Rabies was the real-life nightmare of the Texas countryside, always present in the populations of skunks, foxes, and other animals, especially in the hot months. The accompanying dog might be fatally infected, but certainly would intervene to save the traveling scholar from attack. Some schools are described as having as many dogs in attendance as students.[30]

The last school bus run at Adkins School, 1941. Courtesy East Central Historical Group, East Central ISD, Bexar County. Sadie F. Wade.

Cold, wet weather, however, was regarded as a much more common threat to students' health, and throughout most of the school term, the rural teacher's first responsibility upon reaching the school was to build a fire in the big wood stove that heated the classroom. The idea was that the school building would be warm by the time students arrived. Below, two former teachers describe this ubiquitous experience of the rural schoolteacher, showing why it was a responsibility that had to be met.

In Collingsworth County the winters are very cold sometimes, with the cold, cold wind blowing in from the north and probably at times bringing snow or turning into a blizzard, which sometimes lasted for several days. In those storms, attendance at school was always bad. Most of these came as far as three or four miles on horseback. I rode horseback three miles the two years I taught at Quail. I can well remember how that blizzard wind would burn and sting my face and my fingers would get numb in my wool gloves. However, the weather didn't stop me many days. I wanted to be at school to have a fire started in the big potbellied stove for the children that did make it.[31]

32

The teacher felt that she almost *had* to make it to school to start the fire on these especially bad days. There was no way to notify parents that school was canceled, and the teacher never could be sure that one or more of her students would not show up at the school, miles away from home, cold, wet, and suffering from exposure. Another teacher's account demonstrates a similar level of determination.

> Every day was a memorable experience for me, a seventeen-year-old teacher, in 1917. One Monday morning I awoke to find that heavy snow had fallen. As usual I walked to school. That seemed easy at first, but when the fenced roadway turned, snowdrifts were nearly knee-deep. Should I turn back? I had no intention of doing so! Poe Prairie was a one-teacher school and I was *it!* I must get along and have the room warm before the pupils came.
>
> I found the wood-box empty, but wood was outside under the snow. I dug some out and carried it inside. By the time I had a good fire burning two little boys had arrived. As we stood by the fire warming ourselves, I suddenly felt sick. When I lay down on the recitation bench, the frightened little boys ran home to tell their parents that something was wrong with the teacher. Soon I was riding home on the spring seat of a farm wagon. The day was done. Everything turned out all right, but for some time I had frost-bitten hands and feet.[32]

As teachers walked, rode, or drove to school, they often gathered their students about them. Ora Blackwell did this on foot at Bala School, in King County, in the decade before World War I. Walking two and a half miles to school from her boarding room in the Bala Post Office, she passed by the homes of most of her students on the way. Family by family they joined the entourage.[33] Twenty years later, Essie McCarley and her husband Gordon were the teachers at a two-room school in Medina County. They drove to school in their Model A, picking up a half dozen students as they went, the last and littlest of which Mrs. McCarley held in her lap.[34] Sometimes this free ride from the teacher had a price after all. Fred I. Soape of Panola County tells how the old-maid teacher who taught at the Snap School and lived near him gave him a ride to school each day in her horse and buggy. In return, he had to start the fire in the wood stove and minister to the teacher's horse.[35]

At the close of an all but incalculable number of school days in thousands of country schools, most students made their way homeward without incident, just as they had come. They walked or rode the same paths through woods or pastures, followed the same furrows plowed by helpful fathers, and crossed the creeks on the same makeshift bridges. A significant number of boys now ran their traplines to see if a skunk or raccoon had made a fatal mistake in one of the steel traps designed to provide pocket money for rural youth. Others checked their traps on the way to school in the morning, but these risked the displeasure of their teachers when they arrived at school smelling of the "polecat."[36] Most of the students had chores waiting for them at home at the end of the long day—sometimes long, laborious chores.

There were times, however, when the trip home was more eventful, and almost always the cause was a drastic weather change. Because teachers felt responsible for the welfare of their children on the way home, they were ready to dismiss school when necessary, but they rarely had the benefit of weather forecasts. One student remembered an early release in northeast Texas after the teacher saw a blue norther coming. The student walked home as rapidly as possible, but in her two-mile walk through a pine thicket, the rain turned to sleet and snow and all the little pines bent down with ice.[37] At a Swisher County school, in West Texas, a norther struck so suddenly that the children could not get home at all. The storm came up at about 2:00 P.M. The teacher had the children move all the horses and buggies around to the south side of the schoolhouse for protection, then she and her students held hands and walked to the Murry Evans place to spend the night. They made themselves useful by chasing Mrs. Evans's chickens, which the strong north wind had blown away![38]

In general the weather stories from West Texas have a particularly drastic ring to them, but West Texans, teachers and students alike, were very weatherwise. On a snowy day at the Red Hill School, in Swisher County, one student came to school on the family's Ford tractor. By noon a full-scale blizzard was in progress. The student took some children home on the tractor, while others held on to barbed-wire fences and walked the fence lines home through blinding snow. Nevertheless, "a near tragedy occurred that day because the Kirbys were following the north instead of the south side of the fence line and almost missed their turn."[39]

West Texas dust storms were another hazard, typically coming up without warning late in the day. They were at their worst
in what were known locally as "the dirty thirties," but some struck
decades earlier. Around 1900 in King County, Jack White sometimes had to let his horse find its own way home six miles from
the Union Center School he attended. It would grow too dark for
the boy to see, and because there were no fences to guide him, he
had no alternative but to leave it up to his horse's sense of
direction.[40] A former Swisher County student told how his family
used to sleep with a damp sheet over the top of their four-poster
bed to keep out the dust. School clothes for the next day, freshly
washed, were hung inside another damp sheet.[41] Especially in the
spring these dust storms would come up without warning. At
Simms School, in Deaf Smith County, the dust sometimes rolled
in so thick that the teacher insisted that children travel to the outdoor toilets in pairs, holding hands so they would not become separated.[42] Students recalled that they would get to school on a
beautiful morning, then the dust would start blowing and "it would
get so bad you could not see to read."[43]

The dust storms, and accompanying thunderstorms, could be
deadly. Children at Red Hill School, in Dickens County, were sent
home early because of an approaching storm, but already it was
too late. Eight children of three families were caught in the open
in a great hailstorm. One was killed, and the others were badly
beaten by the hail.[44] A final West Texas weather story from Collingsworth County has a happier ending.

The sandstorms were a threat to the children's safety at times. My
memory is still plain of a little seven-year-old boy that got lost. The
big sandstorm struck the vicinity about noon. It was one of the kind
that blows so hard and the sand fills the air until you can't see very
well. The boy rode a gray mare about two and a half miles to school
by himself. No other child went the same direction. So when school
was dismissed he crawled on the back of his old mare and started east
in the direction of his home. He did not get home by the time his father
thought he should, so he got on a horse and started after him. He
reached the schoolhouse, but everyone else had gone home. So he went
to the county store about one-half mile away and told the men there
his son was lost. In no time at all there were a bunch of men on horses
out in the storm to hunt the boy. One young man had ridden out into
an old cornfield that was very sandy. And all at once he heard a slight

35

noise so he listened and it got plainer. Sure enough there stood the old gray mare all humped up with the boy still on her back. She had gotten lost too since signs in the sand showed that she had been going around in a circle. The man rode up and took hold of the horse's bridle. The boy was crying and scared half to death. The man said, "Son, what are you doing out here?" The boy answered with a trembling voice, "Who am I, anyway?"[45]

One may imagine from all this that the teacher kept a wary eye on the weather at all times. Heavy rains, which could raise local creeks and cut children off from their route home, were obviously a constant preoccupation, and – students being students, then as now – the following story should surprise no one. According to Frances Fish of Menard County, "The kids could really take advantage when they had a new teacher, especially a city girl. One particular school was on a hill between two forks of the San Saba River. Anytime a cloud would form as big as your hand, they'd start gathering up their stuff and tell the teacher, 'We must get across the draw, or it will come down and we'll be cut off.' This ruse would work fine a time or two, so their holidays were rather of their own making."[46] One particular teacher, a city girl teaching in the Hill Country, was so terrified of the usual tree-trunk footbridge over the nearby stream that the trustees cut special poles and left them on either side of the crossing. She used these as supports when she walked the tree.

> One spring day there was a terrific rain-and-hail storm. We stood at the school windows and watched the shingles fall off the roof from the pounding hail. By the time school was dismissed that afternoon, the little creek we always crossed was a raging torrent of flowing hail and water. A group of the fathers were waiting for us at the edge of the water with horses. To my consternation we were mounted on those horses, and they swam with us across the swollen stream. I still remember my feeling of fright which I tried to hide from those staunch, sturdy hill people.[47]

Finally, here is one last coming-home-from-school account from Curry's Creek School near Kendalia. The former teacher is Annie McElroy, and the events described took place about 1920.

> They [the Lux children] lived across the creek from the school. Their daddy had cut a big cedar tree to make a bridge across the creek. There

was a wire to hold on to as you walked across the log to get to school. I walked home with them one afternoon, and we crossed across that log. About two years before I had come to Curry's Creek, Mr. Lux had come on horseback with an extra horse to get the girls because there was a rainstorm and the creek was flooded. He took two neighbor children on his horse, and Hilda and Lonnie [Lux] were on the other horse. They started going across the creek and the horse that the girls were on slipped and the girls fell off. So their father jumped off his horse and caught Hilda, and Lonnie went on down the creek, caught in the flood. He got the neighbor children safely to the shore, then he sent them to get help. On down the creek there was a fork, and he thought that she [Lonnie] had gone one way, so he went that way, but as it turned out she had floated on down the other way. Not far from the fork there is a place called Edge Falls where there is a waterfall, and it drops fifty to sixty feet. By the time some men got to the falls they saw her school bag go over the falls. They knew for sure that she would go over the falls too. Fortunately she had caught onto a limb upstream and hung on. Those men finally rescued her. Lonnie was scared of storms for a long time after her experience.[48]

3. Shiloh to Shake Rag

IN A TIME of primitive transportation, nothing was so important from the perspective of the individual parent as the location of the district school. No matter where the school was placed, its location benefited some students and penalized others. Some had an easy walk or ride to school, while others struggled through deep mud or sand for miles, crossing creeks, picking their way through heavy woods and otherwise paying the price of two to four hours of traveling time each day.

It should surprise no one, then, that the location of the school was the most significant political issue of the era of the common school districts. The one- and two-room frame schoolhouses of the time were highly movable structures, and commonly they were shifted about as district school population changed. The parents would turn out with mules and oxen, jack the school up and put it on beam supports, and off it would go to another part of the district. One observer noted that this happened suspiciously often following school district elections in which there had been a decided changing of the guard. "Quite often when new trustees were elected, the schoolhouse would be moved, perhaps several miles, 'So my kids don't have to walk so far for a while.'"[1] Over the years, some schools were moved not once but several times.[2]

The original location of a rural school was governed by a variety of factors. In the beginning a parent, or parents, wishing an

38

education for their children beyond what they could offer at home, would set up an informal "subscription school," with all participating parents contributing a small amount of money to pay a teacher to hold school for a few months. Sometimes, as in this account from Wise County, the initiative might come from a would-be teacher: "A person who could qualify as a teacher, and desiring to earn a little money and at the same time contribute a worthwhile service to society, would ask parents to sign an agreement to contribute a small sum of money expressing adhesion to a contract stating that his child would receive instruction."[3] Most often these subscription schools were held in a preexisting building of some kind – the home of the teacher or of one of the parents, a local church or business, or a similar location. Settlers who had children and were strong advocates of education either furnished or built their own schoolhouses. One such rancher in Ochiltree County built his sod schoolhouse and partially retrieved the expense by teaching for forty dollars per month.[4]

As rural neighborhoods grew in population in the decades around the turn of the century, parents joined together to build a first generation of rural schools, which merged almost imperceptibly into the era of state support and the organized common school district. From the beginning to the end of country schools, location was always the key issue, since the school needed a solid consensus to exist at all.

Occasionally a pioneer would simply take it upon himself to build a first-generation school. These structures were generally sod dugouts ("soddies") in West Texas, one-room log "pens" with dirt floors in Central Texas, and one-room log or rough-cut frame buildings in East Texas. Because the Pleasant Hill community, in Hansford County, was timber-poor, the first school was a dugout. The schoolhouse constructed by the parents for Miss Wells, their first teacher, also doubled as her "teacherage" (the special residence built by the school district for the teacher, or teachers). It was described as a "half-dugout that was big, deep and wide. The walls were canvas, and the floors were covered. They gathered around the table to study. There was a lamp on the table so they could see to study."[5] Dugouts were a functional sort of structure for pioneer West Texans; for example, one's storm shelter was already built in! They

39

were, however, gloomy, poorly ventilated, and according to early teachers, subject to such vermin as sand fleas, snakes, frogs, and "bugs and spiders."[6] One teacher found a snake curled up in her washbasin when she arose one morning.

Where timber was locally available, one-room log schools were common. One such school was built by Bird Slover in Parker County in the 1860s. Slover, for whom school and community would be named, cut trees, hewed them square with a broadax, and built a one-room structure in which benches and desks, also hewn from logs, rested on a dirt floor. At this very early school older boys carried pistols as protection from Indians.[7] A similar school was located in the Balch community of Parker County. It was a one-room log hut about sixteen by sixteen feet, with one log left out of the east wall to admit light. The roof was covered with two- to three-foot-long boards whose bottom ends were held down by logs to fix them in place. The floors and seats were made of split logs, and the seat was affixed to the walls on three sides of the building. Students used the hewn log walls for seat backs. Harvey Martin, the first teacher, taught fifteen to twenty pupils in this school for several years.[8]

First-generation Tarrant County schools usually were constructed of logs. Some, built without windows, relied instead upon light from the large cracks between the logs and perhaps from torches or lanterns. Seats often were just planks set on logs sunk in the dirt floor. One such school had a crack in its door that was put to good purpose. The schoolmaster, who lived only a short distance away, went home at noon to take a nap. The older scholars were instructed to watch the progress of sunlight from the crack. When it reached a spot the schoolmaster had marked on the floor, they were to sound a horn to summon him back.[9]

Affording us a rare glimpse into a first-generation black school in Bell County, a woman over ninety years old described similar primitive circumstances: "Our seats for sitting in were long, two-foot-by-twelve-foot boards placed on top of two rocks placed at each end of the twelve-foot boards. We used our knees for desks to do our writing. In spite of all our handicaps when compared with today's schools, my school days were golden to me."[10] Many one-room black schools, particularly those in East Texas, retained some of these primitive first-generation characteristics right into the middle of the twentieth century.

Until the very end of the common school era a school might be built at the initiative of a single large landowner, farmer, rancher, or timberman. The Rogers Ranch School, in Caldwell County, for example, was designed to offer basic education to the children of the owner's Mexican tenant farmers. In King County the Gardner School was established to serve the cowboys on the Pitchfork Ranch. The ranch itself donated the land for the school.[11] Cowboys at the JA Ranch in Swisher County donated twenty-five dollars a head to start the Love School, and three men went by wagon to haul lumber from Amarillo. Then "the citizens of the community donated their labor and erected the first school building in the community."[12] Begun by a single enterprise or person, such a school might or might not become the focal point of a permanent community. The Viola School, in Houston County of central East Texas, is reported to have been founded by a sawmill operator whose own name is lost but whose oldest daughter's name was Viola. When the timber in the area had been cut, he moved away and the school closed.[13]

Most first-generation schools, however, represented the consensus of the inhabitants of a rural hamlet or a dispersed rural district. Normally the whole community pitched in to fund the school and to build and staff it. Sometimes, however, start-up money was hard to come by. In 1898, founders of the Shinery School District in north King and south Cottle counties gathered bleached buffalo and cattle bones, sold them in Quanah, then returned with lumber and other materials to build the schoolhouse.[14]

But where should the school be located? If the community was concentrated enough and populous enough, the decision was simple: the school would be built right in town. Often, however, the scholastic population was dispersed and a compromise site had to be agreed upon. It mattered little if the site was "right out in the middle of nowhere," as the saying went. The overriding consideration was to enable the greatest number of children to reach the school with the greatest ease. "Ease" was determined on the basis of not only simple distance but also such factors as the quality of roads or trails and the locations of hills and streams. In Bell

41

County, for example, families living in the Reed Lake area on the west side of Knob Creek CSD took steps to found a new district after frequent overflowings of the creek had repeatedly prevented their children from attending Knob Creek School.[15] The school was quite close, but this mattered little when the creek was up.

After agreement was reached about an appropriate central location for the new school, the parents approached the person owning land there. More often than not the owner either donated the land, deeded it "for the life of the school," or sold it to the school supporters for a minimal value. Such landowners often became formal patrons of the new school. Around 1910 Henry Dunnihoo of Ochiltree County donated two acres of land, fenced it, hauled lumber and other materials from Guymon, and boarded the carpenters while they were building the schoolhouse. If he received compensation for these actions, the account fails to mention it.[16]

The patron might be immortalized by having the school named after him, or there might have to be a compromise on this matter as well. The Liberty Hill School in East Texas was constructed in 1889 at a compromise location in a then-unnamed part of rural Houston County. Timber was donated, and a Mr. Hill volunteered to saw the logs without charge. Others volunteered to cut the logs and haul them to the sawmill, then haul the lumber back to the school site. Then, "much on the order of a barn-raising, all the men of the community gathered on the appointed day and set to work." As the work neared completion, a picnic was held, and there trustees were elected and a teacher chosen. At the same meeting, there was debate over a name. Some favored "Hill School" for the man who had donated the sawing. Others liked "Liberty School," because Texans had won their liberty from Mexico. As a compromise, "Liberty Hill School" was proposed and accepted, and this became the name of the community.[17]

At a similar occasion in Parker County, W. G. Spracklen threw water upon the new school he had helped sponsor and dubbed it "Greenwood School."[18] This impromptu christening marked the beginning of a new community as well. The path from the founding of a compromise school to the establishment of a new community, however, was not always certain. It was the clear tendency, but many factors could intervene. For one thing, when enough of the school population moved away, the school building had to be moved. For example, in King County the Little Arizona School was established in a central location in a field contributed by "Uncle Billy" Dowding. Over the years, families coming into the area tended to locate south of the site of Little Arizona School at a distance judged too far to walk. Because the most important consideration was that the school be placed so that children could get to it without undue hardship, the school was relocated south of the Little Arizona community and was renamed Grace School. Hence, Little Arizona was cut off in the bud.[19]

The whole matter of rural school names is fascinating and instructive. If a school was established in an existing community, it naturally took that community's name for its own. If it was in a compromise location, it might take its name from a nearby geographical feature ("Indian Creek School"), from the person who donated land or built the school ("Aberfoyle School"), from one of his children ("Viola School"), or if all else failed, from the Bible or the biblical virtues ("Shiloh School," "Charity School"). The Grace School discussed above sounds like one of the class of rural school names often affixed to compromise schools well away from pre-existing communities. Sometimes the compromise school origin was made entirely clear, in such names as "Midway," "Halfway," or "Three-Point."

Shiloh School, in Parker County, was named, so it is said, for the "God forsaken country spoken of in the Bible by Jeremiah" — an illuminating name, because there were many Shilohs scattered across the state's rural counties. By 1900 the Parker County Shiloh School had drawn a community around it and had been affectionately dubbed "Red Top School" for its rusted tin roof. As Shiloh's chronicler wrote, "By this time the community was well populated and the school was the center of all community activities. Spelling bees were held once a week and everybody, old and young, participated. Once, the word 'bacon' was given out to Aunt Mary Sharp. She muttered around a minute and then blurted out, 'Well, I can't spell it for thinking about eating it!'"[20]

Diligent local historians, such as Eliza Bishop of Houston County, were often frustrated by the profusion of names they found for a single rural school — or what they suspected was a single school. When the Little Arizona School was moved from one side of the district to the other and renamed Grace School, in all probability the district name remained "Little Arizona." Likewise, the parents from the Little Arizona community who continued to send their children to the old school with the new name probably continued to call it Little Arizona. To them it was still "their school." Sometimes this name change following a move took place not once but several times. District lines shifted frequently, with new districts splitting off, older districts losing pupils and becoming "defunct," and other rearrangements.

A plethora of nicknames compounds the problem of keeping up with rural schools. Frequently when schools developed nicknames (as when Shiloh School became Red Top), these informal names came to hold equal sway with or even displace the formal usages. In the 1870s Chico School, in Wise County, had already been dubbed "Sling Mud School" because of the action of the Butterfield Stage as it passed close to the school building in mud time.[21] The first school at Croton Flat was called "No View School" because it was located in a dense grove of cottonwood trees. Common School District No. 110, in Bell County, was properly known as Cowan School but often was spoken of as "Gander Flat"—to the considerable dismay of Mrs. J. H. Cowan. Some say this name came from the large number of Drake children who attended the school (but a drake is a duck and a gander is a goose).[22]

Some other Bell County school names are listed below, with the formal name on the left and the nickname on the right. Some nicknames became so popular that the official names have been forgotten.

Mitchell	*Dog Ridge*
Cowan	*Gander Flat*
Shanklin	*Hog Eye*
Russellville	*Dirty Bonnet*
Deer Creek	*Buzzards' Roost*
Iduma	*Ding Dong/Hog Mountain*
Maxdale	*Hide Out*
???	*Hop Off*
???	*Shake Rag*

Deer Creek got its informal name from the concentration of turkey vultures that roosted in the brush arbor behind the building very early in the school's history.[23] Iduma School was named for the land of beauty reported in the Bible, but only after the repeatedly frustrated attempts by district trustees to hire a teacher for a school generally known as "Hog Mountain."[24] The formal name of "Shake Rag School" was still remembered by at least one person at the time of the Bell County study of rural schools, but the person, or persons, requested that the real name not be identified — presumably because of the disgrace! Finally, the Hog Eye nickname for Shanklin School is the result of a magnificent hoax perpetrated in 1911 by the students of the school upon their newly arrived teachers. Convinced by the students that the proper name for their school was Hog Eye, the teachers did not catch the trick until they checked county school records in the 1920s. By that time, of course, it was much too late to change, and the school was known as Hog Eye to the end. Some school names hint at extremely bizarre origins. The biblically named Tabernacle School in Shelby County was built, entirely on purpose, right in the middle of a popular local racetrack. Because men went there to race their horses and bet, disapproving local people built the new school in a location intended to exorcise this bad habit from the community.[25]

The story of the "Bootleg School," of Deaf Smith County, a school that never existed, further illustrates the relationship between school and community. When land was being sold by the XIT Syndicate (so the story goes), a dummy school building was moved by land agents to various locations whenever prospective land purchasers were in the area. The phony school building was the essential prop for land agents trying to convince these potential buyers that a community was forming thereabouts. If the school was already in place, could the new community be far behind?[26]

The political process that gave rise to the early country schools is largely lost to history. There is, however, one excellent description of the founding and construction of "Lone Star School," in Carson County, in 1892. The full story was told by Lena Hickox Bishop, daughter of the school's founder, W. H. Hickox. It seems that in 1890–91 Hickox was sending his two oldest children nine miles in to Panhandle to a private academy taught in the teacher's home. The ride was often long and cold, despite the fact that Grandma Morris outfitted the traveling scholars, ages fourteen and eleven, with heated smoothing irons wrapped in paper for their feet and folded newspapers under their coats to break the wind.

In May, 1891, the Commissioners' Court of Carson County directed that the county be divided into eight common school districts, and Mr. Hickox, tired of his children's complaints about the long, cold ride to Panhandle, became convinced that he could form a school. As a first step he circulated a petition, which received the signatures of 100 percent of the district's inhabitants. To receive the state allotment for a teacher's salary, he had to have a certain number of students to attend the would-be school. Finding that he did not have quite enough, "he went nine miles away to C. A. Timmons and not only asked but demanded that they must send their children. They had been debating whether to send them to Boydston or Lone Star School, which I think was farther away."[27] Mrs. Timmons hesitated, but Hickox promised that he would tell the teacher to bring her children to his home overnight when there were storms, when their horse got away, or in the event of other acts of God and chance. Mrs. Timmons finally agreed, though this would mean that Will, Mervert, and Lonnie Timmons would have to ride their single mule eighteen miles every day. With the requisite number of students in hand, Hickox notified the commissioners' court, an election for school trustees was held, and three trustees were duly elected, one of them being W. H. Hickox.

But where would the district find funds for a schoolhouse? Because Texas law in 1891 did not permit bonding of a school district, it was necessary to raise money by private donations. Hickox and the other trustees went forth to accomplish this. Large businesses in Panhandle, the county seat and market town, were heavy contributors. Lumberyards in Panhandle and Claude sold lumber to the district at a reduced cost. Callie Hickox, the oldest daughter of the family, remembered that at age fifteen she drove her father's wagon to haul lumber from Claude. The rest of the money was raised by local taxes, though much of the potentially taxable land in the district was "patented," or railroad, land, given to the railroad by the State of Texas for building track, and therefore exempt from local taxation.

On May 10, 1892, J. R. Blanton and his wife, Viola, deeded two acres of land out of their home section for a school site, but even before that date the young men and school patrons of the new district had been hard at work on the new school. At the same time, trustees searched for a teacher for the coming fall. Finally, the school was ready, and Lena Hickox Bishop penned this excellent description of her completed Lone Star School:

> It was 20 x 30 feet in size, three windows on either side, giving good light. With W. H. Hickox as head carpenter on the work, assisted by Tom Shield, the Lone Star School House was a well-built frame house with siding. It was painted white. The words "Lone" above a large star (the star encircled with red was painted in blue above the door). This was the name of the school.
> Viola Blanton had been given the honor of naming the school; she and Mr. Hickox working for hours to draw this five-point star perfectly before painting it. The windows were fitted with blinds. J. R. Hickox and J. L. Gray painted the building. A fence enclosed the yard. It was built of wooden boards with the one on top laid flat. Walking on the fence was a favorite pastime for pupils. Instead of a gate, there was a "stile"; this was four steps up across the fence. A tall swing was placed in the yard, and a cellar dug, for safety in case of storms, for cyclones were feared.
> The school room was equipped with large blackboards, teacher's table, modern desks for two, and a pot-bellied coal stove. Well-made benches were placed in the back of the room, and wall lamps with bright reflectors were placed so that the building could be used for church or other community purposes. It can be truthfully said that when the school in 1898 was moved, three miles west, to the N.W. corner of the Charlie Kight section, there was not a scratch on the desks, a broken pane of glass, not a board missing from the fence.
> In 1903, the school was moved to Conway and records I believe give it as Conway School although it was in the same district and still the same one-room building until 1912.[28]

Many schools across the state bore the proud name "Lone Star" during the long era of the rural common school districts, but this typical account may stand for the origins of many. When Hickox's school was moved a second time, its name was changed to that of the established community that would be its final home. That Hickox and his family had dreamed of beginning a new settlement was suggested by the action of his fourth daughter, the author of the story of their school, who wrote in her *McGuffey's Fourth Reader* in 1895, "Lena Hickox, Lone Star, Texas."[29]

4. Little Buildings
in the Tall Grass

🂱

ONE WAY to begin a discussion of the physical circumstances of
the country schools is to stand behind several teachers and see
the first day of school through their eyes. For most of these teachers, this was not only the first day of the school year, but the first
day of their professional careers.

My 42 thrilling years of school teaching began in 1920 in Wise County
as a primary teacher of the first four grades with 11 children ranging
in age from seven through fourteen years. The freshly-painted classroom had the following equipment: two brooms, a wood burning heater
(with a wood box for firewood and kindling), a small dipper. A row
of coat hooks was screwed on a board nailed across one wall, and there
was a long recitation bench besides the children's two-seat desks.[1]

On September 5, 1930, I walked up on the small porch of a one-room
school and nervously unlocked the door with a small skeleton key.
Oh, how extremely happy I was! I walked into the room, and there
I saw forty new desks arranged in five straight rows. I walked to the
front of the room, and there was a gorgeous new teacher's desk and
chair. Four windows on the east side and four on the west side—no
shades. On a shelf was a water cooler that would hold about two gallons
of water. A long-handled dipper was hung on a nail underneath the
water cooler for all the students to use. Back in the west corner was
a small closet that contained the year's supply of colored construction paper (approximately 24 sheets, large size), one dozen felt erasers
for the blackboard and a box or two of dustless chalk, one dictionary,
and a new pencil sharpener waiting for the teacher to mount. All my

students were Mexican Americans. I had the first grade through the fifth, no kindergarten.[2]

The new teacher's reaction to what she or he saw on this eventful first day depended on several things. The standard Texas country school was a simple frame structure of one to four rooms, built more or less in keeping with the construction standards of the rural farmhouse. If teachers came from the country themselves, they usually found new surprises. The school building would be clean or dirty, new or run down, but it almost always fell within a familiar range. However, if the school was ill maintained and if the new teacher came from town, as in the second account below, the teacher could be in for a shock!

> A half-mile south and I turned into the school ground. It was brown with dying grass and weeds left to stand since the end of school, red-brown at the back with falling leaves. The schoolhouse looked dusty and deserted. Clean up days would have to be set. I opened the un-locked door to the big room and went in. Nothing had changed in the years I had been away; five rows of single desks faced the blackboard, at the other end of the room a few double desks faced the black-jacketed stove. I went to a double desk and found the initials WAO I had carved years before. Then I tried the pump organ. It was wheezy from dirt daubers and dust but there was enough voice for an open-ing song. The floors had been cleaned and oiled with an oil that smelled of cedar shavings. There was nothing for me to do but open windows and put out chalk and erasers. The little room at the back, for pupils from the primer through the fourth grade, smelled of cedar and buzzed with wasps from a nest under the eaves. I knocked the nest down with a broom and left the door and windows open wide for the wasps to fly out. The water fountain, a varnished oak keg with a shiny nickel bubbler, stood on a rack near the cistern. Under the new school laws the zinc water bucket could no longer be used. I drew water and filled the keg. Then I searched the walls of the two outhouses at the edge of the woods for smut. Still alone, I sat on the front steps in a warm-ing sun.[3]
>
> The building, it was just one big room, and it was very, very poorly equipped. Sometimes the windowpanes were out. I remember once or twice nailing a piece of cardboard over the window to keep the cold wind out. The floors were not covered, and there were splinters, big splinters, in the floors. And no paint. It was unpainted. The walls was naked and bare. It was a horrible-looking sight, I'll be honest.
>
> And there was no equipment. The only thing in there that you could

49

use to work with was a blackboard and a couple of erasers, and maybe a little crayon. But everything else, you just had to kind of devise your own equipment. And there was no water there. We had to carry water from across some of the neighbors' places. The children would carry it in a bucket. They had a few textbooks they had brought us from the other [Anglo] school. They would give the other school the new books and give [us] the old, raggedy, nasty, dirty books! I talked about it so bad one day to Mr. Harris [the county superintendent]. I said, "If it were I, and in my power, I'd throw them back at them! I just wouldn't accept them! They don't give their children those kind of books." I said, "Why bring those old nasty, dirty, and tore-up ones over here?" But they were there when I went there. I guess they had already placed them in the building. Lytton had old-timey desks, some of the first desks ever made, by the looks of them. They were made double, you know, where two sat together.

Oh, snakes was terrible out there! There was holes and cracks in the building; I guess they came in through those. Several times we killed snakes in the building. I'll never forget, they had a little closet built on one side, just a closed-in corner for books. I was pulling some geographies out of the top and something slid over my hand. I said, "What was that?" It was a snake! And he slid off the book, over my head on the floor. And ooh, you talk about coming out of there! One little boy, he said, "Mrs. Byars, why didn't you whip that little old snake? I'm bigger than that snake and you just tore me up the other day."

I was scared of snakes. Every day they'd kill a rattlesnake around the building there, outside. They'd kill him, they'd start piling rocks on his head! [laughs] I remember this particular day, they'd killed one and made a fire and burned him, and I said, "What are you burning him for?" And they said, "Mrs. Byars, don't get on that side of him! If the wind blows smoke from him in your eyes, you'll go blind!" That snake had swallowed a rabbit whole.

I had a coal fire. Sometimes you froze, nearly, before you got the fire made and warmed up. I'll be honest. I was disappointed in what I saw there; I was let down.[4]

The difference between William A. Owens's reaction to his first school in Lamar County and Lula Byars's reaction to hers in Caldwell County (both in the 1920s) is in part explained by segregation and the different standards of maintenance for Anglo and black schools. Owens's Faulkner (Pin Hook) School was Anglo, and Byars's school was the black school of the Lytton Springs District, which was administered by Anglo trustees. If one reads the two accounts carefully, however, it can be seen that the physical cir-

cumstances may have been relatively similar; what is most different is the new teachers' responses to those circumstances. Owens
was a country boy who had once attended the Pin Hook School.
Byars was an Austin girl newly arrived in the countryside and accustomed to better things.

Sometimes, when the new teacher arrived at the school on the
first day, she found encouraging signs of an exemplary community support. Parents often arrived with their children to help put
the school building and grounds in order, often cleaning the schoolyard with hoes and rakes, paying special attention to the sharp
stems of the bitterweed, which, unless chopped off below the
ground, were stiff and sharp enough to pierce children's bare feet.[5]
At the Reeves School near Deadwood, first day tasks were to pull
up and chop the bitterweed, to "draw out" the school well to purify
its water, and to take up, trim, and reset the school flagpole.[6] Sometimes, as at a West Texas school described by Josephine Ballard,
the cleanup activities were even more ambitious:

> The first time I entered Dilworth Ranch school house was on Satur-
> day before the school term was to begin on Monday. As I approached
> the building I saw many people were already there. This was "Clean-
> up Day" for the school. It came each year just before the start of the
> new school term. At this time the entire community turned out to
> remove the dust and grime that had accumulated during the sum-
> mer. The yards were also cleaned at this time. The people brought
> buckets, brooms, rags, etc., and fell to work with vim, vigor and a lot
> of muscle power. Before the day was over the place was clean and shin-
> ing from floor to ceiling. This gave me an insight into the reason our
> county superintendent had said that a teacher would be lucky to get
> into that school. He added that it was one of the best common schools
> in the state. Not only was it a place where children were taught but
> it was an integral part of the community.[7]

The quality of the school building, grounds, and instructional
facilities all depended entirely upon the attitudes of parents and
other local people, as did the cleanliness of the building and its
state of repair. If many rural schools failed to measure up to the
standard of Dilworth Ranch, few were in the sad shape of Ragsdale School in Victoria County. The description below is from a
teacher who had been a country girl—used to a little honest dirt
and hardship, but not to buildings that had to be cleaned out with
a hoe!

Stone schoolhouse at Sisterdale. Courtesy University of Texas Institute of Texan Cultures.

My second school was Ragsdale, in the middle of a large blackland cotton farm in the southern part of Victoria County, Texas.

Saturday, before the opening of school, a little girl and I went down to the school to get it ready for Monday. It was the dirtiest place I had ever seen. She said, "Teacher, I'm ashamed for you to see this." She went home to get a hoe and bucket and cleaned the place up.

The men in the neighborhood would congregate in the building to play cards, drink, smoke, chew tobacco, and visit. There were daubs of black mud, cow manure, grass, and tobacco cuds on the floor. The men would spit on the walls and let it run down, spit on the floors, and through the ink wells in the desk. We raked the filth out and scrubbed it the best we could.

It took me months to get those men to quit spitting in the schoolhouse. I finally came to Victoria and got a sign "Fine to spit in School House." One of the men convinced the others that the law would make them pay a fine.[8]

Lest the reader be swayed too heavily by this atypical account, here is one final description of a very typical country school from southeast Texas a half century ago, this time remembered by a student who attended there for several years.

The schoolhouse, a board-and-batten structure, was built by an uncle who lent the land on which it stood. Some twenty by thirty feet, unceiled, it had only one door, on the south side, but there were nice light-emitting windows on the east and the west. Teacher's desk was centered up front, a pot-bellied, wood-burning stove occupied a place in the middle of the room, and a homemade table for the water bucket stood near the lone entrance. The cedar water bucket that graced the table sent forth a wonderfully pungent smell and cradled the dipper (sometimes enamel ware, sometimes cedar) from which we all drank, blissfully incognizant of the dangers of transmitting diseases.

School furniture was handmade by community fathers. Benches, some six feet long, were made to accommodate several bodies, and long, table-like affairs (wide boards, I think) were made to stand a bit in front of the benches where they served quite admirably as desk tops. A long shelf built beneath the desk top was for storage of books, pencils, tables and slates — we had no chalk boards.

Rows of these bench-desk combinations were arranged down each side of the room so as to leave an aisle down the center. The heavy furniture was strictly wiggle-proof — no matter how much pupils squirmed.

Accommodations for hats, bonnets and wraps were provided by large nails driven into the wall near the door; lunch pails, usually gallon syrup buckets with lids, were placed on the floor.[9]

The first school at Cat Spring. William E. A. Meinscher, copy courtesy University of Texas Institute of Texan Cultures.

According to the monumental *Report of the Adequacy of Texas Schools,* published in 1937, there were still 6,142 common school districts in Texas in the 1934–35 school year, as opposed to 1,011 independent school districts.[10] Of the Anglo common schools, 1,780 were still of the much-criticized one-teacher variety, representing 30 percent of the rural schools and enrolling 10 percent of rural Anglo students. A much higher proportion of black students attended one-room schools. Black one-room schools, 1,006 of them, represented 63 percent of all black common schools and enrolled 39 percent of all black rural pupils.[11] Clearly the forces of standardization and consolidation still had a long way to go in 1935.

Attending one of those black one-room schools in 1924 was Mrs. Wright. She reported that it was a very small (eight by ten feet) wooden shed with a table in the middle and no regular desks. The teacher and her eight students sat around a table in the middle of the little room, and all grades used the same books. Children went into the schoolyard to pick up sticks and pine cones to use in working out the processes of basic math.[12] Another black student described his East Texas one-room school this way:

> The schoolhouse was an old log building, just one room. It had one door and one window, and in the end was a big fireplace that was made out of sticks and mud, like the fireplaces in the houses we'd lived in. That's the kind of chimneys and fireplaces they used then. They called them "stick and cat" chimneys. They made a framework of sticks and daubed it good with balls of mud they called "cats."
>
> There was a blackboard at school, and in one corner the teacher had a barrel where he kept lots of switches of all sizes. He used big ones on the big kids and little ones on the little-uns. We didn't have no desks. We set on anything we could get. There was some benches. The boys set on one side of the room and the girls on the other. We put our dinner buckets down in one corner. There was an old wooden water bucket there, with a couple of gourds that we drunk out of.[13]

Particular counties, and particular common schools districts within counties, had a very high incidence of these one-room schools for blacks. Harrison County, in far northeast Texas, had no fewer than seventy-seven black schools, and fifty-one of these were one-teacher schools. Within the county many of the districts in this tenant-farming area around Caddo Lake had multiple black schools. The Grover District, for example, had a single Anglo two-room school to accompany six black one-teacher schools.[14] This probably was due to the tenant system and the large black population working the lands of absentee Anglo landlords, who lived in town.

School buildings other than wooden ones were very much the exception to the rule throughout Texas. In 1935, 81 percent of the Anglo schools and 99 percent of the black ones were of frame construction, with a few surviving hewn log structures included in both those figures. Most school structures were not particularly old – the 1935 survey found that almost 60 percent of the Anglo rural schools had been built within the previous fifteen years.[15]

The typical Texas rural school was a frame building of from one to four rooms. Many two-room schools had less than a solid wall between them. Sometimes the divider was a partition that

One-room frame school building at Nine, McCulloch County, ca. 1885. Wayne Spiller, copy courtesy University of Texas Institute of Texan Cultures.

pulled out from the side; sometimes it came down from above. Occasionally the partition between rooms was just a wagon sheet, as William Owens found when he visited the Faulkner Colored School in the 1920s. When he complained to the trustees about the inadequacy of this arrangement, they pointed out that the Anglo school at which Owens taught had had similar wagon sheet dividers until quite recently.[16]

Desks in almost all schools were arranged in rows from front to back. Sometimes the desks were homemade affairs, constructed by the parents. As time went by, more and more schools used factory-made desks that often accommodated two students, either side by side or back to back. Tops of the desks often had a pencil groove and a recessed inkwell, the latter figuring prominently in many a disciplinary incident.

A teacher's desk of some kind, and a teacher's chair, were normally at the front of the room, often on a raised stage or platform. That schools doubled as community centers is apparent in the details of their internal construction. The stage at the front lent itself to programs and entertainments of all kinds. The grander schools even had a curtain they could lower from the ceiling at the front of the stage, and salesmen went about convincing local trustees of the need for such curtains. Many of these, like the curtain at Lakeview School, in Swisher County, displayed prominent advertisements sponsored by city merchants from nearby Tulia, Dimmitt, and Nazareth.[17] When one considers that so many schools lacked instructional facilities, toilets, and similar necessities, the

First school building at the Alabama-Coushatta Indian reservation at Livingston. Mrs. E. S. Shill, copy courtesy University of Texas Institute of Texan Cultures.

First school in Crosbyton, built in 1908. Photograph by John D. McDermett, courtesy Pioneer Memorial Museum, Crosbyton.

fact that approximately 60 percent of Anglo rural schools and 40 percent of black schools had a piano on their stage indicates clearly the importance of the country school as an institution of community entertainment.[18]

Many two-room schools had a movable partition between the rooms, to facilitate community gatherings. Small schools with no room for overflow crowds often built special stages outside the building. For Christmas and end-of-school entertainments, the building served as "back stage" for large audiences seated on benches or on the ground. During the day, schools were illuminated by natural light that entered through rows of tall windows. Sometimes these were placed on both sides of the building, sometimes just on the east side, so that the light might come over the students' left shoulders, the direction deemed most appropriate by the professionals at the University of Texas and the State Board of Education. This meant that the fronts of many Texas schools were oriented to the south.[19] Schools often had supplemental lighting of some kind for gloomy winter days and (probably more important) to illuminate school entertainments and other community affairs held at night. Artificial lighting almost always was provided by kerosene lamps.

Often schools had a cloakroom, in which students could place their coats, hats, and lunches (which very often were carried to school in syrup buckets with lids). Sometimes the cloakroom function was filled by a series of nails along one back wall.

Teachers usually found that their schools received very little in the way of instructional materials. All schools would have some sort of blackboard, sometimes on the front wall and sometimes at the back, sometimes of real slate and sometimes of wide boards painted black. There were usually a few erasers, perhaps a metal locker for the school's meager library, and perhaps a map or globe. The teacher was expected to supply the rest of the instructional materials.

Somewhere in the room would be a water bucket, a keg with a bubbler, or some other similar arrangement. Water often was a problem for the rural schools. As late as 1935 only 6 percent of Anglo schools and 3 percent of black ones had running water.[20] In that year 64 percent of the Anglo schools and 76 percent of the black got their water from wells, while 29 percent of the Anglo schools and 21 percent of the black schools trapped their water in cisterns filled from the roof.[21] Despite inroads made by the germ theory of disease, 47 percent of Anglo schools and 91 percent of black were still using cups, often communal cups, from which to drink.[22] At O. T. Baker's school, in backwoods Shelby County, students and teacher drank right from the bucket.[23]

At Hall School, in Caldwell County, Frog Pond School, in Panola County, and many others, teachers and students had to carry their own water to school—a considerable burden for students who must walk (as did Hall students) up to five miles. One informant said that he and other Frog Pond students who found this too laborious often just drank from the nearby mudholes that had given the school its name.[24]

San Vicente School, Brewster County, ca. 1929. Ellen Quillan, University of Texas Institute of Texan Cultures.

At Holliday School, in Ochiltree County, in West Texas, parents at first took turns hauling water to the school in barrels, but range cattle were drawn to the barrel, often knocking it over and seriously threatening to "rub down the schoolhouse." This practice was abandoned, and students began to carry their own one-gallon water jugs.[25] At Armstrong School in Bell County, five different wells were drilled over the years, only one of which supplied any water. Cistern water at this location turned out to be bad, so for the last years of the school's history water was carried from a spring at Salado Creek, four hundred or five hundred yards away.[26] At Hubbard School, in Coryell County, water was obtained from the well of a nearby farm until that farmer sold out to another, who refused to allow the practice to continue. Then the school carried its water from a well fully three-quarters of a mile away. Eventually a well was drilled in the schoolyard.[27]

Obtaining the school's water was often among students' daily chores. At Rogers Ranch Mexican School, in Caldwell County, an expeditionary force of older boys regularly was sent to get water from the rainwater cistern at the Anglo school just up the road.[28] Doubtless at Rogers Ranch, as at the Prairie Lea School that Onita King attended, this was regarded as more of a privilege than a chore: "I remember, we had a tin bucket and a gourd dipper. We didn't have a well on the school premises, so the little boys would have to take the water bucket uptown – a block, across the street. They would go to the well and fill the water bucket and bring it

Interior, San Vicente School, Brewster County, ca. 1929. Ellen Quillan, University of Texas Institute of Texan Cultures.

back. She'd let two of them have the blessed privilege, and sometimes it took them a mighty long time to bring that bucket of water
up."[29] Here is Mildred Abshier's description of water-gathering ex-
peditions at her first school in southeast Texas more than fifty
years ago:

> In early day country schools water supply was a problem. It had
> to be carried, a bucketful at a time, from some home close to the school.
> Two older boys (never girls) fetched the water. To reduce spillage par-
> ticular tactics of transportation were adhered to. A stout stick was
> passed beneath the bail, the bucket of water anchored at mid-point,
> and carriers each grasped an end of the stick and trudged schoolward,
> seeking to keep the load in balance and to avoid sloshing, or outright
> upsetting of the vital contents. At times it took more than one trip
> to get an appreciable amount safely delivered at school—maybe ac-
> cidentally, maybe on purpose. Carrying water was one approved means
> of escaping the schoolroom, even if for a short time.
> Once the water arrived, everyone took turns getting a drink, all us-
> ing the community dipper except those fortunate enough to own one
> of those highly prized collapsible drinking cups. Passing these little
> cups around to be used by friends, no doubt, negated whatever health
> purpose they might have served. We did learn, however, to fold a sheet
> of paper to fashion a temporary drinking cup, and at times we made
> use of these.[30]

Even the matter of abolishing the communal dipper could lead
to trouble for the teacher. There was a strong "social leveling" im-
pulse in these rural Texas communities. If one was "better off," one
had better learn not to act that way! At one school in Bell County
a parent pressed for sanitary drinking facilities (in part because
one neighbor in the community had tuberculosis), and "another
patron was quite angry that other children thought they were too
good to share a dipper with her children."[31]

Like the wood stove, the water bucket often became the inno-
cent prop for mischief. At Williamson Branch School, in Bell
County, drinking water came from a spring under the creek bank
about five hundred yards from the school. Two boys were appointed
each week as "water monitors," who would make a trip to the spring
twice daily, each boy carrying a three-gallon bucket. One bucket
was for the teachers and girls, one for the boys, some of whom were
known to chew a little tobacco filched from their fathers. Once when

a certain boy got miffed at the teacher over some matter, he let it be known among the other boys that under no circumstances were they to drink from the girls' bucket that day: the water monitor had spat in it for revenge![32]

Given these water problems, it is no wonder that students whose schools had access to limitless pure drinking water remember this privilege with gratitude. Wanda DuBose recalled Grice School's excellent well, where boys pumped water into a big barrel with "one, two, three, four, five, six drinking spigots out at the side of the barrel,"[33] and Mildred Abshier remembers the wonderful water of her second school: "Hand operated pumps, the vehicles for getting the water to the surface, brought up great and bountiful gushes of wonderfully fresh water. Taking turns at the pump handle, we drank, one at a time, from the mouth of the pump, each stroke of the handle bringing up a rush of water that often spattered our faces as we drank."[34]

Another perennial problem of the country school was heating the building, something accomplished (or perhaps, not accomplished) in more than 98 percent of the schools by some sort of wood or coal stove.[35] Rural school buildings were designed to admit the maximum amount of light through oversized windows, which unfortunately also meant that the schools were often drafty and cold. As one teacher wrote, "The day we were to dismiss for the holidays everything was covered with ice. The big boys (one of whom I later married) went to the woods and brought back a large live oak tree, completely covered in ice, and set it up ready for our gifts. We decorated it, put on our gifts, in the afternoon took them off, and the icicles were still intact. The big jacketed woodburning stove hadn't furnished enough heat to thaw them — nor our feet."[36]

Earlier we noted how critical it was for the teacher to get to school in time to make a fire and warm the room before the students' arrival. In truly bad weather this was a grave responsibility indeed, because the teacher could never be certain that some children might not show up at the school regardless of the weather. As one teacher said, "It was somewhat exhilarating to arise early in the morning, get a substantial breakfast prepared on a wood stove, walk a mile to school and get a good fire going in the big pot bellied heater before any children arrived with cold feet, fingers, and noses."[37] If teachers sometimes felt that they did nothing but start wood stoves at home and school, this is no wonder. Because just starting the school stove was not enough—the expectation was that she would have the room *warm* when the children arrived —the teacher usually had to get to school about an hour early. In the winter this meant getting there in the dark. One Bell County teacher remembered this experience—getting to school in the pitch dark, lighting the front door with her car headlights so she could see to get in, putting a match to the kerosene lantern, reaching into the dark wood box for a first piece of wood, and on at least one occasion pulling out a snake! Thereafter, this teacher carried her lantern into the "kindling room" and carefully inspected every piece of wood before picking it up.[38]

After the stove was lit, the teacher usually could depend on designated students to keep it going. All rural teachers were their own janitors, dealing with wood and water and normal cleaning and maintenance, but they were expected to assign students to help them with these necessary tasks. Teachers seldom complained about the janitorial aspect of their role in the rural school, but there were exceptions, as this story from Cottonwood School, in Brown County, illustrates.

> Janitorial work, such as sweeping the floor, checking the water supply in the large tin storage tank, closing the windows, and locking up for the day was done by "teacher" before going home. The winter months brought added duties, because a fire had to be started each morning and kept going during the day. After school the ashes had to be carried out and the wood-box filled with wood for the next day. (I complained about this only one time. That was when the trustee, who had a key to the building, took his wolf-hunting friends into the building, burned all the wood, and spit tobacco juice on the floor as they sat around the stove waiting for their hounds to get "on the trail.")[39]

Wood stoves needed constant supervision. Many a rural school burned to the ground because of them, either by a fire started during the school day or else by hunters, drinkers, or others who frequented the building after dark. Many rural children got the terrible and wonderful news, "The school has burned."

64

One school in windswept Parker County tried to increase the heating efficiency of its stove by running the stovepipe horizontally the entire length of the building before it exited the roof. The pipe itself gave off considerable heat, but it was suspended from the ceiling with baling wire, and the sections sometimes came apart, releasing clouds of soot and smoke into the room and driving teacher and students outside.[40] Opossums and other nocturnal animals sometimes got into the flue of the stove. One morning when a teacher at Holub School, in Victoria County, reached her classroom she found one of the older boys preparing to start the fire, but this morning "the fire wouldn't burn and the room was filled with smoke. One of the larger boys . . . took off a grate from the chimney and pulled out the largest live owl that I had ever seen. That was the second morning wasted."[41]

Even in warmer seasons, the wood stove drew the wrath of God. During an April thunderstorm one school's stove flue was struck by lightning, which "traveled down the pipe and seemed to fill the room with a flash of fire. Ashes from the heater were scattered over the room and two children were slightly injured."[42]

Although the operation of the stove was the teacher's responsibility, fuel in the form of wood or coal normally was provided by the school trustees or the parents on a turn-by-turn basis, or else was purchased by the school district. In any case it was expected that the wood should be there for the teacher to use. Normally it was supplied ready to burn, but some trustees and patrons hauled it to the school in pole lengths and issued the teacher an ax for it to be cut into stove wood by the older boys. On other, perhaps not-so-rare, occasions, when school patrons failed to provide adequate firewood, or the winter turned out to be unusually cold and wet, students and teacher had to improvise to keep their schoolroom warm. At Little River School boys walked the railroad tracks to pick up coal that had fallen off the coal cars. Goober Hill students, in Shelby County, fanned out into the surrounding woods to gather fuel for their fire.[43] Around 1918, when Taylor School, in Swisher County, ran entirely out of coal, the teacher declared an emergency holiday, one boy brought the family wagon to school, and all hands spent an entire school day picking up the only available fuel—cow chips.[44] During the 1929 school year Red Ranger

65

School, in Bell County, ran out of wood, the Bell County roads were too muddy to transport more, and in desperation the trustees cut down the school yard shade trees to burn the green wood.[45]

Even when fuel was plentiful, the wood stove could cause problems, often of a disciplinary nature. This last wood-stove incident may have been an act of God or, with a little assist from gunpowder, an act of man.

> When we got to school our first job was to see that the fire was built. . . . Our school yard was covered with big, tall broom weeds. They made a good fire. Each afternoon before school dismissed, in order to keep some of the larger boys out of mischief, we let them go out and gather some of the weeds and kindling to start the fire with. So they filled the stove each day with these broom weeds and kindling. . . . The next morning all we had to do was light it. Well, one morning, I don't know whether it was a joke, but anyway they put too many weeds in the stove. I got down on my knees to light it, and when it lighted the whole door just blew open and all this black got all over me. There I was, two miles from home and all the water there was in the school was in the water bucket. Well, I had to stay at school. I don't think we had much school that day.[46]

The need for adequate toilet facilities was a final problem of the physical circumstances of the rural Texas school, though at a surprising number of schools this was solved in the simplest manner possible. About 4 percent of the Anglo schools and 0.3 percent of the black were blessed with flushing toilets, 84 percent of the Anglo schools and 62 percent of the black schools had pit toilets and outhouses, and 12 percent of the Anglo and 38 percent of the black had no toilet facilities whatsoever.[47] In other words, as late as 1935, some 1,219 schools across the state sent their students out to what one approving trustee referred to as "the bresh."

At Buckner School, in Parker County, the toilet was euphemistically referred to as the "going outdoors place." This was under the nearby creek bluff, the boys going east and the girls west.[48] At Pleasant Grove School, in Mills County, the boys went north and the girls south.[49] At Josephine Ballard's Hubbard School, Coryell County, "There were no toilets of any kind. The schoolground was partially heavily wooded with cedar. The grounds were divided (by an imaginary line) into two parts. One side was the girls'

66

East Gansel School, McCulloch County. The outhouse can be seen to the right of the school building. Wayne Spiller, copy courtesy University of Texas Institute of Texan Cultures.

and the other side the boys'. The privacy of the thick cedars was our toilets for many years."[50] At Tabernacle School, in Shelby County, the building was surrounded by deep East Texas woods. Here, a boys-south, girls-north rule prevailed. When a girl left the school in rainy weather, it was standard practice that she should be accompanied by another girl to hold an umbrella over her while she accomplished her business. Boys were not thought to need this service and went to their section of the woods alone.[51]

Pit toilets — also called "johnnies," "biffies," "outhouses," "privies" — were the common pattern. These were small, rough frame structures with shallow pits below. Many rural schools made do with "one-holers," but some had "three-holers" or even "four-holers." Hanging on the wall of many outhouses was a dog-eared and extremely obsolete issue of the "Monkey Ward" or Sears Roebuck catalog whose pages served as toilet paper.

Some schools lacked a full set of these outhouses. At Mount High, in East Texas, there was only one privy, and girls and boys would alternate days for going first. Goober Hill also had just one outhouse, located behind the school at the bottom of the hill by the spring from which the school got its drinking water. Boys and girls had to take turns going. At Sardis there was a small privy for the girls, but stoic males used a patch of woods next to the stream.[52] According to O. T. Baker, in Shelby County toilets were considered to be for girls and townsmen, and no self-respecting male would use one.[53] Gradually these attitudes changed, and rural school toilet facilities improved. The same Works Progress Administration that funded the Texas School Adequacy Study to count school toilets also funded their improvement, and many new concrete WPA toilets were built at rural schools in northeast Texas in the 1930s. Some students initially resisted using them. Younger children, for example, found them so deep they were at first afraid to approach them lest they fall in.[54]

The outdoor pit toilets were a formal part of the rural school teacher's domain, and she was expected to keep them up. Toilets were inspected every day or so, and lime added to the pit perhaps once a week. As did William Owens on his first day at Pin Hook School, the teachers often checked the walls for graffiti and sniffed the air nearby for the telltale odor of tobacco. Outdoor toilets also attracted "varmints" of all kinds, and as part of her daily preschool round the teacher at Cottonwood School, in Brown County, "checked the outdoor toilets for black widow spiders, lizards, and snakes, then waited for the students to arrive."[55] Sometimes, as in this story from Little Arizona School, in King County, the varmints got completely out of hand.

> To make matters worse, rattlesnakes discovered that these toilet facilities were good places to hibernate in during the winter. There must have been dozens or even hundreds of them bedded down under the floors of those toilets. The boys often amused themselves during recess periods by beating on the toilet floor with stones or poking sticks underneath the floor to further annoy the snakes. Oh, the rattling! The hissing that followed! Sometimes the snakes left their place of hibernation to be chased out and started across the campus by the boys, and many were slaughtered before they could escape the sticks or stones. I remember on one occasion when a huge diamondback came out and started toward me. I thought the end of everything was near, and I was ill for the rest of the day because of fright and running

to try to avoid those venomous fangs for which the diamondback is noted. What a coward I was! The boys were afraid of nothing! How those youngsters escaped being bitten was more than I could figure out.[56]

Many a wayward snake was discovered in many a schoolyard outhouse in the long history of Texas rural education. The attraction of the outhouse for snakes and other vermin was just one of the reasons that country people were not all of one opinion about the need for outdoor privies. Some families preferred to use the porcelain basins (or "thunderpots") by night and the woods around their farmsteads by day. Some even argued that this practice was more sanitary. When this conservative opinion predominated on the district board of trustees, a school might go a long time without getting outdoor toilets. One first-year teacher from the town was appalled when she arrived at her rural school and found no toilet facilities.

> I made up my mind right then and there that when, if ever trustees met, I was going to ask for closets (in the vernacular of the day).
> The Board met in January, three and one-half months after school had begun. I was invited to attend. My father took me to the schoolhouse that night. He waited outside in the buggy. I had told him that I was going to get toilets for those pupils one way or another. He was too embarrassed to go inside knowing how bullheaded I could be when I wanted something. Perhaps he didn't want to see me disappointed.
> Sure enough, the Board said all the nice things they usually do to one's face. They got around to asking me if I'd come back next year at the same salary—$50. Now, I thought, this is the time! I have a dismal description of those poor children coming back into the room after a trip to the brush on those cold, rainy days, shivering, their clothes half "buttoned up," sometimes wet from not making it in time. Then I explained how terrible I thought it was for those big boys to peep through the brush at the girls if for no other reason than to tease them. I asked for "closets." If we couldn't have two, could we at least have one for the girls?

There was a long silence in which each trustee waited for the others to speak, chewing tobacco and soberly regarding the young teacher. Finally, one man spoke for all: "Nope, not as long as all that 'bresh' is out t'are."[57] The brush served as toilet facility for a significant number of Texas country schools right to the end.

5. Reading, Spelling, and Ciphering

🛡

Wʜᴇɴ ᴛᴇᴀᴄʜᴇʀ ᴡɪʟʟɪᴀᴍ ᴏᴡᴇɴs set out for his first teaching assignment at Pin Hook School, he wasted no time in purchasing the "two essentials for a country school teacher, a watch for keeping time and a bell to call the pupils to books."[1] Certainly he needed the watch: Rural schools, with their multiple grades and many required subjects, were a scheduling nightmare. It was a rare teacher who made do with such minimal cues to the time of day as did the teacher of St. James School, near Marshall, in 1917: School began with the ringing of the church bell in the St. James Baptist Church and dismissed when the Texas and Pacific shop whistle blew.[2]

After the teacher stood in the door and rang the school bell, students assembled in lines outside the building and waited until they were told to enter. Mildred Abshier described the general scheduling of the school day and the procedures thousands of teachers used, with minor variation, for assembling and dismissing class:

> Country schools were conducted on a strict schedule, and discipline and orderliness were required. Hours were from nine to four; "dinner time" was a one hour break, cut short by a ten minute bell warning all to get a drink and go to the toilet – if need be; midmorning and midafternoon recesses were of fifteen minutes duration. When entering or leaving the schoolroom as a group, pupils lined up and marched in and out.

70

At nine o'clock when school "took up" and when dinner and recess periods were over, the teacher rang the bell (a little one with a handle), and pupils formed two lines outside the building, facing the door and in the order in which they would reach their seats. Once lined up, quiet and attentive, the teacher gave the order, "Pass." We marched in, in order nonetheless, and stood by our seats until we heard from the teacher, "You may be seated."

When school was out at four o'clock and when time arrived for dinner and recesses, the procedure was reversed. First came the order, "Put away your books." With desks cleared and all at attention, we were directed, "Rise." In response, all rose and stood quietly, awaiting the instruction, "Pass." This was the cue to march outside, in orderly lines, turn and face the teacher who stood in the doorway. Some teachers would not allow pupils to turn and face until the order, "Face," was given. Last would come the magic word, "Dismissed." Relative freedom reigned outside, but inside the story was quite different.[3]

Anita McLean was the teacher for this school at Castell, ca. 1915. Anita McLean, copy courtesy University of Texas Institute of Texan Cultures.

Once properly seated, the teacher customarily took the class through some sort of opening ceremony: the singing of a few songs, the reading of a Bible verse or a prayer, the Pledge of Allegiance or some other patriotic activity. Perhaps the most common opening activity involved the singing of hymns or popular songs. One former student from Bell County remembered singing "those lovely old songs: 'When You and I Were Young, Maggie,' 'Little Brown Church in the Wildwood,' 'America,' 'The Eyes of Texas,' and others."[4] Some rare schools like Lone Star School, in Carson County, had their own school songs. The Lone Star School song had been penned by an outstanding early teacher in the 1890s, "Professor" Role S. Gregory, and began (to the tune of "My Pretty Quadroon") with the following lines:

Oh, who are as happy as we
In our Lone Star School-house on the plain
So happy light-hearted and free
I wish we could always remain.
Our school room is pleasant and light
When the air is not filled full of dust
From the field of our patron, Mr. Kight,
As it is when the wind blows a gust.
CHORUS
Oh, our pleasant school room
Its pleasures will fade out all too soon
And our hearts will be broken in twain
With a sigh for our pleasant school room.[5]

After the opening exercises were completed, class instruction began, and for most teachers in Texas rural schools the first two subjects were reading and math. Very commonly, after all the grades had received a reading and math lesson, the teacher let her class take a brief, fifteen-minute recess, and then reconvened them for spelling instruction before lunch. A one-hour lunch period divided the morning and afternoon sessions. The afternoons generally were confined to a repetition of reading and arithmetic for the younger pupils, and instruction in history, geography, physiology, and nature study for the older ones. A second fifteen-minute recess often punctuated the afternoon session. In the following account, a teacher outlined her typical daily schedule:

We began with opening exercises, and we had the same schedule every day. Every child knew which class was going to be first. I always wrote the assignments on the board. I found that reading was the class I liked to have first, because they were quieter and they were not exhausted from running and playing. You could get their attention. Math, you could have board work. There could be a little activity, and it would be a rest after they'd been seated. I usually had spelling just before lunch. Morning recess? It was much easier to let them have a fifteen-minute recess than to let them go one at a time to the "john," as they called it. After lunch I varied the schedule. Lots of times we'd have reading. They'd be tired, and they were glad to sit and read. Often when I did that I had "nature study" right after lunch. I had some little old books about nature, things in the community. A lot of times on Friday we stayed in the room in the afternoon and sang and played games.[6]

Unquestionably the most important subject in the rural curriculum was reading. In the perception of virtually every rural teacher, reading was the premier academic accomplishment of rural pupils. While teachers allotted a recitation period to other basic subjects on a daily basis, reading often was taught twice daily and sometimes three times. The importance of reading in the rural classroom was likely heightened by the large amount of independent study in which rural pupils were engaged.

The procedure for conducting a reading recitation was typical of instruction in all subjects in the rural school. Usually there was a recitation bench near the front of the room, and the particular grade level designated to receive instruction joined the teacher there for the lesson. Some teachers seated the pupils about the room by grade level and simply moved into the appropriate areas to give them instruction.

There was no predominant method among rural teachers for the teaching of reading. The tendency was to teach reading in the same way that their own parents and teachers had taught them — by sight. Teachers often described their method as "no method," but most of their procedures contained elements of phonics and word families, as well as sight. "Yes, I used phonics. I used flashcards. I used the book. We'd just sit down and talk about it and read it together, work out words and letter sounds. I taught short 'a' and long 'o' type sounds, sure, but I didn't emphasize it. If they

73

asked, 'Why do we say that?' I just explained to them in some words they'd understand. I don't claim to be an expert in teaching reading, but they learned how to read, so I guess it was all right."[7]

Arithmetic was second in importance. In the lower grades the math curriculum was basically the four operations of whole numbers, while the operations of fractions, decimals, and percentage were taught in the upper elementary grades. A large portion of instruction was presented at the knowledge level. Much of the arithmetic instruction was drill work, performed by the students in a variety of ways. "We had to memorize the multiplication tables, but I showed they why – why we say four times four is sixteen. I'd put it down and add it up and show 'em. I did it to let them know it was the short way to say it – made it easier. Just to memorize three times eight is twenty-four, well that's just blind to them. Oh, you've got to have some memory. I wish I had a little more right now."[8]

Spelling was a daily feature of the rural schools and was held in high esteem by the community as a valuable skill denoting an educated person. Spelling was also a skill important to the reputation of the country schoolteacher, as noted humorously by Emma Shirley. "Woe unto the teacher in the older days who couldn't spell down everybody in the country. If she couldn't she had to be plumb across the country to get a school for the next year. I had a friend who missed 'hypostasy' (she spelled it with a 'c') after she had been standing spelling for four hours, and the next time I heard from her she was teaching in Oklahoma."[9] Myra Blount taught spelling in her classes as follows:

> When it came to spelling time, I'd lay my fourth-grade speller here [on the desk], and my fifth-grade speller here, and my sixth-grade speller here. They each had a spelling pad. And I'd give them words for the fourth grade and words for the fifth grade and words for the sixth grade until I gave them twenty words. I made them learn those twenty words if I could. On Monday I gave them the words. Tuesday we worked with the words – made sentences, learned the definitions, and all that kind of stuff. Wednesday we spelled the words for the first time. They wrote the words. Most of the time I didn't check them, but I let a real smart child in the sixth grade check them. Then on Thursday I let them fill in blanks. That's where the board came into use. I'd put sentences on the board and they'd have to copy and fill in with a word from their spelling.[10]

Mildred Abshier remembered that her teacher in a southeast Texas school ran every spelling lesson in the manner of the "spelling bee":

> For spelling lessons, a class came up front and stood in a line near the teacher. Each pupil spelled (or spelled at) the particular word pronounced for him by the teacher. If a word was missed, the next fellow in line got a chance to spell it. When spelled correctly, the successful speller "turned down" the one who missed – that is, stepped ahead of him in the line. Best spellers always were close to the head of the line; those who had great difficulty with spelling often heard, but never relished, the order, "Go to the foot of the class."[11]

History and geography were regular subjects in the curriculum in the upper elementary grades, but neither was taught every day by most teachers interviewed. Both subjects appear to have been learned almost entirely as a result of reading, since few teachers recalled any other activity associated with classes in either history or geography. Nor were music or art reported as regular activities by most former country teachers. The activities were peripheral to schooling – music, for example, was part of the opening exercises each day, and both music and art were associated with programs performed by pupils for community entertainment. The lack of training in these subjects and of equipment and supplies kept most teachers from doing much in these curriculum areas.

The study of science in the early rural schools was the study of nature or of personal health, grooming, and hygiene and was more of a special event than a regular subject. Much depended on the individual teacher's innovative tendencies and grasp of the subject. Certainly some teachers were more willing and able than others to seize opportunities that came their way:

> She [the teacher] would sit in the sunshine and she'd pick a hair from her head and say, "Watch the sunlight catch on that hair," and she'd drop it, and she would talk about what made that hair shine.
> In the spring of the year a little wren came in through a broken window and started building a nest. And I want you to know that we had the best nature study, because everybody watched that wren. It was in the back of the room and if she'd see the wren doing something that she thought we ought to see [she'd tell us to watch]. . . . And we sat for an hour watching that silly little wren trying to get a straw that long through a hole this big. Finally, it made it. The eggs hatched, and there were little fledglings. When the birds got ready

An agriculture class judging capons at Sayers Rural High School, 1925. Courtesy East Central Historical Group, East Central ISD, Bexar County. Leslie Ferrill.

to come out of the nest she told us we were going to have to leave the doors open and let the little birds fly out. They couldn't grow in a school building.

When the birds started to fly, we came to school and a blue jay had gotten in and killed every one of those little birds. He had a great big drop of blood on his beak. So that called for another lesson. We watched the blue jay and we had to do some study on blue jays. Blue jays survive by eating other things. All nature survives by eating something else. The good Lord planned it that way, and further, we were made to get the scriptures and read it. It was unfortunate that our little wrens got eaten, but it did mean survival for the blue jay. Everything she did brought something else in. To heck with books![12]

Field trips were as close as the school door, but teachers had to be careful that they did not do anything that would disturb school trustees, patrons, and parents who took the conservative line that school was for books and books alone. An early teacher at Lone Star School, in Carson County, led his students in "woods botany" lessons out on the surrounding prairie and had them hold hands in circles while he passed a harmless electric current through their linked bodies to demonstrate the powers of electricity.[13] At a much later date, Grace Roberts, of Peach School, in Upshur County, crammed eight students into her car and took them on

76

Sayers School students maintaining their own garden, ca. 1915. Courtesy East Central Historical Group, East Central ISD, Bexar County.

trips to Winsboro to observe the making of cheese and to Grand Saline to see the mining of salt. At other times, as one of Miss Grace's former students told, "We'd just go out and observe nature. When the flowers were blooming she'd take the whole school out. We'd go down to a spring, or go down in the woods or at the back of the school."[14]

Sometimes field trips were entirely recreational in nature, as this black teacher from Caldwell County described: "When we were at Lytton Springs, we'd take a stroll sometimes on Friday evening down here to Stringtown. We didn't all [the] time have a program. Sometimes we'd take a stroll in the woods. And we'd come way over here to a cemetery, walk through that cemetery and read on those stones. Then sometimes we'd take a little lunch and go in the woods and have weiners and broil them on a stick to eat, pop popcorn, and all that. On Friday afternoon we had good woods strolling at Stringtown."[15]

Teachers were expected to buy, borrow, and improvise their own instructional materials. This was not regarded as a hardship by the school trustees, but simply as one of the requirements of the job. Schools usually provided only chalk and erasers for the blackboard, perhaps some construction paper and other odds and ends, and usually a few books for the school "library." Teacher Weldon Hutcheson said, "Actually, you didn't have what you call a library. You just had a shelf over here with a few books, and that was it."[16] Sometimes there were even problems with the basic equipment the school was expected to supply, and this was especially true in the early days. The school Mrs. Frankie Franks attended "didn't have nothing but an eraser and crayon, and half the the time one of those erasers had worn out. We would stuff a little thing about that size with cotton and sew it . . . and erase the board with it. And our board wasn't solid—it was lapboard, tongue-and-groove, and it was painted black. 'Black board,' that's where it got the name, I guess. And you never had enough erasers to go around for a class of ten or twelve children."[17]

In the pioneer schools of nineteenth-century Texas, children used as textbooks anything they had in the house, and teachers were accustomed to dealing with a wide assortment of reading material with which to offer basic instruction. A perennial favorite, of course, was the King James version of the Bible.[18] By 1913, textbooks were available in community drugstores, but first-time teachers, such as Warren Travis White, still had problems: "The first day of school five beginning children showed up. I said to them, 'Tell your papa to get you a first reader.' They asked where; I said at the drug store. Soon they all had books, but each child had a different kind of first reader. That did not bother me: I invented *individual instruction.*"[19]

Every county-seat town had at least one drugstore or dry-goods store that supplied county schoolchildren with the commonly used textbooks. In Guthrie, John Gibson, long-time school district trustee and general store owner, kept a supply of schoolbooks in his store to service the needs of rural schools in King County. Here, as everywhere else in Texas, books were passed down from older children to younger in families and neighborhoods until the books fell entirely to pieces.[20]

The state began to issue free textbooks through the county superintendents' offices in 1919, and this was a great boon to the rural schools and their beleaguered teachers. Now at least textbooks were uniform. School districts used their state textbooks very hard indeed, but after the Anglo schools had used and abused the texts to a certain point, it was a common practice to deliver them for the use of the districts' black or Mexican schools. As Pauline Walker Underwood noted, "The Negroes had their own, so-called separate-but-equal schools, but what a farce they were. Even in those town schools I knew our torn, dog-eared, worn-out old text-books, which were supposed to be put in gunny sacks and returned to Austin each time we received brand-new textbooks, instead, they were hauled over to the Negro school as being plenty good enough for them to use."[21] The reader will recall Lula Byars's passionate protest to county superintendent R. E. Harris over the "old, rag-gedy, nasty dirty books" the trustees had brought over for her use from the Anglo school of Lytton Springs, Caldwell County. It is pleasant to report that Harris soon initiated a policy of new books for all black schools in the county, thus capturing the permanent goodwill of the teachers.[22] Unfortunately, the practice of deliver-ing worn-out books to minority classrooms was common across the state.

Beyond textbooks and building supplies, instructional aids were the responsibility of the teacher, who gradually accumulated a "teacher's trunk" of these aids. As Mrs. J. H. Anderson of Lu-ling told us, "As the years went on I bought globes and maps and things of my own, but for the first few schools I taught we had nothing at school. I had a whole trunkful of things as the years went on. It was my own, and I'd bought it with my money, you see, and I'd just take some of it from one school to the next. I had a globe, I had some books, and I had some workbooks of my own."[23] The average country teacher's salary was insufficient for buying many things, so teachers improvised, borrowed, and scrounged for classroom materials. "I read to them a lot, and I encouraged them to read. I brought books for different sources. I carried magazines to school. Children liked that in those days; they were hungry for anything to read. Just a catalog, a Sears catalog, was a treat, you know. I've always read a lot, subscribed to a lot of magazines, and I scrounged for magazines everywhere."[24] The experienced coun-try schoolteacher had her eyes open for possibilities all the time, as Mrs. Joe B. Coopwood told us: "You'd watch out for all the old

79

magazines you could get – all the old pictures. If the grocery stores had a big ad about something, you would say, 'Would you please save me this mural so I may take it out to the school?' You just collected everything you thought would be possible to give them some activity. And you'd collect all summer. I had a basement of things when I quit teaching, because I was so scared I'd need it for my children."[25]

A wonderful photograph of teacher Alva Stone's Gloria School, in rural Lamar County, hung in the county superintendent's office in Paris for decades and impressively demonstrates the end results of one teacher's inspired improvisation of instructional materials. In the photo, this otherwise plain one-room school is graced with paper birds hanging from the ceiling and several large permanent displays of the Lord's Prayer, the Ten Commandments, the Pledge

The display in Alva Stone's classroom at Gloria Rural School, Lamar County, 1937. Courtesy James H. Conrad, East Texas State University.

of Allegiance, and the Spanish words for one through five. To the left side of the schoolroom is an aquarium built from the window of a Model T Ford, and a sandbox with oats growing in it. In the foreground is a display of the children's art.[26]

Teaching several grades in a self-contained classroom was a sort of instructional juggling act, so complicated that both teachers and students were at times hard pressed to tell how it was accomplished. When William Owens struggled to make out his class schedule on his first day at Pin Hook School, he reflected about how useless his hard-won normal school training at East Texas State University seemed to be. The college courses had been "taught by teachers who had never heard of Pin Hook. They were all town teachers, college teachers, who overlooked the fact that country teachers would have to teach four grades or more and make up lessons for any older boys and girls who might want to come back to school."[27] Like most rural teachers, Owens quickly fell back on the methods he remembered teachers using during his own days in country schools. To understand these folk methods of instruction is to understand much about the nature of the rural school, as well as to grasp some of the things that made it work surprisingly well.

Considering the state requirements for a seven-grade, one-room school, the task of the country teacher was truly daunting. Reading, spelling, language, penmanship, and arithmetic were to be taught every day for all seven grades, nature study for two grades, geography for four grades, and history and civics for three grades. This worked out to between fifty and sixty separate course preparations for each seven-hour school day – a staggering number of lesson plans by modern standards. As a general pattern the teacher dealt with a single class and subject for a brief period of five to fifteen minutes (depending upon how many grades she had) then moved on to the next highest grade in that subject. Hence, if a teacher adhered to the schedule required by the State Board of Education for the seven-grade school, she had more than fifty separate classes for which to prepare, a preparation that often included assigning textbook materials for the next day and grading yesterday's assignments.

The first requirement for managing this complicated scene was

81

a flexible schedule. Frankie Franks explained how she handled seven grades at Lytton Springs School:

> You had to make a schedule, and you made your schedule from nine o'clock to four. And in that you'd have to count your classes and see how many classes you're going to have and how much time you could give to this subject and how much time you could give to this other. That was your daily schedule, and you put it in your [teacher's] register when you got it finally made, one that would work. Every minute of your time was taken. It had to be flexible, because sometimes you would run into snares. In this class, maybe, you'd have to keep them a little long, and you'd run five minutes into this other class's schedule. I always had my arithmetic first, and my spelling came the last thing in the evening. I'd have my English and reading before twelve o'clock. You didn't have lesson plans in those days; you had a plan in your mind.[28]

Teachers varied in how closely they adhered to their own schedules. Mrs. J. H. Anderson believed she should "stick pretty well to that schedule, or else you'd feel that some of the children were being cheated." Lonie Brite took hers even more seriously: "There were so many minutes allotted to each lesson. I had each lesson prepared, even down to the correct spelling—the diacritical marking of words! But then, I had to take time to assign the next day's lesson. I never lost a minute from the time I entered the classroom until the four o'clock bell would ring."[29]

Small wonder that one of the first two things that William Owens purchased for his school was a pocket watch! *A Report of the Adequacy of Texas Schools,* the great statistical survey conducted in 1934–35, was seldom effusive, but it waxed almost rhapsodic about the electric clock as the wave of the educational future, observing that "the electric clock gives order and procedure to the school program. It might be stated that the electric clock is to the school what the storage battery is to the automobile." However, in 1935 only 9 percent of all Anglo country schools had this marvel, and there was only one electric clock in all the black rural schools of Texas.[30]

From the student's perspective, a day in a multigrade rural classroom was a series of face-to-face encounters with the teacher (during which the student "recited" on given subjects) and an equal number of long periods spent working at the desk, preparing for subsequent recitations. Sometimes the class that was "up" (for example, fifth grade) would go to the front of the classroom and take a seat on the "recitation bench," or sometimes the teacher would come to them. Frankie Franks suggested a certain evolutionary sequence in this:

> We went to the board and did our arithmetic on the board, long division or fractions or whatever it was. We did it on the board, and when that five or six got through, they'd sit down and the next six or seven would go and do their thing up at the board. They had a seat they called the recitation seat, a long bench, and everyone came up there and sat down on that seat. "So-and-so and so-and-so, go to the board; the first five here, go to the board. You take number one, you take number two, and work your problem." Long time ago we *stood* in class. I stood in class, too. When we got up to a recitation seat, we *sat* in class. Right![31]

The recitation bench had certain advantages for classroom surveillance. As Onita King told us of her first teacher at Prairie Lea School, in Caldwell County, "She stayed up at the front. And she had a long bench, kind of a picnic bench, up there. And she always stayed facing the class, the whole room. Here was this long bench in front, where you would come to recite, we'd call it. She was clever enough to keep her eyes focused on the whole group all the time."[32] Sometimes personal preferences or physical circumstances dictated an alternative to the recitation-bench strategy: "I had the grades sit together. My little kids sat up to the front, my little primer folks, and the first grade folks, and like that. I didn't have enough room, enough seats, to have a recitation bench, so I let them stay in their seats and taught them from their seats. I'd get up and come down to where they were."[33] A similar procedure was followed at the Enterprise School, near Center, where one beleaguered teacher taught eleven grades. Students were arranged by aisles, each grade having its own aisle, and the teacher moved from grade to grade, aisle to aisle.[34] When students were grouped by rows, the youngest were often seated by the windows so they would have the best light in which to work. Likewise, in the winter, they were often given the privileged place closest to the stove.[35]

The teacher either moved the grades to her while she taught each subject, or else she moved to them. She coped with this staggering number of classes by using four different strategies (strategies that tell us much about why the rural school functioned as well as it did): (1) combining grades for a single subject, (2) employing peer teaching, (3) encouraging "instructional spillover" from older grades to younger by allowing the latter to "listen in," and (4) relying on students' personal responsibility and parental support for an effective homework program.

Combining grades was a common practice. When Warren Travis White signed on in 1913 to teach Enterprise School for a six-month term at the excellent salary of ninety dollars a month, he found that he was to have eight grades and seven required subjects. "Now the perplexing problem of making a schedule of classes was taken to Mr. George J. Mason, my high school superintendent. Fifty-six classes were on the program. Mr. Mason took a drink of water, cleared his throat, and commented. 'Too many classes!' We were able to combine groups until we had only fourteen periods. One recess, each morning and each afternoon, with a dinner period long enough to play a game of 'town ball' constituted our recreation and free exercise."[36] More than thirty years later, at the Africa School, in Shelby County, the teacher was grouping several grades together on the basis of educational level, not just age. Twenty-five of twenty-six teachers surveyed in a recent oral-history study said they regularly used this practice.[37] Some subjects lent themselves more conveniently to combining grades. Teachers often combined grade levels for poetry and literature, and the shortage of supplementary readers often required that the teacher read aloud, sometimes in whole-class instruction. Discussion and questioning were carried out with groups of two or more grades. History and geography also were taught in combination, especially in the upper elementary grades. Here are two teachers' comments on the practice:

> How did I manage? Sometimes I'd combine. Say, I'd have the fourth-grade lesson one day and the fifth-grade lesson the next for both classes. We did that in reading, writing, and arithmetic.[38]

> I joined much of the reading — those who were capable after I saw them for a few days. I saw the levels they were reading on, or the levels their math was on. At first they all did math together on the chalkboard and let me see where they were. So it ended up with about grades

one through three having their reading lessons together and the fourth having the more advanced reading. Yes, it was ungraded. I might have a third grader reading first-grade material for at least a period of time.[39]

Whole-group instruction was a natural extension of this practice of combining grades. Oral reading (by the teacher) of narrative and poetry usually was a whole-group activity. Many contests devised by teachers for drill work necessitated the use of the whole class simply to have enough participants; the teacher matched the level of difficulty of each question with the capacity of the pupil to whom the question was directed. Classroom spelling bees and blackboard arithmetic games were commonly of this kind. Preparation for public programs and entertainments, always a whole-group activity, often superseded regular instruction. Pupils were engaged in decorating the room and in learning parts to deliver at the community gathering.

A second common strategy for coping with the multigraded classroom was the practice of having older pupils help younger ones. This "peer teaching" went on daily in most of the country schools. Rural teachers often stated that the rural school could not have worked without the use of peer teaching following recitation periods. The consensus was that the practice not only benefited the younger child receiving the help but also strengthened the learning and self-image of the older peer teacher. This practice of caring for younger peers was a part of the "hidden curriculum" of the country schools of Texas. Like the sharing of agricultural labor among the farming community and the Christian ethic of helping your neighbor, peer teaching was directly related to socialization, interdependence, and the building of a familylike atmosphere in the classroom. Children in rural schools could depend on their peers as resource persons and helpmates. Later, or perhaps even at the same time, they assumed the same responsibility for those coming after them. Peer teaching, an embodiment of the spirit of cooperation, was seen by rural teachers as an important element of schooling. In the following passages, several teachers tell how and why peer teaching worked:

> I don't believe any rural schoolteacher ever taught without help from the older students. That's the truth of it! I don't believe you could

handle that many grades without a cooperative effort from every-body.[40]

The kids in the sixth grade would teach the first grade how to read. They'd go sit by them in the desk and show them the words and how to say them. The boys would teach arithmetic. I had a whole lot of teacher helpers around when I was teaching in a one-room school. It would be accurate to say the children did lots of teaching.[41]

The older ones usually had to help the younger ones. If they got their own work and were making good enough grades, the older children always helped the small ones. I used them that way all the time when I taught. You see, in those days there wasn't any band, there wasn't any competitive games or anything extracurricular for them, you know. And when they'd get their own lessons they'd be bored if they didn't have something else to do. I think they really enjoyed helping the younger ones. Sometimes, when some younger child was having some learning difficulty, maybe even where the teacher didn't find it, an older child could. She [the teacher] needed the help, and anyone that had the time could give it to her.[42]

In Lonie Brite's class, in Caldwell County, a child who was doing seat work and needed help had only to raise a hand and an older student would move to assist. The teacher's permission was not required. "You'd be surprised how quietly these children could move around the schoolroom and do things, not ever causing any confusion. And R. E. Harris [the county superintendent] approved of that! Sometime a child could explain a problem in a different way than a teacher did, and it was a good learning experience for both children."[43] Teachers reported that the children's motivation to help others was very strong.

Sometime I'd let those children who were pretty good readers to help this child with his reading so that when he come to me he probably will be able to read just by repetition – you know, reading and reading and reading. They [the peer teachers] would try to imitate the teacher. I had children I couldn't, like, teach long division. So I said, "Well, I'm going to change this now. I'm going to let some of these children try it." And they did a pretty good job of it. The one that was doing it, he enjoyed it, and you know, all of them would want to do that, some of them that couldn't even do it. They's want to help this child when they couldn't even help themselves.[44]

A third strategy that country teachers used – or, perhaps more accurately, simply allowed to take place – was the natural process of "instructional spillover" from higher grades to lower, something that helped grease the wheels of overburdened education engines in the rural school. Since several levels of instruction (most of them "out loud") were going on in a single self-contained classroom, children who were interested or unusually advanced in a subject could listen to what was going on in higher grades and learn as much as they could. Conversely, students who were behind had a ready source of review. As a former Menard County student described this process, "It was an incentive to prepare your own lessons and homework so you could listen (eavesdrop, so to speak) as the higher grades recited about such fantastic subjects as Physical Geography, Beowulf, Plutarch, Thomas Paine, Algebra and Geometry."[45] According to Stella Murphree of Caldwell County, "A child over here is in the fourth grade, if someone over here in the seventh grade is studying something he's interested in, he's learning too. I learned that way. I listened to multiplication of fractions in the eighth grade when I was in the fourth or fifth grade, and I learned what they were doing. Children learn from other children; they learn so much from their peers and those above them."[46] Another teacher, Emma Ohlendorf, told us, "I was so eager for them to learn that I didn't mind if one in a lower grade would know something that one [in] the upper grade didn't know. And if he supplied it, I didn't mind him speaking up. Now, that is one of the advantages of having more than one grade in a room, because you can always listen and maybe pick up something. I know: When I started to school, there were seven grades, and whenever my work was finished, I loved to listen to the upper grades."[47]

With all these levels of instruction going on in the same room, the rural school created a complex learning environment that in part compensated for its relative poverty in teaching aids and other material props of instruction.

> At Lytton Springs I taught from the first to the seventh grade. That was everything and everybody. I had around forty-eight children, and I got around to everything every day. I always figured that a child learned more in those – I guess you call them self-contained classrooms – you know, where everybody's in there. This child in the fourth grade will learn what the fifth grade is getting, you see? If he's got a mind where he can keep up with his lesson and listen too. And so you could develop some pretty good students out of a school like that.[48]

Indeed you could, and there are numerous instances of children showing up at the start of school for their next grade and being promoted to the grade beyond because they already could read the books and do the work. When Marguerite Page reached the seventh grade in her rural classroom in northeast Texas, the teacher found that she had listened in with such effectiveness that she had already mastered the texts. She was passed immediately to the eighth grade.[49] In Central Texas another student who attended a country school through the tenth grade before going to town for high school reported that she scored the highest grade in the school on the tenth-grade accreditation test in U.S. history. "I had never done one assignment all year, other than to sit there and listen."[50]

Sometimes this process of listening in reached even beyond the school. James C. Daily attended Broom School, in the "sand hills" region of Shelby County. Because he had observed closely the school texts and homework assignments of two older brothers and one older sister, he could read the entire textbook used in this school by the time he first attended in 1917.[51]

Finally, effective home study and close parental support greatly enhanced the effectiveness of the country schools. In her student days at a one-room school in Falls County around 1912, Annie Jay Cane walked five miles home, did her evening chores — sometimes until as late as 8:00 P.M. — then lay on the floor to do her homework and study by light from a candle or a pine-knot torch.[52] Former teachers and students both affirm that rural students often spent a considerable amount of time doing homework, that their parents often helped, and that this helped compensate for the hectic scheduling in the rural classroom. Students were assigned homework to prepare for the recitations of the following day, and by and large they did it.

In most households parental support for home study was strong. Rural adults unquestionably had more influence on the conduct of the local common schools than do parents in today's larger, more bureaucratic independent school districts. Most rural parents in the early decades of the century had a personal acquaintance with the teachers of their children. The emerging technology of the twentieth century was slow to filter down to the rural schools. Consequently, the largely unchanging character of the curriculum and the routines of schooling gave parents a comfortable familiarity with their children's learning environments. The close-knit political structure of the community afforded parents quick and easy access to trustees and substantial influence in school affairs. The additional time invested by parents in encouraging home study was a logical and natural consequence of the closeness of these parent-school relationships and the home-oriented rural life-style of the day.

Rural teachers readily acknowledged the contribution of rural parents to the task of schooling. Bessie Sanders observed that when a child was slow or behind in a particular subject, parents would spend more time helping him or her at home, sitting around the fire and working as late as needed to get the task done.[53] Elsie Hamill described how her father helped her learn to read: "My father sat me up in his lap, took the book and opened it and read it, and then told me to read it. I don't know how we learned it. He just read it, and then I read it. It wouldn't surprise me if my students' parents did the same. In that day and time, the parents enjoyed reading those books to their children."[54]

Two other factors that contributed to the effectiveness of home study were the independence and self-discipline of rural pupils and the relatively few distracting influences in the average rural home. Before television, in the infancy of radio, the *McGuffey's Fourth Reader* could be the best show around.

The country school, with its long periods of seat work between recitations, forced rural students to direct their own learning and to concentrate in noisy and difficult circumstances. This stood them in good stead when they went home to study, as these two accounts indicate:

> The teachers and pupils soon learned that much of the work had to be done by the individual student. The teacher must be the guide and leader in classroom learning, but in common schools with more grades than one in a room, the pupil had to learn to work without constant teacher supervision. That is a big plus for these schools, as the very vital lesson of self-reliance is learned early and that makes all learning easier.[55]

> I think there are a lot of advantages where there is more than one grade in a classroom. And I think this thing of teachers saying they

can't teach where there is another interest group going on is the biggest piece of foolishness. It's like saying you can't study unless you get the room quiet. I never would have studied at home. There were nine of us children, and I was the second one from the bottom. If you think our household ever got quiet for anybody to study! . . . It is the craziest thing to indulge people to allow themselves to think they can't concentrate if there's other activities going on. That's perfectly foolish. As I look back now, [I think] we had a glorified system of supervised study – at home and when I taught in the rural schools. We were supervising the study, not so much hearing lessons.[56]

The rural students' capacity for self-reliance and concentration was one thing that helped them study at home, and another was the lack of competing sources of intellectual stimulation. Physical stimulation, however, was not hard to come by. Walter Neuenberg's experience must have been the common experience of many rural children after their trek from school to home in the evening: "I remember when I came home from school in the evening there was so much work to do. During that time my father was waiting for me in the field. We had wheat and oats. We pulled corn, hauled in the hay, and if the harvest was put up, I had to help Mother take care of the chickens. We had cattle, hogs, milked a bunch of cows, had our own butter, eggs and pork."[57] Is it any wonder that young Neuenberg was ready to escape to his schoolbooks and homework after chores were done? Sometimes the social facts most important to our understanding of a past society or system of education are so simple that they go unexpressed. But in the following passage Susie Bell Anderson expresses the inexpressible:

> In those days, they didn't have any TV. They didn't have any ball games to go to, or anything. They just went home and went to work. Changed their school clothes, hung them up behind the door, and went to work – feeding hogs or cattle or chickens – maybe even chopping cotton or picking cotton after school. Next morning they'd get up and take those clothes down from behind the door and put them on and go to school. Maybe they'd wear them a week like that. School was really a vacation to them, as much as anything else![58]

School and schoolbooks were an important source of amusement and often the only available refuge from the workaday world at home. Some students were even sorry when the school year ended. Weldon Hutcheson said, "Over here at Elm Grove I'd always check out the history books I would be studying through the next year and read them through the summer, because I wanted something to read."[59]

Those work-filled country summers could wear long, even with the aid and comfort of next year's "second reader." In this account the Reverend Charlie White captures more than a little of the feel and essence of the lost world of Texas rural education.

I was looking forward to the beginning of school. I was almost ten. This would be my fourth year. Of course, just having school four months a year, and not getting to go all the time at that, I didn't get along very fast. I could read a little now, and spell some, and add and subtract. I liked reading and spelling best, but I wanted to be good at arithmetic because I knowed if I could figure good couldn't nobody cheat me. I had been promoted to the second reader, and Mama was so proud of me she brought me a new book.

And that new book liked to a been the death of me. There was an old tree out behind our house, that the wind had blowed part way over, and you could walk up to it and set up among the top limbs, maybe ten or fifteen feet above the ground. Isabel and me set up there a lot and just talked, and sometimes she'd read to me. She could read better than me. She had older brothers and sisters that could read and sometimes they'd help her, and she got to go to school more than me because I had to stay out lots of times to help Mama.

Us children was all up in that old tree a lot. We'd always climb up there when Mama let us feed the hogs, so we could drop the corn down to them and they couldn't get at us. We had an old sow we called Wiley that was real cross, especially when she had pigs. We was all afraid of her. So we'd go up in the tree before we started calling the hogs. We'd call, "Pig, pig, pigooooo, pigooooooo. Pig, pig, pig, pigooooooo." We didn't feed them much. Just enough to keep them coming to the house, so if Mama wanted to kill one she could get close enough to it to knock it in the head. Mama wasn't afraid of Wiley, especially when she had an ax in her hands.

Well, one day Isabel and me was setting up in the tree, and she was reading to me out of my new second reader. Old Wiley had some little pigs, and her and them was nosing around down there under the tree, hoping to find something to eat, I suppose. I don't know how it happened, but Isabel dropped the book. The pigs come over and started to rooting the book around, and I couldn't stand that happening to my new reader, so I jumped down to get it. Old Wiley come a tearing at me when I jumped down among her pigs. And I guess she might of got me if Isabel hadn't broke off a piece of dead limb and throwed it and hit one of the pigs. When the pig squealed Wiley

The seventh-grade graduates of Adkins School. Courtesy East Central Historical Group, East Central ISD, Bexar County. Sadie F. Wade.

turned around to see what was wrong with it, and that gave me time to get up out of her reach. Isabel and me just set up there, breathing hard, and didn't say nothing for a while. But I had saved my book.[60]

The testimonies of former students and teachers in Texas country schools and the data gathered by the 1924 school survey attest to the general effectiveness of the schools in imparting the basic skills of reading, arithmetic, penmanship, and spelling. If a student managed to attend school with sufficient frequency, the strategies of instruction in the multigraded rural classroom would do their job. For many, however, that was a very big "if" indeed; thousands of the state's rural students, some of whom wanted very much to attend school, failed to do so regularly enough to learn to read, write, and cipher beyond the most minimal level. Seldom was this their fault, the fault of their parents, or the fault of the school districts; rather, it was an unavoidable consequence of the requirements of survival in a rural agricultural society. William Owens's family may serve as a case in point. A few days after Owens, the third son, was born, his father died. The family spent his growing-up years moving from tenant farm to tenant farm in rural northeast Texas. Owens's mother often chose one tenant situation over another if it had a good school nearby. She did heavy chores, such as plowing, to give her boys release time for school, and she scrimped and saved in every conceivable way, but very often the hard facts of life on a tenant farm kept her children out of school or took them out early. Attendance could not begin in the fall until after cotton picking was over, and planting the fields had to take precedence over the last of the spring school months. Owens's experiences typify those of many Texans in the 1920s and 1930s: "Linden was a good school, but soon after Christmas we were staying home again, cutting sprouts, burning brush, working at anything we could to get the land ready for planting. We had not stayed in school long enough to get promoted, or to get report cards, but that could not be helped. We were renting the land, and we had to make it pay more than the rent. All of us had to go to the field.[61] And again, at another school a year or so later: "All that day I packed into my head what I could, studying with the feeling that this was my last time to study. I had seen what had happened to Monroe and Dewey [Owens's brothers], now out of school, and was happening to Cleaver. They were not in school now. They would never be in school again. All the talk of school was lost because we had to work too hard to make a living."[62]

The workings of the rural schools were themselves adjusted to the rhythms of life in an agrarian society. In 1916 the State of Texas mandated a six-month school year, tied directly to the Compulsory School Attendance Law. By this law, "Every child who is eight years and not more than fourteen years old on September 1, 1917, will be required a minimum attendance of 100 days in the public schools."[63] However, neither the enforcement of the six-month school term for districts, nor compulsory attendance for children, was given serious consideration by state, county, or local authorities. Strict enforcement was an impossibility. The 1916 law

93

was more an institutionalization of ideals, or the legalization of a future goal of school reform. Considering school conditions in the 1920s and 1930s, compliance by the general public in sending their children to school would have created insurmountable problems. "Local school authorities frankly said that they did not have the buildings or the teaching staff necessary to care for all the children of compulsory school age. Therefore, they did not endeavor to enforce the act."[64]

Disregarding the educational laws, many rural districts ran school terms of only four to six months, with black and Mexican schools averaging on the low end of this range. Absenteeism for agricultural work was anticipated by all, and many a county superintendent counseled new teachers, "Now, don't worry if the boys aren't there at first. They'll be in class by Christmas." These teachers would find, as did one teacher in Bell County, that "after the first two months, with cotton-picking season over, my enrollment jumped from ten to eighteen, giving us more help with housekeeping chores, more players for the ball games, and more pupils in each grade."[65]

The rural schools were administered by farmers and ranchers to meet the needs of the sons and daughters of farmers and ranchers, and it is no wonder they were sympathetic to the rhythms of the agricultural year. At Callan School in the 1930s, "During harvest time it was not unusual for school to start early in the morning and turn out about 11:00 A.M. so the pupils could go home for lunch and then work in the fields all afternoon. Sometimes if the weather was just right for hog killing, school was suspended for the day and all hands fell to in rendering fat, grinding meat, stuffing sausage, and slicing thin strips of lean meat for jerky. The larger boys were let out from time to time to help with livestock work."[66]

Every common school district had its share of "scholastics" (in the state's nomenclature) who either never attended school, or did so only briefly or sporadically. However, it is impossible to study the memoirs, interview transcripts, and letters that form the primary sources for a history of Texas rural education and not be impressed by the lengths to which parents and their children would go so that the children could stay in school. Families such as William Owens's tried desperately to give their children the rudiments of a basic education. Charlie White's mother, also a widow, gave up her easy job as maid to a family in Shelbyville to "make a crop on the shares" so her children could start school in the fall. She bought their slates, pencils, and dinner buckets and carded, spun, knitted, and sewed school clothing.[67] Children in many families had to take turns going to school. A woman in northeast Texas, for example, told how she had to stay out of school until age ten to help her mother at home, during which time her mother tried to give her the rudiments of reading and writing. After attending school for several years, she had to quit to let her little sister go to school in her place. Beginning at that time she had to do heavy field work, including plowing and picking cotton.[68]

Families such as White's, right on the edge of subsistence, often had trouble obtaining the penny pencils, paper, crayons, Big Chief tablets, and schoolbooks they were expected to bring to school. Just how difficult this could become was indicated by one East Texas woman who told how her family was so poor it could afford only one pencil a month for five children. When her mother broke it into five pieces, there was always a scramble for the piece with the eraser. The children salvaged sacks from the garbage to use for writing paper, which they erased several times and reused. Lunch for this family was, without exception, corn bread and syrup.[69]

The end product of all these hardships, necessary periods of agricultural work away from school, and family persistence in the cause of education was a significant minority of much older children in many country schools who read and ciphered well below their chronological age but who stayed in school to get as much education as they could. A former student at Summers Mill School, in Bell County, put words in the mouth of some hypothetical old-timer from his school to this effect: "When I was promoted from the third to the fourth grade, it made me so nervous I could hardly shave."[70] Hinkle Schillengs remembered many older students at the Good Hope School that he attended. Young men of eighteen and twenty were not uncommon, and "I remember the guy who broke my nose with a wet baseball was twenty-three."[71]

Despite all the family's difficulties, William Owens was ultimately successful in finishing grade school and attending normal

School at Simmons, Live Oak County, 1909. Mrs. Bryant M. Collins, copy courtesy University of Texas Institute of Texan Cultures.

school to become a rural schoolteacher himself. Charlie White, however, was not so lucky, and his painful experience probably represents those of many rural Texans.

After that, when Mama sent us to church I'd stay under the clay root. I got to hiding my new second reader under my shirt and I'd study it while I waited for the others to come back. I was anxious for school to start so I could learn enough to read all the stories in it.

I practiced reading in the evenings, too. I'd put pine knots in the fireplace, to make it blaze up so I'd have light to see by. We didn't have no light except the fireplace. Mama sewed by light from the fireplace. Sometime I'd write words in the ashes with a stick, like "cat," or "dog," or "house," and try to teach Mama to read a little. . . .

School started out real good. The teacher said he could tell I'd been studying because I read better than the others. Going through the woods on the way home that evening, seemed like I was so full of myself I didn't know what to do. I run, and jumped, and kicked, and felt all bouncy, like a ball. . . .

But on the third day of school that year Mama couldn't get out of the bed. I know she tried, but she just couldn't make it. Everybody said it was the rheumatiz, and I suppose it was.

She called me and said when I got through eating breakfast to come there, she wanted to talk to me. I went and leaned against the wall at the foot of her bed, all pleased with myself because I'd had Frank help me and we'd got in lots of wood and water while Liza cooked breakfast, so Liza wouldn't have nothing to do but take care of Mama till we got home. I figured we'd already done what she was going to tell me to do. I sure wasn't ready for what come.

She said, "Charly, it looks like you're gonna have to quit school and go to work."

I pushed my hands hard against the wall behind me, and tried not to let her see how my insides was churning up and down.

She said, "Mr. Tom Barlow talked to me the other day about getting you to work for him, but I said no, I wanted you to go to school. Now I can't work, so I guess you'll have to. You can do it. You're a big boy now. You're ten years old."

O-o-o-oh, I hated to quit school. And just now when everything was going so good. But I'd a done *anything* for Mama, of course. So I went to work for old man Barlow.[72]

The oral-history tapes, county histories, and schoolteacher memoirs that constitute much of our evidence about the rural schools of fifty years ago contain few accounts of people who were able to attend the schools only sporadically and did not make of their schooling what might have been. But here, with a last word, is Will Chandler, who spoke of his feelings about his education at Levelview School in Baylor County:

In that one-room unpainted schoolhouse is where I got the meager book learning I have. No fault of the teachers, however, I didn't get to attend school regularly. Of course, my not getting an education didn't stop the world from going 'round. I have survived the blows, and it has never faded from my memory. However, it has been very embarrassing and disappointing at time, causing me many a heartache. However, I am proud to stand up and tell it to the world how I appreciate what little education I do have; and it was taught to me by teachers who only knew how to teach the three R's away back yonder when men were honest and God ruled the country.[73]

97

6. Syrup Buckets and Flying Jennies

MOST TEXAS COUNTRY SCHOOLS punctuated the instructional day with fifteen-minute recesses in the morning and afternoon and a one-hour break around noon. During the latter, a few children took their time with their dinner, going down to a creek or into a nearby grove for a picnic, but the vast majority bolted their food and rushed into the serious business of play.

More often than not, children carried their dinners to school in a syrup or lard bucket. As Ruth Cook Nash, of Buckner School, in Parker County, said,

> On the inside, between the doors, was a low shelf for the water bucket [a cedar bucket and tin dipper]. There were nails on each side of the entrance for the boys' hats and the girls' bonnets and wraps. Under those were shelves for the lunch pails, usually syrup buckets with a bail for easy carrying, and a slitted lid to keep the food fresh. If weather permitted they usually ate outside by the side of the house....
>
> School didn't start till November and that was "hog killing weather." Everyone had hogs, so there was fresh pork, usually sausage and biscuit sandwiches. There were always boiled eggs, usually a glass of syrup or preserves, with a big lump of butter. My sister and I usually had a fried butter pie for dessert.[1]

All the way across the state, in northeast Texas, Hinkle Schillengs reported a similar dinner, one in which "we didn't even know what sandwiches were." Schillengs had a lard bucket in which

98

to carry his dinner – usually biscuits, butter, and syrup for the main course, with sweet potatoes, eggs and bacon, sweet cakes or "tea cakes" for dessert, and buttermilk in a fruit jar.[2] For Bertha M. Stephens at Quail School, in Collingsworth County, dinner "usually consisted of a cold biscuit with a slice of bacon between it or a piece of ham, a teacake [homemade cookie] or two, and an apple or peach or what fruit might be ripe in the orchard at home. I knew one little boy and girl that brought a small [snuff] glass full of sorghum molasses, a chunk of butter in it and a piece of cornbread for each. They carried it in a little bucket and it was about the same lunch every day. . . . The children nowadays would say that is a story, but it is the truth!"[3]

Dinner-bucket foods in the section of northeast Texas studied by Bill O'Neal and his students ran the gamut of East Texas country fare: "turnip greens, corn bread, black-eyed peas, fried squirrel, fried chicken, buttermilk carried in a fruit jar, sweet potatoes, gingerbread, rice pudding, syrup cookies, home cured ham and fried pies."[4] Here, as elsewhere across the state, biscuits or corn bread from breakfast that morning or supper the day before, along with some kind of meat, were the mainstays. Quite often several family children attended the same country school. Usually their dinners came in a single large bucket, and the oldest child was in charge of the bucket and distribution of the food.[5] This practice could lead to discord. At Arcadia School, in Shelby County, for example, Eva Grant and her two sisters carried buttered biscuits, syrup, bacon, and fried squirrel in a large, communal syrup bucket, and Eva reported that her two sisters often griped at her about her eating behavior, specifically about her leaving crumbs in the syrup. Irritated, she got one of her father's old axle-grease buckets, cleaned it out by scrubbing and boiling, and made a pretty dinner bucket of her very own, which aroused the envy of her sisters and the other children.[6]

School dinnertimes drew interested visits from the dogs that accompanied children to school each day, or that lived in the neighborhood of the school.[7] Dogs were common scavengers, but in Kerr County one school was on the daily round of a large flock of turkey vultures. A former student reported that the "buzzards" would circle overhead during the noon recess, then swoop down in droves after the bell had rung and the children had gone inside. He remembers them hopping about, hissing at each other, and devouring every last scrap of food the children had left under the trees outside.[8]

Occasionally teachers and parents worked together to serve children hot food. The teacher at Piney Grove School in the Gill community near Marshall put two big lard cans full of water on the wood stove until the water boiled, then the children held their dinner buckets in the water until the food was warm.[9] Mrs. C. Underwood described a more elaborate system devised by her husband for a school in Tom Green County: "My husband knew how to do things, how to figure them out. First we sent notes home telling the parents that if they wanted their children to have hot food at lunch they would send soup, cocoa, beans, stew, or whatever in fruit jars labeled with the child's name. About thirty minutes before noon, my husband (the principal teacher at the school) lighted the fire in the oil stove under a big tub of water where we set the fruit jars on towels in the bottom of the tub. So, we had our hot lunch program!"[10]

Many parents occasionally sent some delicacy as a special contribution to all the school's dinner buckets. Near Lone Star School, in Carson County, a bear wandered out of Palo Duro Canyon and was shot while trying to cross to the brakes of the Canadian River. The kill was made near the Timmonses' dugout. Mr. Timmons dressed the bear, and Mrs. Timmons cooked it up and "fried a piece of bear meat for every child in Miss Cappie's school and sent it to them in a tin bucket."[11] At some schools parents became more regularly involved in the dinner programs. At Sardis School, where the school motto was "Take what you have and get what you want," parents put the school credo into action. Taking turns the mothers came, one each day, bringing canned goods from home and preparing a hot dinner for the children.[12] The Dawn School, in Deaf Smith County, had a similar but even more elaborate and well-organized arrangement: "The women of the community got together each summer and canned food to be used. They picked up enough potatoes from the fields to last until spring, and when corn was in season they served fresh corn. Many families donated food, and each child was required to bring one dozen eggs a year. The community held cafeteria benefits to raise money. Pie suppers were a popular method."[13]

Not all the parents chose to participate in the Sardis School "hot lunch program," and their children continued to carry cold dinners in the familiar tin pails. The reason was not given, but perhaps the families were too poor to put on a proper show when it was their turn to feed the class. In a cash-poor agrarian society, where the range between relative poverty and relative affluence was not very great, there was a great deal of social sensitivity about public displays that emphasized these distinctions, and this even extended to the contents of children's dinner buckets at school. A good many former students reported that they had felt ashamed to carry simple corn bread for dinner, as opposed to the flour biscuits that most of the other students had. The lunch of corn bread and syrup carried by the poorest children was often looked down upon. Conversely, if most of the children at a school carried corn bread in their lunches, a student might be hesitant to reveal her mother's fine light bread biscuits – as was one student at Hebron School in Bell County.[14] To bring something as grand as an apple or an orange to James School, in Shelby County, was regarded as even worse "showing off." Mouths watering, the other students gathered closely around the social transgressor as he tried to eat his prize and probably made him very sorry he had brought it to school.[15] Teachers knew to be careful when commenting on the contents of students' dinner buckets, but town-raised teachers sometimes made mistakes. When a new teacher from Belton asked her rural students where they got the lovely "white butter" on their bread, she was informed that it was hog lard.[16] A teacher in a remote Hill County school also committed a *faux pas*. The "chicken" in the children's spring dinners turned out to be wild turkey, killed out of season.[17]

Sometimes food created special problems for teachers. One little girl's father told her about a certain man in the Deadwood community who stole other people's hogs, theirs included. Incensed at this, the girl began to watch the man's children at the Reeves School they attended, and sure enough, his children always had good ham and pork sausages in their dinner buckets! Several times she recruited other kids to help her chase and overpower the children to get her rightful pork back—much to the consternation of the teacher.[18]

One new boy came to the Emery School with only a jar of peaches to eat, as Elsie Hamill described: "I never will forget one country boy who lived way down below me. His name was James Hainey, and [he came from] a very, very poor family of about five or six kids. He rode his horse to school, and the very first thing those kids [at school] did was to get some long switches and hit his horse, and they almost made the horse throw him off. . . . I believe he came one more day. He had peaches for his lunch because they canned peaches. He got his little jar of peaches to eat, I assume. Anyway, they called him 'Peaches,' and they made fun of him, and he didn't come to school after that."[19]

William Owens told a classic story of the social significance of corn bread in the dinner bucket:

> I had to go to school, but I did not want to. My shoes were worn out and I would have to go barefooted. We were down to corn bread for breakfast and I would have to take corn bread in my dinner bucket. The money we had saved up had gone for the doctor and medicine. Monroe and Dewey were at work in the woods cutting crossties for the railroad, but the money they made had to go for seed and to the blacksmith for sharpening sweeps. It would be corn bread for breakfast till more money came in.
>
> It was bad enough to go back to school barefooted. It was worse trying to hide what I had to eat. As soon as the dinner bell rang the other boys and girls took their buckets and paper sacks and went to the benches under the arbor to eat and talk and sing "Oh, Bury Me Beneath the Willow." I would take my bucket, hide it under my coat, and going toward the privy and around it, slip out of sight in the woods behind the school ground. There, hidden in the bushes, I would cram down my corn bread and fried meat in a hurry so I could get back for playing.[20]

Although some children sat on benches or logs or wandered into the woods to enjoy a leisurely dinner, more often the food was gobbled down so that the balance of the hour could be devoted to play. Playground equipment was often nonexistent or, at best, primitive—perhaps a rope swing or a "flying jenny." A flying jenny was a board or one-half of a split log nailed or spliced over a tree stump. A child sat on one end while other children began spinning the log on the stump with ever-increasing speed. As one former student put it, "If a kid wouldn't ride the flying jenny, they just weren't with it!"[21] As O. T. Baker emphasized, the flying jenny was "kind of dangerous."

> You cut off a tree, made some kind of a spindle, and took another tree and split it in the middle—forced it open there where it would fit on this spindle, and poured a lot of soft mud in there to make it move around pretty good, and you had a flying jenny. This left the horizontal log about three feet off the ground, and it probably would stick out about eight feet past the pinnacle on each side. If you got two or three big boys right there in the middle, using all their strength to pull that thing around, it gathered pretty good speed! The idea was to get two or three boys on each end of this pole and see how far you could throw 'em off, or if the guy was going to ride it, see how long he could stay on. And it would really whiz. It took a pretty good

Highland School students on homemade seesaws, ca. 1920. Courtesy East Central Historical Group, East Central ISD, Bexar County. Carmen Leal.

rider to stay on that thing. It was not uncommon to fall off, and if you didn't fall pretty agilely, well, you might get bumped on the head with that pole. If it hit you, they might have to drag you out of the way.[22]

Another child-created apparatus was the "jumping board" or "daredevil seesaw." A board or plank was placed over a log and a child stood on the down end while one or more children jumped on the other end of the plank to see how high they could make him go. This could be dangerous when the board split, as sometimes happened. A rural teacher had to keep her eyes open for these innovative but health-threatening play strategies. Once, at the Heldenheimer Colored School, in Bell County, the new teacher was preoccupied with getting her classroom in order on the first day and had allowed her students an extended recess outside. The area had received heavy rains for several days before, and when the teacher finally thought to look out the window to check on her pupils, she discovered the big boys clad only in their underwear, riding railroad ties down a raging torrent of water in the nearby ravine.[23]

At Sardis School, in Shelby County, the children rode a flying jenny, in this case just a board nailed to a stump, but they also made use of the young pine trees surrounding the playground. Several boys would help to bend a tree over to the ground and hold it while another child climbed into the top. Then the holders let go, and the rider rode – or was thrown.[24] At Willow Creek School, in the German Hill Country, a variation on this game involved willows instead of pines. Boys climbed into a willow, sometimes several of them on different limbs, and then the bigger boys tried their best to shake them out. "All went well as long as each boy had a tree or limb to himself, but all too often the bigger boys wanted to climb onto an already occupied limb and shake the smaller kids out, about the same way we knew how to shake an opossum out of a tree. There were plenty of 'dropouts' in the game, but fortunately we usually landed on all fours, like a cat. The sand and the Bermuda grass were soft, so our landings were not much of a jolt."[25]

Students at an early Carson County school in West Texas developed another sort of riding game. The "broncs" were the big boys and the little boys were the "bronc busters."

The school ground contained a number of "corrals," staked off with foot-palings. The broncs . . . would be driven into the corral. They would pitch, kick, jump, run and act as much as possible like real broncs. The little boys would toss their lassoes – everybody carried a lariat rope. When the broncs were roped, two or three would hold him until the rider got seated, his feet locked firmly around the boy's chest or stomach. The best riders never grabbed the coat collar of the bronc. Sometimes the wilder broncs would pitch for fifteen minutes in intense efforts to throw their riders.[26]

Not all these "play-like" games were so vigorous and life threatening. At the Rock Creek School, in Menard County, the little girls rode stick horses about the playground – properly sidesaddle, because the teacher was convinced that to ride astride was unladylike.[27] These same little girls pulled broom weeds and piled them over and around sawhorses and low-hanging limbs to make play houses, and the girls at Maple Springs School in northeast Texas did the same thing with pine straw in a thicket across from the school, hanging "pretty pictures" on trees and branches.[28] At Little River School, in Bell County, the children played revival or camp meeting. Pauline Allison was always the preacher, and her new converts were baptized in a pile of oak leaves.[29] At one school in Shelby County, "the boys would pull up logs in place for school and church. A boy would preach while the other children would sing and shout."[30]

Some recess activities were entirely idiosyncratic, linked directly to unique local resources. Bland School students, in Bell County, dug in the nearby "Indian Burial Grounds," and those from West Hamilton School, Shelby County, used a kitchen knife to carve soapstone blocks from local cliffs.[31]

Mostly, however, children played the traditional games of the playground handed down across many generations of childhood: Annie over, wolf-over-the-river, red rover, drop the handkerchief, blindman's buff, alley alley oxen free, leapfrog, hide-and-go-seek, hide and switch, kick the can, tin cannelina, goose and gander, tag, pop the whip, ring-around-the-rosy, little house on the hill, Little Sally Walker (and other ring plays), chicken in the crane crow, stink base, the flying dutchman, cross line, and fox and hounds. Then there were such games and athletic pursuits as jacks, hopscotch, jump rope, horseshoes, wrestling, foot races, spin the top, mumble-peg, and marbles, which in rural Texas was not only played "for keeps" but often "for blood" as well. Rural schoolteachers did not have to encourage these activities; all they had to do was stand back and allow nature and the ancient culture of childhood to take its course.

Some games were complicated, and some were wonderfully simple. In the East Texas version of fox and hounds, "one kid would take off running, and a pack of kids would come running after him." That was the whole game! Always popular with the boys was mumblepeg. Depending upon how the blade landed, the knife artist was awarded twenty-five, fifty, seventy-five, or one hundred points. The first boy to accumulate five hundred points was the winner, and at Round Timber School, near Seymour, the low man among the players had to pull a wooden peg out of the ground with his teeth, "and get a mouthful of dirt to boot."[32] In the passage below, O. T. Baker describes how tops was played at his Shelby County school around World War I.

> Playing tops, we had a ring. We might start off with a token top in there. The idea was to wrap your top up real tight and throw it in spinning position and hit it [the token top] with your top and knock it out of the ring. If you knocked it out of the ring, you got the top. But if your top didn't come out of the ring itself, you had to stay there. Course, everybody had two or three tops, and you might wind up with a dozen and somebody else not have any. A pretty good top man could hit the other top and split it in two. You'd throw your top in there and if it didn't hit the other top, just started spinning, you were fair game. Anybody who wanted to could plug your top while it was spinning. Some of these old boys would file their spinners like a chisel, and if they hit that other top they could very easily just split it right half in two. You got some pretty good respect if you were able to cut up two, three tops, and this was what you aspired to do. I made tops out of dead peach trees.[33]

Students at schools in the Texas-German Hill Country played a few exotic games derived from their German heritage but similar in spirit to many more common games. One of these German exotics was "sow driving."

> We played games in the morning and afternoon recesses and during the noon hour. We called one of these games *Mummela*, but in other

106

parts of the German Belt it was called *Sautreiben* ("sow driving"). Before playing this game we dug a number of six-inch holes or pits in the ground in a circle, one hole for each participant, less one, and one larger hole in the center. All the players had three-foot sticks or pegs, and they stuck them into the center hole and marched around mumbling, "Mummela, mummela, mummela." Outside the hole was a crushed tin-can ball. At some moment in the circular marching and chanting a signal was given, and all the boys made a dash for the outside holes and stuck their sticks into the holes. The odd player, who failed to make good his claim to one of the holes, was "it." His task was to knock the angular ball or "sow" into one of the holes on the outside or into the center hole. Everybody defended the territory with his stick or maul, provided he did not get mauled first. If the can landed in one of the holes or if the attacker stuck his stick into it while the defender tried to beat the can away, the loser was "it," and so it went on. I don't remember what the rewards or the spoils of the battle were, probably none, but the penalty was that you got your shins smashed.[34]

Organized team sports were late in coming to the country schools of Texas, though they certainly reached most of them in the end. The county meets of the Texas Interscholastic League were of huge interest to rural students, teachers, and parents by the 1940s and 1950s. An early ball game was the widely played "townball," a rural version of cricket, the game from which American baseball developed. "Townball was our main game for which we chose sides. Since we had no store-bought balls or bats, we made our own. For balls we unraveled large socks and wound the ravels around a small stone until it got about as large as a baseball. It was then securely sewed to keep it from unwinding. (My mother made many of these.) For bats we used a strong stick or a board which we had shaped like a paddle so we could hold it."[35] At another school the ball was made of rags wrapped with twine from flour, meal, or fertilizer sacks, and the bat was a piece of plank. Somewhere else the ball was constructed of auto inner tubes cut into strips and wrapped to make a rubber core, then covered with yarn from heavy sacks with twine wound over that. None of these balls would go as far as a real baseball when struck and so were more suited for use in town (hence, the name) and in schoolyards as well. Townball just had two bases – home base and a base located where second base would be on a conventional baseball dia-

Utzville School students playing a game of townball, 1915. Courtesy East Central Historical Group, East Central ISD, Bexar County.

mond.[36] W. Silas Vance has offered an excellent description of how townball was played at Lucky Ridge School in Wise County about 1920:

> Most of us at Lucky Ridge never saw a basketball or football or volleyball or tennis ball or golf ball or a store-bought baseball. Our constant game, in and out of school, was townball.
> Often considered the forerunner of baseball, townball was a less rigidly regulated and more individualized game. Historians have suggested that baseball replaced it before the end of the nineteenth century, but we were playing townball at Lucky Ridge down to at least 1920. For us it had certain distinct advantages. First, any number could play, from teams of four or five up to fifteen or more. Second, it didn't require any equipment except a ball and bat, and we didn't have any, not even a catcher's mitt. Third, the poorest player could take part with some success and enjoyment, since the pitcher had to deliver the ball with an underhanded pitch and usually served it as gently as possible to smaller boys and girls. Fourth, since a team remaining "in bats" and "in town" (as we said, "at bat" being used only for an individual player) until every member was put out, the inept player was not the serious handicap he would be to a team in baseball.

Townball differed from baseball in several other ways. A batter could be caught out on either the first bounce or fly, and a runner was put out by throwing the ball between him and the base he was running to. A runner after once leaving a base could not return to it. The only fixed positions were those of the pitcher and a catcher, and sometimes a "pigtail," as the boy was called who was put behind the catcher to stop any balls the catcher failed to stop. The rest of the players on the team in the field took positions wherever they chose. Fielders would commonly shift about, right and left, up close and back, according to the quality of the batter. The better players did practically all the ball handling. And when batting, they survived and went on scoring for their team after the poor players were liquidated.[37]

Gradually, as the century progressed, sportsmen and innovators such as T. L. Devlin, a teacher at the Elkins School, in Swisher County, brought competitive athletics ("ball sports") into the educational backwoods. Devlin got a basketball and constructed a hoop and a court to play on. "The goals were made of steel buggy tires for hoops which were suspended on backstops of one-by-twelves and held up by a four-by-six post."[38] Schools sometimes found money for uniforms for both girls' and boys' teams, and at Cedar Creek School, Bell County, the "red bloomers and white blouses" which the girls' basketball team used were especially prized.[39]

Some schools had trouble raising the money for these things. O. T. Baker's one-room Shelby County school was issued one basketball a year, and it was played with until it was absolutely used up.

We only managed to have one basketball a season. You know, in those days when you got the basketball it was deflated when you got it, and you had to insert a bladder, and most nobody could blow hard enough to pump it up very hard. In those early days nobody had an automobile in the area, so we had to go with a pretty flat ball — just blow it up as hard as some big boy could puff it. . . . We would play with the ball until we wore it through and the bladder got punctured, and then we'd take the bladder out and throw it away and stuff the old casing [of the ball] with newspaper. And we'd play with it more or less like a beach ball — we'd just throw it. Then, when we wore the ball out totally, it it was time to start playing some other games.[40]

The Educational Survey of 1924 bemoaned the general lack of recess paraphernalia in the state's rural schools. Many of the country schools scrimped and saved, raising money at bake sales, box suppers, cake walks, and the like to provide at least a minimum of athletic and recreational equipment for their children. Perhaps no school went further or worked harder in this respect than Wolf Ridge School, ten miles northwest of Gainesville. Wolves were long gone from the area, but it did have a convenient plague of rats and mice.

> My second and third years of teaching were in this two teacher school from 1926 to 1928. . . . The six or seven month school left little money for supplies, and playground equipment was not even considered. One box of chalk was stretched to last all year. Pieces of linen braided together made a jump rope. A rock carefully wrapped with strips of string made a ball for Annie over or stick ball. However, the big boys especially wanted a basketball – an impossible dream.
>
> A scourge of rats and mice over the county prompted Gainesville Chamber of Commerce to offer prizes to the school that brought in the most rat tails – $15 for the first prize, $10 for the second prize, and $5 third prize. There were no exterminators or effective rat poison in those years. Here was a chance for a basketball. The children and members of the community took up the challenge to decrease the rat population. Eighteen hundred rat tails won for Wolf Ridge.
>
> With the supervision of a trustee and the work of the big boys, the goal posts were set, the basketball court outlined and a dream realized.[41]

7. Heaven's First Law

🕮

IN THE COUNTRY SCHOOLS of the 1920s and 1930s discipline was seldom a serious problem for either students or teachers. Many teachers reported that disciplinary incidents were rare in their class-rooms and that when discipline was necessary, parents usually were supportive. Built by slaves in 1859, the old Rock Church School, in Bell County, had over its blackboard a statement that succes-sive generations of rural parents and teachers would stand by: "Or-der is Heaven's first law and must be had at all times to succeed."[1]

Lonie Brite responded to "confusion" in her schoolroom in Cald-well County by quietly sitting down at her desk and fixing the in-stigators of confusion with a piercing gaze. "I just looked at them. Looking at them you'd be surprised how quickly they got quiet. So, then I just got up and went back to work."[2] Lula Byars com-bined an effective system of classroom and campus monitors with a similar kind of psychological control: "I don't ever remember hav-ing to discipline anybody out at McMahan but twice, and I made them stay in. I never had any problem like that with the children, 'cause I always told 'em—I think I'd scare them to death, nearly, in the beginning—'Now, look, I'm not going to harm you, but I'm not going to let anyone harm me.' They'd look at me and say, 'What you mean, Mrs. Byars?' I'd say, 'Children, if you're too grown to be obedient, then you don't have any place in the schoolroom.' And I told the parents that too."[3]

111

Sometimes teachers did resort to what Herman Allen referred to as the "board of education" or in Frankie Franks's case, the strap:

> In those days we used the strap, and I had a boy that didn't want to take a whipping, so he went home. Walked out and went home. In less than an hour his mother was back there with him. She told me, "Now, here's this young man. I brought him right back here, and you whip him or whatever you want to do, because these children been telling me how he's been showing out down here. You just take him and whip him." You thrashed one out pretty good, and that settled the room out for maybe three or four days. You didn't have to do it every day.[4]

Weldon Hutcheson, telling of another classroom-discipline incident in which he was personally involved, placed the issue in historical perspective:

> Generally speaking, I always had teachers that I liked. There were few teachers who were disliked. People respected them. When I went to school at Elm Grove, we had only one teacher, and that one teacher was teaching grades one through seven, all in the same room. I don't know how she handled it! For things like reading and arithmetic classes, and things like that, she called one of the older children to assist the younger, because that was the only way you could get it done. How did she handle the discipline problem? Well, I'll tell you, she didn't spare the rod!
>
> In those small schools, there would be one or two get a whipping just about every day. Because, in the first place, you were sitting all crowded up, especially in the winter time. You had one stove right out in the middle, and what you ended up with was all these kids seated on these benches around the stove; that's the only way you could keep warm. Course, every now and then we'd get in a little problem there. I know I had one little situation there one time. I didn't get too many switchings while I was in school, but there was one old boy who was getting it continuously because he didn't give a darn about anything. And she says one day, "Anybody speaks three times today gets a whipping." I had had it about twice, so he decided that I was going to get one. I was sitting right on the end of the bench, and when he sat down there he reached around and stuck a pin in my leg, and when he did, I hollered. The first thing that popped into my mind was, "I'm going to get a whipping, but I'm going to make it worthwhile!" And I jumped up and hauled off and knocked him right off his bench. So we both got a whipping.
>
> . . . You seldom ever had a case of a youngster taking to fight the teacher, or anything like that, and we had some big old boys in that

112

school. They took it because they were taught that we had to obey orders. They also expected, when they disobeyed and caused any problems, that they were in trouble when they got home. The point I'm trying to make is that you were taught to obey authority. When he or she told you to sit down, well, you set down![5]

Many of the teachers interviewed for this history spent the latter stages of their professional careers in the town and city schools, and they testified almost without exception that classroom management and discipline was much less of a problem in the country schools where they had attended and begun their teaching days. What, then, is the relationship of this testimony to what we may call the "myth" of the rural school, where "big old boys" harass the teacher and force him or her to fight or flee? Are these folktales pure hyperbole, or do they have some basis in historical fact? As we will see, the teachers do seem to be essentially correct in their characterization of discipline in the country school, but the myth has some basis in truth as well.

Many of the latter-day rural school teachers interviewed for this book had heard the stories about teachers being "treed" by their older students, but by and large they regarded them as tales of dubious validity. Ochee Holt told of hearing one of these "horror stories" about a school at which she got a job, and of what she found when she got there:

Some people heard that I got a job in Stampede. Someone said, "My lands, you're going out to that school? That's where the boy pulled a knife on the teacher the year before." His name was Boyer—it was a name I knew since my mother used to live out there. I gave him a good look the first day of school. I guess school had been going on two or three months, and he said, "I been wanting to ask you something. Did you ever hear anything about me?" I said, "Yes, I heard something one time." He said, "Was it about a knife?" I said, "Yes, but I don't believe it." He said, "Well, I just wanted to tell you what happened." The teacher was getting after him, she was really eating him up, and he crossed one leg over and started to sharpen his knife on the sole of his shoe. It was a common thing. He said "It never entered my mind that I would harm her."

Maybe that did frighten the teacher. It was always just stories, just like this, that could give the school a reputation that there were boys over there pulling knives on the teachers. We'd go on possum hunts with those children![6]

113

Confrontations could occur, however. In 1928 Emma Shirley, writing a *Dallas Morning News* article under the nom de plume of Clara Weems, described one of her early experiences:

> I have always looked upon those [dinner] pails as deadly weapons since the day I tried to whip a boy because he refused to learn the seven times table. He was sixteen or seventeen and larger than I, yet I was trying to do my duty toward him and make him worthy of the ballot when his sweetheart, a husky girl of fifteen, landed me in the head with her red schoolhouse dinner pail. I saw all the planets in the heavens and heard them singing in melodious harmony. The next day the couple rode over to the county seat and married, and I never saw them again until twelve years later, when they and their ten children moved into the community where I was teaching. I gave up a good salary that year and hunted for six months before I found another school, and this is the first time I have told the reason.[7]

Clara Weems's pail incident was humorously described, but it probably held little humor for her on the day it happened. Fifty years later Shirley was interviewed about the incident and was able to put the whole issue of student challenges to rural teachers in historical perspective. In the process she made a telling point that is borne out by a wide array of primary accounts from the country schools: Women teachers rarely had serious physical confrontations with their pupils.

> My getting hit with the lunch pail and the man who taught with a pistol on his desk that I wrote about was not a commonplace thing. You know, a woman teacher, I don't believe the kids would go against a woman teacher as much as they would a man teacher. They wouldn't resent her as much. I found a great regard for women among the rural boys and girls. Boys would just be fighting, and I'd go out in the schoolyard and take hold of one of them's shoulder, and they wouldn't hit me. They might now, but they wouldn't then – seems to be a different view of women, or of schoolteaching. I never had any trouble with big boys.[8]

It is worth noting that even Emma Shirley's dinner-pail incident tends to support this generalization. The male member of the sweetheart pair was taking his licking with docility when his girlfriend assaulted the teacher with the pail. Things were different for men teachers, however, and this was true from the very earliest days of Texas rural education right up to the era of consolidation. The tale of the woman teacher assaulted is a rare one, but not so Shirley's other account: "The man with the pistol was Mr. Holbrook. He told me the kids were so bad that he could not teach them. He had a German luger he'd gotten in WWI. He just laid it on the desk and said he intended to teach this school. And he taught it, too. He didn't have any more arguments."[9] Here is the full account of Mr. Holbrook's epic confrontation with his male students, as described by Shirley in the *Dallas Morning News* story in 1928. Holbrook's name has been changed to Duncan. This story is also humorous, but the reader is invited to look beyond the humor to envision just how serious this affair really was. The echoes of numerous similar confrontations come down to us in the records of early rural schools.

Most of the school teachers I know today are women, while a few years ago many of the young men who aspired to be doctors, lawyers or preachers taught school a year or so in order to get money to go to professional schools. The older boys in the country districts resented the intrusion of these personable young gentlemen into the midst of their susceptible sweethearts, and many a young school teacher found himself in fights with the boys before he could see any reason for the ill feeling.

One Mr. Maurice Marion Duncan was employed to fill the vacancy left by Miss Priscilla White, who married the only widower in the neighborhood and left me in the middle of the term with the whole school to teach. Miss Priscilla had been very successful because the big boys wouldn't fight a lady, but the young man who had preceded her must have had a time of it because it was reported that he had left the district with one arm in a sling and one cheek full of birdshot. The big boys—and by big I mean six-foot, two-hundred-pound, 17-year-olds—swore they wouldn't let any man, much less one named Maurice, teach that school. Mr. Duncan appeared on the scene the next Monday, and he was every bit of five feet tall and must have weighed 125 pounds. Marv Dillard, one of the biggest boys, pitched a note with the ease which only a skilled country lover can know toward his sweetheart, when Mr. Duncan, like a shot out of a cannon, beat the note to its destination and caught it as it landed upon her desk.

"If you open that," Marv shouted, "I'll whip you all over this place!" Mr. Duncan very calmly unfolded it, Marv made a lunge, Maurice dived for one of Marv's feet, turned him over against the stove and scattered stovepipe and soot from one end of the room to the other, while the scared children ran for the doors and windows. I saw the rest of the fight myself, as I turned out my room when I heard the others running out because I thought there must be a fire. Maurice grabbed Marv by the ear while he held Marv's thumb in his teeth. He kept Marv's left arm pinned to the floor until he finally managed to get on top of Marv and walk around him like a big bale of cotton until the big boys pulled him off.

When Marv came to, the little Maurice was holding a pistol as big as he was on him and ordering him to fix up the stove. When the stove was set in place Mr. Duncan called in the pupils and announced:

"I came out here to teach this school and I'm going to do it if I have to do so at the point of this pistol. You boys know you are bigger than me, but I'll have you understand I'm going to teach this school."[10]

Needless to say, the rogue school and its big old boys were cowed at this point, and the new teacher was in full control. Emma Shirley went on to say in her story that Mr. Duncan/Holbrook became a successful politician in the region and that "Marv Dillard told me some years ago that he always voted for Duncan every time he ran for office because he was still afraid to oppose him."

In the first decades of Texas education, the period from roughly 1870 to 1910, most of the schoolteachers were men. The reasons for this are not entirely clear. Perhaps the woman's place was still too firmly in the home, or too few women had received the requisite education, or the bad old days of the frontier were still too close. The documentary sources have little to say on this matter. Schoolteaching was simply thought to be a proper job for men, who often were granted the honorary title of "professor." The task was sometimes rather akin to breaking wild horses, and occasionally whole schools would run entirely out of control and require special "bronc busters" from outside the community.

Local traditions relate that something like this happened at the Panhandle School, in Carson County, in the 1890s, where the bad boys had managed to humiliate and run off every teacher who tried to teach there for almost a decade. A trustee from the beleaguered school met a Frank Elston on a train trip and became convinced that Elston was just the man to tame the bad boys of Panhandle. This trustee, Sig Wheatley, persuaded Elston to come to Panhandle to teach school and then returned to convince the other trustees that here was just the man to take over their school and "keep order and make the pupils like it."

The board hired Elston sight unseen on Sig Wheatley's recommendation. Meanwhile, the defiant students of the community learned of the coming of the new schoolmaster and made plans to offer him a warm welcome. The crisis at the school, which lasted two memorable days in 1898, focused on a duel for control between teacher Elston and the informal leader of Panhandle's wicked students. Elston wore out six switches on this lad, or so the story goes, but broke his spirit only when, on the second day, he picked him up bodily by coat collar and seat of the pants and threatened to throw him out the school door down a long flight of steps. Resistance crumbled at that point, and Frank Elston taught Panhandle School from 1898 to 1904, later becoming county judge.[11]

Fragments of similar stories come down from the early days of Texas rural education, all involving men teachers. At Okay School, in Bell County, around 1900 a strict male teacher who dressed somewhat as a dandy "reprimanded two boys severely one afternoon," and the next day when he got to the school he found a donkey wearing the school bell wandering around inside. The place was a mess, "the teacher was angry, and a big disturbance followed. After that the teacher wore a long Bowie knife at his side."[12] In the early days the armed teacher was no real exception; in a number of accounts from the 1890s teachers were described as reinforcing their authority with knives and pistols.

The game could get very rough, indeed. At Veal Station, in Parker County, a boy stabbed and killed his teacher, a Mr. Cooper.[13] At a somewhat later date a teacher accepted a position in southeast Texas at a "small school where teachers had often been run off by teenage boys." The teacher lived with a family near the schoolhouse, and one night he and the other teacher heard catcalls coming from the vicinity of the thirteen cords of firewood trustees had stacked near the school. The other teacher fired two shots in the air, which in no way impressed the catcallers, who redoubled their howls. Then the first teacher took the pistol and fired two shots directly at the stack of firewood. That did the trick: "Such a noise we heard as the intruders scrambled through the barbedwire fence! We had no more trouble that year."[14] The local bad boys had gotten the message.

117

Another violent incident was reported from the Sulphur River bottoms of East Texas, but this time we see the affair from the big boys' point of view:

> We was purty mean in school. Me an' another feller made one six months o' school an' never missed a whippin'. We wore these britches up to here, an' black stockin's. He pulled 'em loose from my leg an' I pulled 'em loose from his where the blood was stickin'.
>
> Wasn't nobody put no wood in the schoolhouse. We'd hep the teacher cut some, 'cause we didn't want to freeze. We'd hep him an' then turn around an' do ever' mean trick just to aggravate him. Me an' some other boys, we went down there one evenin' after school. We got his bell, an' all the trinkets he kep' down there, and we destroyed it all, carried 'em way down on the branch an' tore it up an' throwed it away. We went back up there an' tore up his desk; an' then we taken our pistols an' shot all the brick off, one brick at a time off the top o' the house. I don't guess we was very mean, just mischievous. We would fight—yeah, we'd fight, but we just called that playin', you know.[15]

Wood stoves were dangerous, and hunters, card players, and other community irregulars frequented the country schools at night, but these structures still burned to the ground with suspicious frequency in the early days. Were local big boys, like those from the Sulphur River bottoms, simply taking things one step further? There was a story from Bell County about a boy who fell in love with the daughter of one of the trustees of the Liberty Hill School and asked to marry her. The father replied that his daughter was still too young, and besides, he wanted her to go to school for some years more. The young man then left to burn the one-room structure to its rock foundation, assuming, it is supposed, that if the school was the problem this might serve to eliminate it. Years later he did marry the girl.[16]

Male teachers seem always to have had more discipline problems, but these conflicts were at their worst when the teachers were young. The root cause seems to have been what Emma Shirley suggested in her *Dallas Morning News* article—sexual jealousy from the big boys who "resented the intrusion of these personable young gentlemen into the midst of their susceptible sweethearts." What with having to miss school for work, the oldest boys were often nineteen to twenty-one years of age, and the young teachers were sometimes no older. Is it any wonder that the young men of the countryside often resented teachers' assertions of authority? At the very least these young male teachers were tested. Here are two such cases.

At Guthrie School, in King County, there was a change of teachers, and the new teacher was a young man with several years' teaching experience. Some of the older boys from Guthrie decided to "try him out" to test the severity of his discipline. One boy got two whippings in one day. The first was mild, and the boy made the mistake of remarking, "Don't believe you got the dust out of my pants that time." The second whipping, which followed immediately, was decidedly immoderate – so severe, in fact, that the former student remembered it well after half a century.[17]

A former Caldwell County teacher, Herman Allen, told us this story:

> Usually I tried to get there to build a fire. I built many and many a fire! The first year I taught, this old boy – we used coal, and we had a good fire going, and he threw in some paper from the wastepaper basket. He was a big old boy, about my size; I was six months older than he. He went back to the stove, opened the door, and put the wastepaper in there. I didn't know why, when there was a good wastepaper basket up close. He turned around, and about the time he turned around, "KABOOM!" It blew the door off the stove. He had emptied a shotgun shell of gunpowder in the paper and blew up the stove. Well, we had a little session at recess about that. I called my principal up to witness, and he witnessed me giving him fifteen licks. And just as I was ready to quit, [the student] said, "That's enough!" Well, I'll leave that story right there. We had a fistfight later. I had to have a fistfight to stay on my job; I knew what I had to do. He was as large as I was, and anyway, I kept my job. In fact, I was the only one reelected to teach the next year. The other teachers were fired.[18]

Male teachers also seemed to have more precarious relationships with parents and trustees. Just as older boys bridled under the authority of the young man, the teacher bridled under the authority of the older trustees, who ran the school and often told him what to do and how to teach even though at times they were barely literate. At Little River School, in Bell County, a father came with a whip to pay the teacher back for his vigorous disciplining of his children, and was only reluctantly talked out of it.[19]

William Owens lost his second school at the end of one year

119

because of mishandling a single discipline incident. After catching a boy smoking in the privy, Owens at first procrastinated, though all the students and the trustees agreed that a whipping was appropriate. Then he finally whipped the boy's hand with a ruler, something looked upon as a "cruel and unnatural" punishment at this particular school, where switching was the customary corporal punishment.[20] For this, and for some other more political reasons, the trustees declined to renew his contract.

Sometimes the discipline problems male teachers had with their students broadened to a general conflict with the community at large, and every time this occurred, the teacher's job was doomed. One such incident took place in 1915 at a small two-teacher school:

> The upper grade teacher-principal was a young man twenty-one years old, with two years' college work; in fact, he had been to the University of Kentucky. He dressed in the latest fashion, and his soft, white hands showed that he was obviously a stranger to manual labor. Just his very appearance antagonized the farm boys. Furthermore, he catered to the older girls who were seventeen or eighteen years old; the boys resented this. He was a good athlete, but he always *had* to win.
>
> Discipline was extremely lax with older pupils, but the principal punished younger children severely for minor rule infractions. One Friday he whipped two little boys severely with a piece of mesquite limb. This infuriated the community. The following Monday morning, as the pupils gathered in the yard, I could sense restlessness and tenseness. Ordinarily the younger children lined up at one end of the building, and the older ones at the other. However, this particular morning, when I brought my pupils in, some of the older group were in my room, while others looked out of the door of their own room. All at once the older boys and girls started throwing eggs (some of them aged) at the principal. When he tried to escape through a door, more eggs would stop him. Eggs dripped from blackboards, desks and walls; but chiefly they dripped from the principal. He finally maneuvered to the middle door and while wiping egg from his face, asked me, "Shouldn't we dismiss class?" I replied that his room seemed to have dismissed itself, but that I would continue with mine. He left hastily while a few of the determined boys pursued him, pitching eggs as they ran.[21]

It sounds very much as though the informal support of the whole community was behind this Monday morning egg party, especially in light of the events later that week. At a meeting of the school board, parents, county school superintendent, and county attorney the young teacher was fired for his cruel punishment of the younger pupils, and the egg throwers were let off with a stern reprimand and an order that they scrub the school building until not a vestige of egg remained. This young college man had violated every unspoken rule of the rural school. A foppish city boy from another state, hardly older than the older students, he had played up to the big girls, thus ensuring the wrath and jealousy of the older boys. That was bad enough, but he had evidently disregarded the unwritten rules of discipline by underpunishing the big boys and girls while overpunishing the young ones. In the end even his co-teacher offered him little support. His behavior antagonized the whole community, and the whole community rose up to throw him out.

The old stories of confrontations between male teachers and their older male students contained more than a grain of truth. There were, however, a variety of reasons why the average rural school and its female schoolteacher had few problems with discipline by the 1920s and 1930s. To begin with, parental support for the teacher was usually close and direct. Parents and teachers all accepted the principle that order is essential for instruction; they were in firm accord with the Rock Church School's dictum on "Heaven's first law." Children's behavior in the school reflected on their families, and the school was the only vehicle for the development of the public social behavior of children in many country communities. Both to preserve the family's reputation and to afford their children practical training, parents wanted children to demonstrate respect for authority and institutions and conformity to a rather uniform moral code. In this process, teachers and parents became necessary partners.

The solidity of this adult alliance of teachers and parents on the question of classroom order is reflected in a general rule of thumb reported from all across rural Texas: "A whipping at school means a whipping at home." In the small, face-to-face world of the country community, where everybody knew everybody else, there was absolutely no chance that news of a child's transgressions at school would not reach his parents—many times even before he got home that same evening. As one former student put it, "I'll

Grades one, two, and three, seated in the preferred style, at Sayers School, 1954. Courtesy East Central Historical Group, East Central ISD, Bexar County.

tell you what! Daddy, my parents, told all of us, if we got a whipping at school we'd get one when we got home. The teachers had to whip some of the children sometime, that's true. I don't know if the other parents told their children they'd whip them if they got a whipping at school, but Daddy always did us. I was always so afraid that I'd get a whipping at school that I was afraid to hardly talk. I don't remember them having a problem with discipline at Grice."[22]

One teacher at the Smith-Owens School, in Harrison County, formalized this customary relationship with an exchange of notes, a procedure that must have deterred many of her students from wrongdoing. For minor infractions students were made to stand on one foot for thirty minutes. For major ones they were switched and made to carry home a note requesting that they be switched again. Then, more often than not, they carried a second note back to the teacher, saying something like, "Please feel free to whip him again if he doesn't behave."[23]

Many teachers managed students by using forms of psychological control where physical punishment was rarely needed, but the success of this technique often was based on the threat of a whipping at home. Sometimes, as in the following incident, this threat was all that was needed:

> It was at Prairie Hill right after the war. Little fella came in, and he didn't speak good English. He was awfully timid. This poor thing came in from the playground, and he was just crying his heart out. I went to talk to him. He said, "I just feel so bad." I asked if he was sick. He answered, "No." "Well, what's wrong?" Finally he sobbed out, "I'm German! The big boys won't let me play because I'm a German." I told him that every one of them out there, their grandparents or great-grandparents came from somewhere unless they were Indians. "Don't cry about that." Then I said, "Would you like for your mother to come to school?" He said tearfully, "She can't come because she's sick, but anyway, she's German too." I felt so sorry for him. I told him, "You just wait and I'll straighten this out."
> So when lunch money was taken up I put it all in a little box and gave it to the German boy and told him to take it to the lunchroom ladies. Then I landed in on that bunch. I told them how ashamed I was. And I said, "I'm going to tell your parents. I know them, and I'll let them handle you." One little boy said, "Oh, they'll kill us!" I went on and talked to them and asked them how they'd feel. I just ate them out. And when recess came the same little boy who said his parents would kill him, put his arm around the German boy and said, "Come on, let's go play some ball." And that was the end of it.[24]

In forming an alliance with parents for control of the classroom, a teacher had to be sensitive to the traditions of discipline at the school and in the community. These traditions varied from school to school and community to community, and to a degree teachers had to make their actions conform to the local customs and expectations. At one school a teacher who almost never had to use physical punishment nonetheless knew very well when it was required. Discipline was moral training, and rural communities not only expected the teacher to enforce community mores, they demanded it as an important aspect of employment: "There was an attic above the classroom, and I sent one of the boys up with some books to store that we weren't using. After a few minutes, water started coming down the walls. I had to wait three days before I had good enough control of my emotions. I was very angry. Then I gave him a whipping. I remember seeing that boy years later when he was a man, and I thought maybe that wasn't such a terrible thing to do [laughs]. But we did have a toilet outside."[25] Another teacher said, "I only spanked two kids during the two years I was at Valley View. One I spanked for taking out his pocket knife and carving a hole in the bottom of his desk where he kept his books. He ruined it. I took the wooden piece out and made a paddle from it and gave him a spanking."[26] Possibly neither of the teachers involved in the incidents above could have kept their jobs if they had not taken action. As Elsie Hamill told us, "I wouldn't have had my job if I hadn't had good discipline. That day and time it was expected. I never did really want to whip children, but I used the paddle if I had to."[27] In clear-cut incidents of violation of the behavior code, the teacher was not only free to impose severe punishments but often felt compelled to take action in line with community expectations.

> It was right after lunch. I told them to get out their pencils and papers, and we were going to have a writing lesson. There wasn't a pencil in the room! One child had had 50 cents on his desk, and that 50 cents was gone. I said, "Just all of you stand up, and we'll see if we can locate those pencils. Those pencils don't have feet. They can't walk." So they all stood up – except one little girl. I said, "Honey, what's wrong? Why aren't you standing up?" Another child said, Miss Onnie, she's got something under her blouse." And you know, she had all the pencils in the room right there. Her daddy had a store down the highway. There wasn't any use at all for her to steal those things. I did what I thought I should do. It was just plain stealing. I paddled her.[28]

Parents and trustees had few external cues by which to judge the quality of teaching in their school, but discipline and the caliber of school programs and entertainments were two of them. At some places the willingness and ability to administer physical punishment was an absolute requirement for being rehired.

> I wanted to succeed, so I began listening to what the residents of the community said they considered to be a successful teacher. At the

supper table one night the man in whose house I was boarding for $20 a month came to the point when he asked me if I had spanked any kids this year. The behavior of my fourth, fifth, and sixth graders was above reproach, so I had to say, "No."

He said, "You won't be considered a good teacher if you don't do some paddling."

Knowing that he was on the school board and that the rehiring was drawing near, I began to work out a scheme for measuring up to what was expected of a good teacher by spanking at least one pupil. So I said to my sixth grade class, thinking the bigger the kid I spanked the more enhanced my status would be, "If anybody misses three words in spelling tomorrow, he will get a spanking." The biggest boy in the room, who was the son of the man who informed me of my short-comings, missed three words and gave me my chance to demonstrate my spanking ability. He got the spanking, and I advanced one notch up the ladder of success and was reelected for another term of seven months at a raise in salary from $70 to $80 per month.[29]

Although this matter of disciplining the trustees' children was always a delicate issue for teachers, the trustees usually gave their teachers strong support in disciplinary matters. And when discipline caused a teacher to come into real conflict with a parent, that support was needed.

When I was teaching at Bodark I had a problem that often happened on the road to school. Somebody had cut down some trees and left great big stumps. So, I put one little girl on this stump and one little girl on this stump and so on—every play period they had to sit on a stump. Every morning I got a note from mama. "Don't you make my children sit on a stump another day, or I'll come up there and pull your hair." I told Mr. Phelps, the people I was living with at the time, that I was going to come home after school time baldheaded because this woman was going to pull my hair out. Mr. Phelps said, "You be sure those children are sitting on those stumps tomorrow." So I made them set there just as long as I said they were going to have to. You know, she never did come. I said they were going to set there for a week, and they set there for a week. Then, at the end of the year, we were having a little party and this woman came in and worked just like a Turk. And I didn't hear anything about it.[30]

On one occasion a teacher who had a rule that both children involved in a fight would always be punished had to whip two boys, one of them a trustee's son. "So that night someone knocked on the door, and there was Mr. Persky. He said, 'Miss Willib, you spanked my boy today.' I said, 'Yessir, Lee got into a fight.' Then

125

he said, 'Don't you know you're not supposed to spank a trustee's son?' I said, 'No sir, I didn't know that.' I'm sure I was speechless about that time, and he began to laugh! He says, 'That's the best thing you ever did.'"[31] The following incident showed just how swift and comforting trustee support could be when a really serious issue arose with a parent:

> In those days I never was very much of a whipper, but I did whip one little boy. After I whipped him he ran off and went home. . . . When he came back, he had pin scratches all up his legs to his knees – he looked like he'd run through a briar patch. But he went home and told his parents that that was belt marks that my whipping had left on him. So they came up there and jumped on me about it, and [told me] if I didn't pay them fifty dollars they was going to take it to court. Well I wasn't but seventeen, and I was scared to death! Word got to the trustees, somebody went and told them what had happened, and they just took the harness off their mules and got on them bareback and came to the school to help out! It was the same afternoon. They got this boy out and looked at him, and they said, "Don't worry, Miss Bell, a thing about it. They can't do a thing, and besides, that's blackmail." I was so scared. I always had wonderful cooperation.[32]

One can almost see the faithful trustees riding muleback to the teacher's rescue! To sum up, during the 1920s and 1930s most female teachers had little problem with discipline. The parents were close, concerned, and generally supportive of the teacher; the students were accustomed to acknowledging adult authority; and when real trouble arose, the trustees were ready and willing to help deal with it.

Other factors also worked in favor of classroom discipline. For one thing, having many a student in class year after year, teachers had very detailed knowledge of those students' natures, characters, and family backgrounds. With this knowledge came an increased ability to nip discipline problems in the bud or to intervene quickly to solve problems that did emerge. As Weldon Hutcheson said, "I had the advantage of knowing all those youngsters, and knowing their peculiarities, and that gave me a better opportunity to try and be of help to them. . . . If I had a problem with one of them I could go talk to the parent, 'cause I knew the parent. Generally speaking, we were friends, and I knew that that parent wanted that kid to accomplish something. That's the reason why

126

I say that many of these kids that were finishing back then in many respects got a better basic education than those that are going through now."[33] Or, as Susie Bell Anderson put it, "The big advantage is that the teachers know the children. They know what their difficulties are, they know if they have problems at home, and they know if they are going to have to have extra attention at school. In the smaller schools you usually visited in the homes. You knew if they had any problems there, and maybe you could smooth over a lot of those problems when you were in school."[34] Teachers had the knowledge, time, and commitment to help students work out personal problems that showed up at school. Sometimes the teacher could go beyond a disciplinary symptom, addressing instead the cause of the problem:

> I had a little boy that . . . I encouraged to enter junior declamation. He was very backward, but I got him to memorize his speech. And I would tell him – he was timid – I'd say, "Now, you go home, and to-night after you get those chickens fed and that cow milked, you climb up on that rail fence, and you sit upon that fence, and you say your speech loud and clear to those cows and things." He was embarrassed to talk to his people in the house. And I want to tell you, I took him and won the county declamation with the little old fellow! I was proud of that. Some good can come out of Nazareth, is what I'm trying to say.[35]

Successful interventions like this were always based on close, personal knowledge of both the children and their families.

There is some evidence that in these days before the serious enforcement of compulsory school attendence in rural Texas the real behavior problems never showed up at school. Families kept out of school those children who were retarded, troublesome, or who, in the opinion of the family, lacked proper aptitude for schooling. These children never attended school or else were withdrawn after trouble developed, partly for the good of the child and partly for family honor. The result was that country teachers only rarely had to deal with the severe behavioral problems that modern teachers know so well.[36] When they did, they often did not fare much better, as these two accounts attest:

> I had quite a time at Griffin. I had one little boy who was just ter-
> rible. I didn't know what to do with him. I'd put him in the cloak room

and shut the door because I couldn't teach with him in there. He jumped up and talked and interrupted. One time I shut him in that room and left him in there and forgot about it and left him in there and went home [laughs]. I called the other teacher, and the other teacher went over there, and he said he'd already raised the window and got out. He didn't act any better after that.[37]

I had a kleptomaniac who went by the blacksmith's shop on his way and picked up the blacksmith's eyeglasses and came on to school with them. Course I didn't know this, but I knew that he was a "klepto." He was always taking the kids' pencils and things, and the only way I could make him give it back or tell me was to start spanking him with his belt. I'd make him take off his little belt, and I'd start spanking him. (I wouldn't do it that way now if I had it to do over.) Anyway, Dick, the blacksmith's older son, I suppose he must have been eighteen or nineteen, came up to me and said, "The only person we saw come through was Clemo." So I called him out. I said, "Now, you took those glasses." He began to cry and say, "Oh no, I didn't! Ever' time anyone takes anything you lay it on me!" And so on and so forth, until I think, "I guess I'm wrong this time." But anyway I got the belt and started spanking him, and I told him I was gonna spank him until he told what he had done with those glasses. So he said he had threw it in the outhole of the boys' toilet! Dick had to go get a big long wire and reach down in there and finally grab those glasses [laughs].[38]

Discipline is a fascinating topic for the historian of the country school, but the problem in discussing it is that we may give the impression that life in these schools was just one disciplinary incident after another. Of course, this was decidedly not so. The average rural school ran smoothly and serenely from fall to early spring. Mostly what was heard inside were the peaceful noises of the daily round – children's voices at the recitation bench, the shuffling of paper and creaking of desks, the drone of an occasional passing wasp, and the sharp pinging of the metal roof as it heated in the sun. Only very occasionally was there the sharp crack of the switch upon buttocks of wayward scholars.

Among average rural teachers in average schools, discipline then as now depended in large measure upon the personality of the teacher. Like Lonie Brite and Lula Byars, in Caldwell County, and like Wanda DuBose's favorite teacher, "Miss Grace," at Peach School, in Upshur County, some teachers were like "the barnyard cat/that keeps a pack of leaping dogs at bay/by concentrating/and looking a certain way." Miss Grace was a worthy case in point. She ruled not only her own classroom, but the miles of country lanes that led from her students' homes to the school. Anything that happened from the time children left their front gates in the morning until they returned to them in the evening was within her jurisdiction:

> Miss Grace was a real pretty lady in her twenties. She had beautiful black hair and pretty blue eyes, and she wore a beautiful blue coat in the winter time. She was the typical Southern lady – so gentle and kind and never used any kind of slang or raised her voice. And that was the way she ruled those big, rough-type boys that she taught. Her voice was so kind, yet when she said something, she meant it! I mean, you better not question it, 'cause when she said, "You do so-and-so," so kind, if those boys didn't do it, she'd whip them. She'd just really whip them with a belt. She'd take them to the cloak room and whip them, and they didn't try to fight back or anything. And she was always taking us on picnics; if you were good, she'd always reward you.
>
> She almost whipped me one time. You see, if you had a fight on the way home from school before you went into your gate at home, she still had the authority over you to whip you when you came back to school, no matter what the fight was about. The word would get back to her every time. It never failed.[39]

Even in the normal country schools, Texas rural schoolchildren did not behave like little angels; the Miss Graces of the land needed their carefully escalated regimens of punishment. At the ironically named Fairplay School in the 1940s, students would crawl under the schoolhouse to smoke and emerge to rock the girls' privy whenever one went inside.[40] Boys would dip girls' pigtails in the inkwells set in the top of their desks, flick ink from their pen staffs when the teacher's back was turned, or tie girls' braids to the back of their desks so that when they tried to rise their heads would snap back.[41] At Good Hope School near Center, love notes were passed around the room, and when they had served their purpose were "dropped down the wall through a knothole, where they remain till this day." A favorite sentiment was,

> A ball of mud on a stick of wood
> A kiss from you would do me good
> The road is wide, and you can't step it
> I love you, and you can't hep it.[42]

Students leaving Adkins School in a disorderly fashion, 1941. Courtesy East Central Historical Group, East Central ISD, Bexar County. Sadie F. Wade.

Wood stoves mysteriously blew open their doors many times in the history of Texas rural education, often with the assist of a small quantity of black powder. One teacher at the Missouri Avenue School, in Ochiltree County, spotted a student playing with something in a tobacco sack and commanded him to throw it into the wood stove. This was a mistake, as the sack was full of .22 shells, and "It sounded like a battle!"[43] Another teacher smelled a horrible odor one morning and found a small boy holding his cold, bare, horny foot against the wood stove to burn the manufacturer's name into the callus of his heel.[44] The Tabernacle School was struck by a clever biological time bomb one winter day. Students on the way to school had found a hornets' nest full of hibernating hornets, had plugged the entrance with a small piece of ice, then had hidden it in the school. When the teacher got there and started up the wood stove, the room heated, the ice melted, and hornets boiled out, and school was over for that day.[45]

One ancient discipline problem for the country schoolteacher came from outside, the "school taunter." These were young free spirits from the neighborhood who came by the school to mock their imprisoned counterparts inside. This sound of a free voice was invariably infuriating to the boys, who would rush outside to the attack despite anything their teacher could do or say:

> I drove the oxen and the two-wheeled cart to go to the water mill and such. In them days, it was a great insult to say, "You have bread and rotten egg for supper." I was going to the mill one day, past the school, and I said that to the children. I thought the teacher wouldn't let them come out, but I made a mistake, for they was just like yellowjackets pouring out of the hive. They threw sticks and stones at us, and that surprised the ox and he ran. The road was rough and that cart had no spring and the corn was scattered on the road. Marster whipped us for that. Not hard, just a couple of licks.[46]

The irony of this account from before the Civil War was, of course, that the voice taunting the schoolboys from outside was that of a slave, and the prisoners were the sons of his masters. Nonetheless, his words still stung.

The expletive "school butter," which may have had sexual overtones, was used as a school taunt in various areas of the state, but whenever it was used, the taunter had better get ready to run or fight. At Carson County, cowboys from the 6666 Ranch would occasionally stick their heads in a school and holler, "School butter!" and one former student described the usual result: "That taunt from anyone was a sign for the instant dismissal of school. Every boy and the biggest girls let out chasing him. If he was on a horse, they mounted theirs and chased him until they caught him. If he was afoot, they chased him for miles. A good booting was proper punishment for the 'school butter' taunter."[47] According to Otho Harrison of Baylor County, "school butter" was treated even more seriously there. Around 1910 a "smart alec from Seymour" drove by the Cache Creek School in his buggy and yelled, "School butter! School butter!" As this former student said, "that was the biggest insult that could be offered. . . . The big boys from the school grabbed horses from a wagon and gave chase. They ran the offender some four miles, caught him, and brought him back. Then [they] laid him across the wagon tongue and whipped him viciously

with belts, then took off his trousers and made him walk around
the house twice. After a few 'gentle pieces of advice about his conduct,' they let him go. No more 'school butter'!"[48]

Although it does not fall into the category of conscious mischief, a discipline problem for some Texas teachers was the boys'
attempts to earn pocket money by laying traplines along their
routes to and from school. Traps were normally run in the morning on the way to school, and since one of the chief furbearers of
the 1920s was the skunk or "polecat," success on the trapline could
lead to trouble at school. Several students and teachers have commented on the peculiarly unwholesome odor of skunk-impregnated
overalls under the influence of a wood stove. A number of students
told of having been made to go home or to build a cedar fire outside the school and stand in the smoke to deodorize their clothes.[49]
Sometimes trapping led to even bigger trouble:

> I was the meanest boy that ever attended Armstrong School. I trapped
> for wild life and on the way to school one morning I took a skunk
> out of one of my traps and buried it. The odor was apparent at school,
> and the teacher sent me home. I was so furious I wanted to get re-
> venge. The next night I caught an ol' possum alive. I hurried to school
> before the teacher arrived and put the live creature in her desk drawer
> where she kept her roll book. After the pupils had been seated and
> she was to call the roll, she pulled the drawer open, the possum jumped
> out, and began running about the room. What a commotion! I ask
> you, was I smart, mean or bad?[50]

A traditional disobedience far older and more significant than
trapping was the custom of playing hooky (or playing tricks on
the teacher) every April Fool's Day. This custom, reported from
all across Texas, evidently was quite old. In the 1890s R. T. Smith,
at Cottonwood School, was familiar with the practice from his boy-
hood school in Tennessee and so was prepared when all his students hid out in the nearby creek bottom. Professor Smith just
locked the school so they could not play any tricks on the inside
and went home for the day.[51] One year on the first of April at the
Red Hill School, in Swisher County, the students played hooky and
rode over to disrupt classes at the nearby Vigo School. The next
April Fool's Day, "to keep the kids from playing hooky and getting in trouble, the whole community declared a holiday and went

on a picnic to Palo Duro Canyon.[52] At North Elm School, in Bell County, it was the tradition to lock the teacher out of the school on April Fool's Day, and the teacher showed up with candy and fruit to try to coax the students to let him in. Another time this teacher found a big farm wagon in the school building; students had taken it apart piece by piece and assembled it inside.[53] Sometimes the community planned a surprise of its own for those children that ran away from school on April Fool's Day. For example, at Cache Creek School, in Baylor County,

> One April first the boys and girls decided to run off at noon. When the teacher rang the bell, the kids ran to the spring where they entertained themselves with various games. Around two o'clock several women came with lots of ice cream, cakes, cookies, apples, bananas, candy, etc. When it dawned on the runaways that something was going on at the school house, they sent a delegate to ask if they could return. The answer was that they could return, but could not share the goodies. About two-thirds of the kids were bitterly disappointed.[54]

April first "Hooky Day" was a modest affair of an hour's dinnertime on Bread Tray Mountain for students at Pleasant Grove School, in Mills County. However, this cost them dearly when they returned. Their innovative teacher made each student lift larger and larger rocks on the school grounds until he found the largest rock he thought each child could handle. Each student had to carry his special rock during the morning recess and the noon dinner hour for the week that followed the illicit picnic.[55]

Apparently, the Pleasant Grove community saw nothing wrong in this punishment. Teachers had to be careful to use punishments that were within the traditions of the school, that were acceptable to the community at large, and that did not arouse the ire of parents because they seemed to ridicule the child and, by extension, the child's family. Beyond that, teachers were limited only by their imaginations in devising appropriate modes of discipline to fit the minor and major crimes committed under their jurisdictions.

When Charlie White got to his first school, he saw prominently displayed a "switch barrel" full of many sizes of switches, one to fit every child. After his first transgression, fighting with a bigger boy, "I thought I got whipped plenty hard, but I didn't get it like that big boy did. Looked like when the teacher hit him with that

133

big stick he almost lifted him right off the ground. I told Isabel, 'I'm gonna try to learn to behave myself before I get big enough to get whipped with a stick that size.'"[56] Many teachers used switches, often adding the psychological punishment of requiring the lawbreaker to go outside and select from the trees and shrubs surrounding the school an instrument appropriate for his discipline. If he failed to select one sufficiently large the teacher would go out to choose another, and that would be unfortunate indeed, as teacher-selected wands invariably were very large and strong.

Often veteran teachers evolved a calibrated series of punishments, whipping being only the last resort. One pioneer teacher at Mount Vernon School, in Bell County, used four punishments in ascending order of magnitude: (1) The transgressor would be made to stand on one foot for a period of time. (2) If a boy disobeyed, he was made to go up and down the rows of boys and girls asking if he could sit with them until someone allowed him to do so (this was considered very humiliating). (3) The roof of this unceilinged school was supported by posts, and a child would be made to climb up a post and stay there for a specified period of time. (4) As a last resort, the child would be sent outside to cut a switch and was whipped.[57]

Beyond the punishments of the flesh were a wide range of psychological sanctions. It was very common to make children stay in during recess, or else just sit on the sidelines and watch. Boys who got into a fight in one school were made to "kiss and make up," something surely regarded with horror. One teacher made her students sing a little song about "How Dumb I Am" while they stood in the corner. Standing with one's nose in a ring on the blackboard was a common punishment, far more usual than teacher Frank Chudej's making his students kneel on a rock. The forced memorizing of something very dull and instructive, such as the Preamble to the Constitution, was favored by some.[58] One Shelby County teacher simply made her students sit on the floor under their desks.[59]

One final approach was to develop something in one's school program so interesting and motivational that the threat of its being withheld was sufficient sanction. For example, O. T. Baker's first teacher in Shelby County kept Baker and the other first-year students in line by threatening to withhold a cherished privilege normally exercised during the last fifteen minutes of every school day – the right to fight red wasps with pine tops under the school eaves.[60] In Caldwell County, Onita King developed a similar "behavioral" approach to classroom control:

> You have to have something to use to help you with your discipline. If I hadn't been a disciplinarian I don't ever think I could have endured teaching in a small school like that. I always played baseball with my boys, and I want to tell you, they had to walk the line if they wanted to get to play baseball! In later years in the other one-room schools that I taught I had so many Latin Americans, Mexican boys, I used baseball as a large tool to discipline with. If they didn't study their lessons, and if they didn't behave themselves, they didn't get to play on the baseball team.[61]

8. Spelling Bees
and School Closings

A GREAT MANY COMMUNITY ACTIVITIES took place in and around the country schools. There were Friday afternoon spelling contests and public recitals that the community attended. Major school programs at Thanksgiving, Christmas, and "school closing day" drew large audiences to hear student recitals, plays, singing, song-and-dance performances, and a variety of other things. Rural schools were the functional centers of their communities, and the countryside was starved for any kind of entertainment, even the simple Friday afternoon spelling bee: "Most time, on Friday afternoons, the children liked to have something like an assembly. They would want to have recitations, and nearly every Friday we'd have a spelling bee to see who could spell the best and stay up the longest. We'd have it for the parents and the public to come in. You'd be surprised how they would come. They'd just flock to the school."[1] The significance of the country school for entertainment can hardly be overemphasized. This was a time when, as one of our grandmothers once told us, persons would come for miles in Nacogdoches County to see the flames shooting out of her family's brick kiln at night. Communities looked to their schools for entertainments, and woe unto the teacher who failed to put on good ones. Even when no community programs were planned, schools often were under surveillance by community members hopeful that the teacher and students would do something, anything, amusing. Mrs. H. M. Gunn told us how starved for action her community was: "You'd see 'em over there at the store standing there watching us at recess. We'd play kick ball, and those old men would come over there and stand at the store and watch us, and they'd come over there when we got all three rooms together and sing. We'd see 'em standing outside, watching and listening. You know, German people love music."[2]

Weldon Hutcheson of Caldwell County was one of the very first teachers interviewed in the Common Schools Oral History Project of the University of Texas, but even after hundreds of descriptions of school entertainments, his account still best captures the spirit of the times and the vast gap between then and now:

> Here's something you may have trouble conceiving. Normally there was some kind of community activity that went on at least two or three weekends out of the month, because everybody had to supply their own entertainment. People enjoyed getting together. They might

Girls volleyball team at Sayers Rural High School, 1924–25. Courtesy East Central Historical Group, East Central ISD, Bexar County.

Gathering for a school program at Camp San Saba, McCulloch County, ca.
1890. Wayne Spiller, copy courtesy University of Texas Institute of Texan Cultures.

get together and have a singing, and so on like that. Twice a year
at the school you'd have a school play, and you'd have a Christmas
pageant at Christmas, and usually have a Christmas tree.

Well, gosh, you wouldn't have room to seat everybody, because everybody came! They didn't have nowheres else to go, and after all, they
either had kids, grandkids, or nieces or nephews in school anyway.
Out in those little old country schools, usually, every darn kid that
was in the school performed. At a Christmas program there'd be songs
and maybe some kind of a little skit. You know, we were rather easily
entertained back then. Then, sometimes, there'd be some kind of a
little comic something done. In other words, those little first graders,
well, they got up and sang some kind of damn little old song, just
to give them something to do. And then somebody'd memorized some
little ditty and get up and say it, and everybody would just set there
like they were having the biggest time!

You see, you're talking about times that's just so different from now
that there's no comparison. People just didn't get out and go very
far, and any activity that was in the community, everybody turned
out for it. The center of the community was the church and the school,
and of course in the church, you didn't have any of these social activities like you have in them now. That was in the school. If there
was any community meeting, it was held at the school, because that
was the only place to hold it. In the summer, when you'd have any
of these political races, usually you'd have some kind of an affair, and

138

all of the candidates from local offices would be down there and every one of them would speak. Usually that meeting was at the school, because that was the only building.[3]

As Hutcheson noted, schools were used for many community purposes besides the education of children, and their internal arrangements showed various adjustments to those other purposes. Country schools also functioned as meeting halls and club rooms and polling places and as the centers of every conceivable sort of rural entertainment from the turkey shoot to the three-act play. Many schools had a stage at the front of the room, and "for every stage there had to be a curtain."

> If there are any merchants living, I'm sure they can tell a story about the country school curtains. There were traveling printers and artists that went from school to school trying to sell a new curtain to the school board. To pay for the curtain, a group of community patrons descended upon the county merchants asking them to take ads (at a certain price) to be printed on the curtain. When the curtain was finished it looked something like a patchwork quilt. There were many small blocks with the names of different firms handprinted in each block, and a few hand-painted flowers and landscapes added for attraction. When the first program was held, the whole community viewed the curtain with pride.[4]

Many a two-room school was divided, not by a proper wall but by some kind of movable partition pulled down from the ceiling or out from the sides. For example, Midway School, in Parker County, "was built with big square columns in the center, where big doors were attached that could be raised to make it a big one-room for community programs, church on Sunday, Saturday evening singings, Sunday community dinners, and on Christmas a huge big live oak that would be cut and brought in by the fathers and decorated by the mothers and children and teachers."[5]

As we have seen, more than one-half of the Texas rural schools in 1935 had a piano, but music as such was seldom part of regular instruction; the main purpose of the piano was to serve as musical accompaniment for a variety of community programs.

At the Oslo community, a Norwegian settlement in Hansford County, the school was the first community building erected by the Anders L. Mordt Land Company. Mordt, himself a recent ar-

139

rival from Norway, placed advertisements in several leading Norwegian language publications in Iowa, Illinois, Wisconsin, and Minnesota. The schoolhouse was built in 1909, the same year the first settlers arrived at the site. The Oslo community school became the center of everything. Used for religious services, picnics, spelling bees, programs, Bible school, pie suppers, and the meetings of the Young People's Society, it also served as living quarters for recently arrived families until they could build a home.[6]

The Newark School was built in Wise County around 1900. This two-story structure also served many purposes, including regular Sunday services for the Church of Christ, gospel meetings and debates during the summer, and the pie suppers, box suppers, and plays of the regular school year. In the partitioned room upstairs the principal teacher shared space with the Woodmen of the World.[7] Likewise, when Lula Byars's McMahan School was not having one

Students of China Grove School in costume for a school play, 1926–27. Courtesy East Central Historical Group, East Central ISD, Bexar County.

of its famous programs, the building was in use for alternating Sunday services of the local Methodist and Baptist churches, special community "planning sessions" of all sorts, visits from the county agent, and meetings of the County Home Demonstration Club.[8]

In Protestant communities fractured by religious differences into several warring camps, the schools were often the only neutral ground. As they did at McMahan, the denominations alternated Sunday services in the school buildings in the early days, then after their churches were built, used the school for all community-wide secular functions. As an elderly lady in the Red Rock community of Bastrop County once explained to us, "Churches divide a community, the school brings it together." No matter what fine lines of personal differences or theological belief divided neighbors in a time of deep religious faith, the country school was always a place where people could come together.

Lula Byars mentioned that McMahan School was used for "special community meetings of every kind." One of these kinds of special meeting was probably the sort of conflict resolution, or "kangaroo court," described by Wanda DuBose in Upshur County:

> They used the school to vote, and they used the school for any kind of community activity. It was where they met. If there was a disturbance and they had to get together and talk and have sort of a kangaroo court. Like if somebody shoots somebody else's dog and they were upset about it, instead of taking it to town to the sheriff, they'd just get together, and some of the older men would hear the case and try to reconcile it that way. I remember an incident where somebody shot somebody's rooster, 'cause he went over and ate up their garden, and they met in the schoolhouse for that. It was the only place where they had a building to go where it wouldn't be somebody's home – sort of a neutral place.[9]

As community center and neutral ground, the school was the natural launching place for any program of community improvement. Regarding themselves as guests of their communities, teachers usually, but not always, waited for trustees and other community members to take the lead on such innovations. Some teachers made full use of their position at the center of community life. Here is one such instance from the teaching career of the remarkable Lula Byars of Caldwell County:

141

I'll tell you something else we did out there that's still going on. The colored cemetery was right next to the white cemetery out there at McMahan. Well, the colored cemetery was so woolly and wild looking that I said to the children one day, I said, "You know how many of you all have people in that cemetery right up here on the hill?" And they all were holding their hands: "My grandmother's buried there! My daddy's buried there! I got an auntie buried there, Mrs. Byars!"

And I said, "You know what, you all tell your parents that I want to talk to 'em about the cemetery and see if we can't set a day aside and clean off the thing up there. I'm ashamed of you all's cemetery!" The children went home and told their parents exactly what I had said, and Mr. Thomas (one of the trustees) came over to the school. He said, "Mrs. Byars, Charles came home the other day and told us what you had said about that cemetery." And I said, "I'm glad he did, Mr. Thomas; it's a disgrace before God for you all to let the cemetery go like that. You follow 'em to the grave, and then you leave 'em and forget about 'em. You at least ought to have enough love and respect to keep them clean!"

I said, "Let's set a day aside and all go to the cemetery and see if we can't clean up that place some." All the children brought hoes, rakes, and everything that next week, and here come the parents, and we cleaned it up so it looked like a different place. And I told them, "It takes so little, if everybody would take part." We'd meet at the schoolhouse, and all the parents would come. They'd meet us there at the school on a Saturday morning sometimes two or three times a year. And, Honey, we'd clean that cemetery![10]

Mrs. Byars had the McMahan community in the palm of her hand with school programs that were the talk of the countryside. Small wonder that the school patrons were willing to clean up their cemetery for her.

Some community activities in the rural school building were informal, unauthorized, and at times illegal. After school hours and in the summer card players, whiskey drinkers, wolf hunters, and other followers of the sporting life gathered there. Many a tramp spent the night in a rural school. The buildings were seldom locked; when they were, usually it was a simple matter to raise a window and climb in. Teachers often complained about the dirt and disorder left behind by these night owls. Generally, though their wives might decry it, school trustees and other community males winked at these "men's club" activities, because they were disallowed at home and could be held nowhere other than in the school building. Like the Moon School, in Cottle County, however,

142

several schools were burned down by the nocturnal carelessness of persons unknown.[11]

There is little doubt, though, that the main secondary purpose of the rural school was to stage community entertainments. Teachers who had grown up in the country knew this very well, and city teachers found it out very soon after they came. Trustees and parents paid little attention to the technical side of the teacher's instructions in the three R's, but they looked very closely at two aspects of job performance – discipline and community programs. When William Owens's first Christmas program at Pin Hook School was a big success, he breathed a huge sigh of relief, knowing he had passed one big test of his teaching abilities. A person who had known him a long time came up to him after the program to give him the ultimate mark of approval, saying, "I knowed you'd be a good teacher."[12] The person may have known it, but only with the successful school program was it an established fact. A teacher at Bembrook School, in West Texas, described her feelings on a similar occasion: "May 30, 1925, was the real test of my teaching ability. The end-of-school program was ready to begin. Would the kids forget their lines, would the Coleman gasoline lamp go out, would the wigs stay on, or would the audience like the production? All these questions went through my head when the curtain (bed sheets) went up. But as the dialogues were said, the songs were sung, and the lamp stayed bright, my fears were gone – I was a good teacher, because as many said, 'She has put on a good program.'"[13] The first grand occasion of the yearly round at nearly all country schools was Christmas; the second was the end-of-school affair. And there were many others as well. In fact, sometimes it seemed that schools seized upon every conceivable occasion for a community program. (We have seen that even the humble Friday afternoon spelling bee could draw large audiences.) One night a month at Oxford School, in Parker County, the school would hold an "exhibition," where debates, plays, singings, speeches, and dialogues brought the benefits of the world of culture to a rural public; elsewhere in the county the New Hope School held an affair at the other extreme of schoolroom entertainments, the "Opossum Roast." Dale Roark, a teacher at New Hope in the 1930s, was even dubbed "Official Opossum Roaster."[14]

At the Crossville School, in Bell County, one night a month

143

was "parents' night." The students put on a program or a spelling bee, and then the parents played dominoes and other games until quite late.[15] As Josephine Ballard summed up the varied programs at Hubbard School,

> We had singings both in the schoolhouse and in private homes. One girl played the organ, and she or her sister led the singing. She boasted that she would take her group and sing against anyone anywhere. . . .
> Each summer there was a revival under a brush arbor on the schoolground. There was usually a stand where cold drinks and ice cream would be bought. As I look back I think the young people looked forward to these revivals more as social events than as spiritual ones.
> The schoolhouse was really the center of the community. It was our one building for everything. We had no organization of parents and teachers, but they worked together for the good of all. We had box suppers to raise money. The women and girls made beautifully decorated boxes and filled them with all kinds of delicious foods. They were auctioned to the highest bidder who then got to eat with the owner of the box. We organized a club which we called our Literary Club. Twice a month on Friday night we had a program for the entire community. Maybe it was a play or perhaps a lively debate between two debate teams of students. Sometimes the parents debated the students. We also had spelling bees and arithmetic contests.[16]

Hubbard School's Literary Club had counterparts at many country schools, often with an emphasis on dramatic productions of one sort or another. At Shiloh School, in Parker County, for example, the school "Literary Society . . . was carried on like a Community Theater or Straw Hat theater – going on through the summer months. A program or play was presented every Friday night."[17] Three-act plays became so popular at Armstrong School, in Bell County, that the young people of the area continued to produce plays for the community long after they were out of school.[18] At many places adult school patrons were not just a passive audience for these dramatic excursions. A teacher at a black school in Central Texas said,

> Once during the year I'd a program with the adults. We had a play there through the adults, and, you know, those adult people learned their parts. Some of them couldn't read, and their children would teach them. When we had that program, if there was a little old two-cent quartet around there somewhere, we'd get them to sing, and it went over big.[19]

Students of Ernestine Edmunds at St. Hedwig celebrate Thanksgiving, 1918. Ernestine Edmunds Collection, San Antonio Conservation Society.

Often at such dramatic productions, literary affairs, and box suppers, some of the family men and young bloods of the community gathered outside the school building to talk, socialize, smoke, and perhaps have a drink or two. Things seem to have gotten a little out of hand at one such literary society meeting in the Maxdale District of Bell County. The school had burned the year before, and the literary society was meeting in temporary facilities donated by the community Primitive Baptist Church. Meanwhile, outside, two young men got into a fight, and as a result one of their saddle horses was shot to death. Literary society or no, this was too unseemly for the Primitive Baptists, who threw the school out of their church building.[20]

Many school entertainments were designed both to entertain the community and to raise money for the school. One woman from Bowen School, just across the Arkansas line, reported that Bowen used the following events to make money in 1928: two Friday afternoon spelling bees a month; one play a month (usually a comedy); and pie suppers, box suppers, and cake walks at irregular intervals.[21] Box suppers were particularly popular as school fundraisers, and Susie Bell Anderson remembered well the box suppers at her Hall School:

145

The girls and single women all brought boxes filled with food for two. I remember that my mother was quite artistic; she made me a big box in the shape of a star and covered it with gold paper and put some handmade crepe paper flowers on top of it. The others would have pretty boxes, too. There'd be fried chicken and cakes, pies — such as that — food for two. The young men would bid on these. They weren't supposed to know [which box], and sometimes one would spend a good deal of money, think he was bidding on a certain girl's box, and it would be some other lady's. The parents and older people came and would sit there and watch the bidding.[22]

Some schools were more successful than others at this money raising. In later years Mrs. Anderson took a job at a Czech and German school in the vicinity of Seguin. When she first arrived, she was astounded at the size of the school library, the excellence of its teacherage, and the remarkable array of instructional materials Laisner School's teachers were provided with. At the traditional supper held in the fall of the school year, she found out Laisner's secret strategy for fundraising:

I was principal. We were getting ready for the supper, and I was supposed to be making all the arrangements for it. Well, the morning of the supper, a great big beer truck drove up and began to unload beer. I went out there and said, "You weren't authorized to bring this beer out here!" He said, "Oh yes we were." And I said, "Well, who authorized it?" He said, "One of the trustees. Why, they've always had that; we've always drove a truckload of beer out here to these suppers!" People from all over the county came and from even farther away. Their sausage was delicious, and they had all that beer, you know. And they had bingo, cakewalks, and so forth.[23]

Sometimes there were very interesting, if one-way, relationships between black and Anglo schools in the same and adjacent districts on the matter of school programs. In many places the pattern was clear: the white trustees and other members of the Anglo community felt free to attend the entertainments at local black schools, but blacks were seldom if ever welcome at Anglo programs. Sometimes the white audiences came right inside for the black Christmas programs or school closings, but at other places they kept a somewhat greater social distance. At Lytton Springs Colored School, "Those whites would come out there in their cars, and stay in their cars and turn their headlights on so they could see

146

what was going on on the stage. I know they were out there. Over half of our audience was white."[24]

The Anglo school in one district had a custom of holding weekly "devotional" programs, and one teacher made it a practice to invite the black teacher to bring her students up to the Anglo school and put on the program for her. This was in the nature of a command performance, one the black teacher evidently did not think she could refuse:

> The devotion would be some singing and two or three poems, or something like that. They sent the bus down there and got us, then all them mothers would be there to listen at this program. She would have us come and do this devotion for her, instead of her and her children, whenever her time came around. All the mothers from the white community would come up there, but none of our folks didn't go but me and the children. We sang "There Is a Church in the Valley by the Wildwood," "Jesus Wants Me for a Sunbeam," "Joy Bells Ringing in Your Ears," "Glory, Glory, Hallelujah," and all those kind of songs. Well, that'd throw my schedule out of line, you see![25]

At the tiny, one-room McMahan Colored School, the resourceful Lula Byars somehow managed to put on a community film series, much to the delight of her large, triethnic audience. Clearly McMahan School had the best show in town.

> The ladies were the nicest things to me while I was out there. You know, in the country, out in the rural schools, on school closing day they'd have big dinners and things like that. The white ladies would come with their big baskets, and one or two would bring dinner in a tub! They would take part in everything we had out there. . . . I'd have programs all the time out there, musical programs and first one thing and another, and they'd all come. We had more Caucasians out there than we had black folk. I had a friend in Smithville that one time ran a movie house in Austin. I got in touch with him, and once a month he would come and bring picture shows to the school. They would all come, and oh, they had a time! All the folk, not just the colored, 'cause they didn't have anything like that noway to go to. Everybody would come, white, black, Mexicans, all. Everybody seemed to enjoy it immensely. It was in my school, that same little building. And people would be standing all on the outside, looking in the windows, in the doors, everywhere, because the building was small.[26]

All across Texas, the grand spectacles of the performance year were expected to come at Christmas and on school closing day. On these two occasions the teacher made her mark. She might approach them with delight or with loathing, but she knew that her community would judge her on the basis of how well her programs went on these two days. All over the state, teachers responded with ambitious and elaborate entertainments. These amused and astounded rural school patrons and made such indelible impressions on the minds of students that even in the 1980s many of them remembered parts of their school program recitations. One black school in Central Texas expanded its closing ceremonies to three days to meet popular demand. Trustees at Hall School and many other places customarily built special stages outside the school buildings for each school closing, tearing them down after the performances. Lonie Brite somehow managed to stage "wordless Tom Thumb weddings" in full costume, with Mexican bands to accompany. Another school enjoyed "Musical pageants two and a half hours long. They danced, they waltzed, they would speak! I would show them how I wanted it done, and if they didn't do it exactly right, we went over it again, until, when I drew those velour curtains, fine piano upon the stage, they did it!"[27] All this made a great impression upon the schoolchildren. Sometime around 1895, as a first grader, S. L. Davis of Austin walked out into the center of the stage at St. John's Colony School and recited the following verses to a packed house:

> Some of the boys in our school,
> Whose elbow I cannot reach,
> Are ten times more ashamed than I,
> To rise and make a speech.
> Oh, I guess they were afraid some girl,
> Who was just about their age,
> Might laugh and criticize their looks,
> When they came on the stage.[28]

Frankie Franks remembered not only many of her own recitations from the school programs of six decades ago but also a verse recited by one of her cousins, which she believed to be a "good, wise poem for anybody today." The poem began with Longfellow, but its moral was even more direct:

> I shot an arrow in the air,
> It fell in the distant, I know not where.
> The farmer said it killed his calf.

148

I had to pay him four dollars and a half.
I bought some poison to slay some rats.
The farmer said it killed his cat.
Rather than argue across the fence,
I paid him two dollars and fifty cents.
And that's the way with random shots,
They never hit in the proper spot.
The joke you spring you think so smart,
May leave a wound in somebody's heart.[29]

The Christmas program made a lifelong impression on many students: "The community Christmas tree party, always held in the schoolhouse, was a time of almost unbearable excitement when we were small. The first glimpse of the lighted tree would even outshine our expectations. It would be so tall it seemed to reach beyond the ceiling, and so brilliant it outshone the stars. No child was overlooked on that occasion."[30] Teachers' and students' testimony was full of wonderful recollections of Christmas programs in the country schools. Here is one from Josephine Ballard's Hubbard School:

At Christmas time we had a program by the pupils from both rooms, with manger scenes, angels, songs, plays, and such together with Santa Claus and the biggest Christmas tree we could get through the classroom door. It was like a holiday when the teachers said we were going to the mountain to get a Christmas tree. We had plenty of cedars to choose from, so we always got a big beautiful one. After it was chopped down the students and teachers dragged it to the door. The trunk was sawed smooth and boards were nailed to it, then to the floor. No Christmas tree stand would hold our tree. Most of the time some of the community men came to help and supervise putting the tree up. There were few decorations except homemade ones like popcorn on strings and chains made of red and green paper. Gifts were not wrapped. Handkerchiefs, scarfs, and such were spread over the branches. Dolls, trucks, and such toys as we could buy, were tied on the tree. . . . Dishes, vases, and other glass articles were set under the tree.[31]

The teacher at the two-room Goodcreek School told of a memorable Christmas program financed by an extraordinarily successful box supper that just preceded it.

We had this money, and we wanted to have a Christmas program. We didn't have any kind of a stage. The school board members bought some lumber and built a stage, and we proceeded to work on this pro-

149

gram. We worked for weeks. We had what we thought was a real program, one that involved every student. . . . We went out in the woods and found the nicest, biggest tree you could find. For the stage we bought green cotton material and made a curtain. Then we had two dressing rooms curtained off to one side. In one of these we put the Christmas tree and didn't let anybody see it until we were ready. We worked at night getting the tree ready. We didn't have enough money for presents, but we did have enough to put candy in little mesh sacks for every child in school. Well, there happened to be a gentleman in the community who was wealthy, and he had a great love for all the kids. He decided that that year he would buy all the children in school a toy. For every girl, and I think there was nineteen, he bought a big doll. And for the boys there was marbles and balls and whatever they liked. Nobody knew anything about it. That night the building was just full. I will never forget the reaction that I had when we opened that curtain and here was this beautiful tree! Were the kids surprised! That is the highlight of my life.[32]

If Christmas was big, the school program that accompanied the closing of the school at the end of the year was usually even bigger. Without the unifying symbols associated with Jesus' birth, Santa Claus, and the Christmas tree, the programs for school closings were more variable than those at Christmas. Because they were so ambitious and the anticipated audiences so large, they were almost all conducted outside. As Wanda DuBose described, in parts of East Texas school closings often combined the usual sorts of school presentations with a day-long "Texas stew":

At Grice the men of the community usually came real early in the morning of the last day and they had a couple of big washpots. And some folks would donate chickens, some butter, some tomatoes, potatoes and corn, and things like that. And some people would bring squirrel and whatever meat they had, wild game if they had it. Or they might go out and kill it that day. So they'd come and sit there all day long cooking and then late in the afternoon everybody began to come in and have their supper. And it was really good![33]

Three hundred miles to the southwest, Lula Byars moved her act outside the school and staged "little dramas, little short plays, little playlets, singing, recitations, things like that. And we would have little drills, you know, little fan drills and flag drills and things like that. We'd have to have them on the outside. The building wasn't large enough. I'd have my piano sitting on a truck outside. I'd always be up on the truck to play."[34]

Weeks ahead of time at literally thousands of country schools across Texas, parents and trustees began to prepare for the school closing. While teachers planned programs and rehearsed children, mothers made costumes from flour sacks and crepe paper and everything they could get their hands on. At the same time, men brought in lumber and built elaborate outdoor stages that often were linked to the school buildings so that the schools themselves could be used as "backstage." Then, sometimes for two or even three days, the show would go on. At times these early school programs seemed almost unbelievably elaborate. As a case in point, here is one former student's report on the remarkable school programs at Carson County's Lone Star School around 1900:

> I remember one drill especially: the Sword Drill. Anna had made our costumes of dark blue cotton, and caps, trimmed in red military braid [flat tape]. W. H. Hickox had whittled the wooden swords into shape using heavy wire to twist and shape the handles, then covered the wood with tinfoil taken from cigar boxes (D. O. Wolf, a veteran of the Civil War, just could not believe they were not real). Anna, Floyd, and Lena were the soldiers; Lester was the drummer boy. . . .
>
> The school had bought a very small organ (one pedaled with the feet), and Mrs. Younger played the marches. It was a varied program of recitations [readings], songs, and dialogues. I wish I had space to go into detail about the drills, readings, pantomimes, etc., many of which were done in costume, to show you how much could be accomplished with so little to do it with and how whole-hearted the people and the pupils entered into it. It seems there was endless practice and memorizing at home and at school from one recital to the next, which were done at the close of both fall and spring terms of school. I remember one lovely pantomime drill where the girls wore angel-costumes and the teacher read "Sandalphon" behind the curtain. A colored spot light thrown on the last pose was made by a match being touched to a pan of colored powder at the far end of the room.[35]

Many schools ended the year with picnics at favored sites in the nearby countryside, a picnic that for the students at Round Timber School, near Seymour, was graced with ice-cold pop and the pleasures of wading in the Brazos River.[36] At Gilbert J. Jordan's Willow Creek School, in the German Hill Country, the school closing picnic began with a parade from the school to traditional picnic grounds in the pecan bottoms about a mile down Willow Creek. The wagons, hacks, and buggies in the parade were decorated with bright-colored crepe paper, and "some of the boys and a few girls on sidesaddles rode their horses decked out with ribbons and paper flowers on saddle and bridles. Then we moved in a gay procession, led by mounted flag bearers, to the picnic grounds, singing, shouting and talking." Parents, older and younger brothers and sisters, and most of the rest of the community were already in the bottoms. A wooden stage had been built in the pecan grove, and after the schoolchildren arrived they staged an elaborate program of poems, songs, and skits they had learned in school. The youngest children (whose language at home was German) recited such traditional German poems as "Klaus ist in den Wald gegangen, weil er will die Vöglein fangen" ["Klaus has gone into the woods because he wants to catch the birds"] and "Fuchs, du hast die Gans gestohlen" ["Fox, you have stolen the goose"]. "There were also recitations of English poems, such as Longfellow's 'Under the spreading chestnut tree the village smithy stands.' Some pupil usually orated the 'Concord Hymn' and tried to impress the Texas ranchmen with this poem about the 'embattled farmers' of 1775."

Recitations, songs, pantomime acts, and other presentations were followed by political speeches from the candidates of the year, but by that time most of the children had escaped to the refreshment stand for soda pop, lemonade, chewing gum, popcorn, and homemade ice cream. The men and older boys chewed and smoked, and, as Gilbert Jordan observed, "To this day, the smell of cigar smoke out in the open air reminds me of school picnics in the pecan bottoms, and to this day I think smoking and chewing tobacco are outdoor sports. At noon our lunch was served on the ground." In the afternoon there were footraces, tree-climbing contests, the pitching of horseshoes and dollars, wading in Willow Creek, and a traditional baseball game, which was always held in a nearby pasture. "When the game ended, the picnic was over and we left. Going home at the end of the day had a touch of sadness about it. We were leaving our playmates and going home for a summer of hard work on the farm or ranch."[37]

9. Professors and Schoolmarms

F OR MANY PEOPLE, the commitment to schoolteaching came very early in life; some of these people told us they could not recall a time when they had not planned to become a teacher. In fact, some combined their own school assignments with fantasies of future teaching careers:

> When I was in the third grade, about age eight, I wanted to be a schoolteacher. . . . I'd get a piece of chalk or two from the chalkboard and bring home with me, and I'd play school out in the yard until dark. We had two fireplaces. One was yellow brick, and one was red brick. And the red brick was slick – I could write on that. So that was my blackboard. And I'd get the rake and a broom and a shovel and an axe and a mop and put 'em in a circle under the ash tree. Those were my students. The mop was very unruly. I would grab this mop and a switch, and I'd really whip him with that switch. Then I'd set him back down on the ground. Then I'd put arithmetic problems on the chimney, and I'd put the answers. I'd write my spelling words that we had in school. That was one way I could learn them.[1]

Many were like Ochee Holt, who "just grew up knowing I'd be a a schoolteacher."[2] Often there were long family traditions of schoolteaching. As Doris Green told us, "I was the fourth youngest child, and all the others had been teachers, and I was dying to teach school."[3] Mrs. Robert Page had seven brothers and sisters, and they all taught school.[4] Velma Adams "came from a fam-

153

ily of teachers on both sides of my family. My aunt was a pioneer Texas teacher."[5]

Some got a very early start. Charles Gregg was taught to read by his mother before he started school; by age seven he had already helped a cousin learn to read. "I decided then to become a teacher,"[6] he said. By the time students had reached the fifth or sixth grade, the peer-teaching customs of the country school already had apprenticed the brighter ones to the teaching craft. They might have several years of this sort of practice teaching behind them before they graduated from the rural school at grade seven or eight. This aspect of the ungraded school should be kept in mind when we consider the accounts of girls age sixteen or seventeen becoming classroom teachers. For many, this was just a formalization of what they had done in their peer-teaching days.

Getting a certificate to teach was another matter. Texas teacher certification could be acquired in either of two ways: by passing a written examination or by acquisition of credit from an institution of higher learning. The majority of Texas rural teachers were certified by third- and second-grade certificates earned by written examination. First-grade and permanent certificates, though they could be earned by examination, generally were obtained through institutions of higher education.

Examinations to certify teachers were administered five times each year in the county courthouse by the county superintendent and two appointed examination board members. Both appointed members were required to have first-grade certification or higher. Persons desiring to take the examination were required to submit character recommendations from "three good and well-known citizens." The county examination board graded the third-grade examinations.

An applicant for a third-grade teaching certificate was administered a written examination in spelling, reading, writing, arithmetic, English grammar, geography, Texas history, elementary physiology and hygiene, the laws of health with special reference to narcotics, school management, and methods of teaching. Those persons in search of a second-grade certificate answered questions on all the subjects listed above and on United States history, elementary principles of civil government, English composition, and physical geography. The seeker of a first-grade certificate dealt with all subjects covered for a second grade and in addition "physics, algebra, elements of geometry, the Constitution of the United States and of Texas, general history, and the effects of tobacco and alcoholic intoxicants upon the human system."[7] The examination for a permanent certificate was even more onerous, and it was no wonder that most teachers preferred to obtain it automatically by successful completion of a degree at an approved college.

The third-grade certificate, which allowed a person to teach grades one through six for a period of two years, was the entry point into the profession for most rural schoolteachers. The problem most faced, however, was the gap between the level of subject matter provided by the average seven- or eight-graded country school and the requirements of even the third-grade examination. One way to fill this academic gap was to go away to an accredited high school, but for the country student, getting into such a high school was not often easy:

> No one in the district had ever gone higher in school than the eight grades taught at Hubbard. I had different aspirations. I had no idea how I would accomplish it, but I intended to finish high school — maybe even go to college. Most of the students were glad to finish the eighth grade and be out of school forever. One girl and I wanted to continue our education. We began planning ways of accomplishing our desire. We began with the school trustees. We asked them to add the ninth grade to the Hubbard curriculum. They were willing but had to consult the teacher. She, being interested in doing anything to help the students, agreed. I promised to give her all kinds of help, much of which I was already doing. So, we had nine grades in school instead of eight. This was one hurdle passed in my search for a high school diploma. When I finished the ninth grade I entered Gatesville High School and made good grades from the beginning — I made the A Honor Roll.[8]

Making "the A Honor Roll" is easily said, but in another letter teacher Josephine Ballard described the real price she had had to pay for a high school degree and a teaching career. She was boarding in Gatesville to attend high school, and before her first year was over, her father, "an average-income farmer," was struck by a severe drought.

> It looked as if I would be unable to finish high school after all. I was determined. I persuaded my parents to allow me to work with some

155

family in Gatesville for my room and board, thus enabling me to attend school. They finally consented.

I found an elderly couple that wanted help. I moved in with them and began work. My chores were many and varied. They including rising at four o'clock each morning, cooking breakfast, washing the dishes, and cleaning the house. This I did by daybreak. Then I milked the cow and led her to the pasture to graze. I then walked across town to school.

After school I brought the cow in from the pasture and milked her, gathered the eggs, and fed the chickens. By then it was time to cook supper and wash the dishes. We then sat by the fire and talked, listened to the phonograph, or read. Sometimes I went straight to my room and studied. . . . In 1926 I got my high school diploma.[9]

One large group of rural teachers attended enough high school to pass the third-class examination, took a first teaching job at age sixteen or seventeen, then pursued additional certifications by attending summer institutes between school terms. Most of these teachers never saw the inside of a college or normal school. That road to the permanent certificate was long and hard, too. The following is a typical account:

When I finished high school at seventeen I took state examinations which qualified me for a second-grade certificate for two years. I taught these two years and then took state examinations for a first-grade certificate, a four-year certificate. During the six years that I taught on these certificates I went to school twelve weeks each summer and took correspondence courses in between so that I would have enough credits to add up to two years of college work and a permanent primary certificate. That piece of parchment was like gold in my hand. I was so proud.[10]

The summer normal institutes played an important role, helping hard-pressed and underpaid teachers to attain higher certifications and advance their careers. The purpose of the institutes was to provide short-term training related to the written examinations for certification in a variety of locations statewide. Institutes were conducted by county superintendents and visiting college faculty, with many college and normal-school professors acting as lecturers. Regulated by the state's Department of Education, the Summer Normal Institute usually lasted five weeks. Regulations required each Summer Normal Institute to provide adequate buildings, library, laboratory, and boarding facilities and to employ special instructors of recognized teaching and administrative ability, one of whom had to be a specialist in primary methods. Warren Travis White remembered his "summer normal" from about 1920:

> Now do not confuse my "summer normal" with any state institution. Each summer several superintendents, principals, and teachers, under the leadership of another superintendent who knew his way around, in most part college or university graduates wanting to make some extra money, would organize a "normal." It was not difficult to get approval of the state superintendent because country schools needed teachers. A graduate of a good high school had rather good qualifications for these teaching jobs, but he mut have a valid certificate.
>
> In the summer normal the curriculum consisted of conventional high-school subjects, primary and elementary methods, and management. There was also a conglomerate of what seemed to me to be "ethereal phantasy" which probably had some of the elements of later pedagogical psychology. After six weeks of this rather concentrated capsule of learning, carefully guarded examinations prepared in Austin were sent to the normal for administering to the candidates for certificates.[11]

The summer normal institutes should not be confused with the one-week teachers' institutes often held in the county seat towns before the beginning of each school year. These doubtless played some role in helping teachers prepare for higher certification, but their main purpose was "in-service" training for the county systems. Teachers had mixed memories of these usually obligatory functions. For some they were a cross to be borne; for others they were a chance to socialize with peers before the usual professional isolation of the school year. Sometimes, however, things that rural teachers heard in a one-week institute stayed with them throughout their careers:

> We used to have to go to the institute before school started. We had about a week that we had to go to Goliad every day. We kind of got the framework for our work every year. I remember several of the things he said. He said, "Now, don't let your children drink from a stagnant pool. I know that you don't have much time to work with each child, but at least keep abreast of things as they happen. You can give them something interesting." I thought about that all through my teaching year; that's something that stayed with me. And another thing he said, "I think a dedicated teacher gets paid in three ways.

157

First of all, the salary, and it's small. Then you get paid by the love of the children. Then, I hope there'll be a star in your crown for being faithful."[12]

A second group of rural teachers, their numbers increasing as time went on, attended some sort of institution of higher education – a normal school or a college. There was a progression of educational requirements for teacher certification, but for many years these stopped short of demanding a bachelor's degree. The normal school provided training beyond high school, training that required less time and less commitment on the part of the teacher candidate. The idea of an interim educational program designed for teachers had been implemented in 1879 with the founding of Sam Houston State Normal Institute, in Huntsville. As a normal school it issued only teaching credentials, not degrees. The role of the normal school as part of the interim educational program was expressed at the opening of North Texas Normal, in Denton, in 1903: "The Normal is neither a college nor a university. The statute creating the institution declares its purpose to be 'for the special training of teachers.'"[13]

One of the functions of normal schools was to provide remedial high school training for those rural students that still needed it. "Sub-college" programs admitted pupils from the unaccredited rural high schools and prepared them for the advanced subject matter of teacher certification. When rural students came, as they often did, with no high school background whatsoever, the entry exams for the subnormal programs could be traumatic: "The entrance examination was our first introduction to our college life. I had had no high school work and the exams were a farce as far as my passing them was concerned. The authorities let me see some grades: 19 in Texas History, 27 in arithmetic, etc. But I made freshman entrance – they did not send me back home. They didn't turn anybody away."[14]

Elsie Hamill came from the same general family background as William Owens, and both attended East Texas State Normal, at Commerce, about 1920. Both had come to the same conclusions about teaching careers for many of the same reasons. As Hamill said, "It was a basic love for me to go to school. The second thing for me was that it was very hard work and hot work to go out there in the field and work. So I thought it was really a life of ease to go to school and get out of that hot field."

For Hamill, as for Owens, however, the building of a better life required a lot of hard work, some of it back in the cotton field:

> You could go to Commerce and they had a subcollege there. If you went to school there a year, you could get a three-year certificate and teach. . . . We light housekept, several of us, using the same little apartment, cooked and whatever. I went that year, but I ran out of money the first six months. I didn't have enough money to go that fall. So I went down to Troy, Texas, where my uncle lived, where he had a blackland farm, and he had a lot of cotton. I picked cotton, and then I went from there to my other uncle on the plains at Levelland and they were pulling cotton out there. By the time Christmas came I had a hundred dollars, and I went back to Commerce to go to school.

After Hamill's cotton-picking money ran out, she managed to get a job as a domestic servant for the school's dean of women and so made it through normal school.[15]

This hardscrabble existence at the regional normal school was a common experience of many rural teachers. Essie Adele Haynes described how she cooked, ironed, and tutored for room, board, and school supplies at Southwest Texas State Normal, at San Marcos:

> Well, I was very fortunate, was very happy. I cooked the breakfast for Mrs. Kinsel and her husband and Mr. Kinsel's brother [who] was there, a very old man. I cooked breakfast for the four of us every morning, and I'd do the dishes before I'd go off to college. I didn't have to cook the lunch, but I did prepare the evening meal. I ordered all the groceries over the telephone. I did the ironing for all the family. She hired her washing done. A woman came and washed out under the tree in a big number-three tub and hung them on the line. And I found different ways to make money. I ironed for a family across the street, she had five children. I did the whole family ironing for twenty-five cents an ironing. I also read to a blind girl for twenty-five cents an hour paid for me by the state. That was my money to buy pencils and notebook paper, which I needed for my studies. I stayed there, and I loved it very much, but I had to work pretty hard.[16]

As these hardships suggest, even the teachers who could begin their teaching careers with attendance at a normal school or college rarely were able to remain continuously in residence. Much more commonly they attended for a year or so, took their precious

Trustees of Saltrillo School, 1931. Courtesy East Central Historical Group, East Central ISD, Bexar County. Nola Schroeder Ristow.

third-class or second-class certificate, and went out to find a school. Subsequent advancement through higher and higher certificates, perhaps culminating in a university degree, typically went on as opportunities permitted: a summer normal attended this year, correspondence courses taken the next, a summer's attendance at the nearest normal school the following year, and so on. The salary commonly bestowed upon the country school teacher allowed no other option.

Getting the first teaching position could be a real problem. Many trustees cared little for the quality of the teacher's certificate or how many years of college she or he had, but they did care about teaching experience. As we will see, at various places and times district trustees went to some trouble to recruit teachers for their schools, putting out the message through personal friends and family networks, writing letters to state normal schools and placing ads in newspapers. This sort of recruitment was most common in the 1910s and least common during the economic depression of the 1930s, but it was never the norm. In normal circumstances, job seeking was up to the teacher, and was a laborious process of traveling from district to district and trustee to trustee. Here are two variations on the usual story of obtaining a first teaching position, one from an older college man and one from a young woman just out of high school:

> I applied for a one-teacher school near my home [Grayson County]. There were three trustees and it became necessary for me to contact each one individually. I found them plowing in the field across from their home – they called it the "fur piece." I trudged across the plowed ground just like the candidates did in seeking votes. They were courteous to me but would not say much. Each man asked me "How much 'sperience do you have?" I had to tell the truth and say none. They were not concerned. One trustee said, "I don't know you, but I know your family name." I got the job. (What's in a name?) The contract called for $60 per month. I was to furnish the coal to heat the schoolhouse, and get tuition for any pupil under eight years of age [for] $1.50 per month, and $2.00 for any pupils over 17. I got three unders and no overs, which about paid for the coal.[17]

> At the end of this last public school year for me, I took an examination in the county superintendent's office and received a third-grade certificate to teach. At the superintendent's suggestion, I applied for a small school ten miles "back in the woods," down east of Franklin.
> Mama let me wear one of her long dresses to look more mature. Brother took me in the buggy to see the first trustee. I had to go to the cotton field to see him. During our conversation I took his hoe to show him that I knew how to "chop cotton." This proved almost a catastrophe when the hoe got tangled in my long dress. He was understanding and soon put me at ease. Then he suggested going with me to see a second trustee, a Mr. Cavitt. . . . These two told me that I could have the school and that they would see the third trustee.[18]

Although most trustees were farmers, and farmers were naturally in the field, this matter of impressing them by demonstration of cotton-chopping prowess was most unusual. Many teachers told similar stories about "trudging across freshly plowed ground wearing my best and only patent shoes and silk hose for interviews with a succession of trustees."[19] The three trustees that separately interviewed Lillian Danton Milam of West all asked the same three questions: What were her qualifications? What religious denomination did she belong to? Could she play the piano?[20] Another board of trustees met with a teacher applicant in a joint interview and asked her to spell "asafetida" and to tell them whether she would relinquish the school at the end of a three-month period if the board felt she couldn't handle it.[21] Although the second teacher flunked the test of spelling "asafetida," the answers of both teachers must have been otherwise satisfactory, because they got their respective jobs.

Sometimes, as in this account from Willie Faye Wiley, a job applicant had no problems with two of the three trustees, but had to return to the third more than once to wear down his resistance.

> The roads to each of the homes of the trustees were almost impassable. Two of them were so nice to me and gave me the school on my first visit. One trustee made me visit him three times before he consented to try me for just one year. The one and only question he asked me was: "Are you a looking for a place to flap? The teacher before you was a flapper and we don't want another flapper out here." Well, I have never been able to understand why nor how a flapper could flap in the wilderness of which I was about to become "a lone ranger."[22]

Most trustees were polite and courteous to job applicants, though they must have endured a steady stream of these interrupting each day's work. Some, however, must have relished this chance to show smart college men what they thought. William Owens ruefully observed, "I learned fast that there was no one tougher, harder to talk to than the trustee of a country school, especially a trustee with a job to give out. . . . School-hunting time was a busy time for farmers, and most of them resented having to stop work long enough to talk to anyone who wanted to be a schoolteacher. One told me scornfully that there were more schoolteachers than Baptist preachers. He let me know that he had little use for either."[23]

When Owens got his first job at Faulkner School District, he did so in large measure because he was personally known to the trustees, and this was the case in the majority of instances of first employment reported. Most country teachers began their teaching careers in or around their home counties in places where they or their family names were personally known. Given a crowd of candidates with hard-to-judge credentials, local trustees naturally favored young women or men with known family connections to the area. Candidates with connections sometimes could even unseat competent incumbents that had none. After one year William Owens went on to another community some distance away but failed to be rehired after a generally competent teaching performance. The board of trustees had changed and now looked with disfavor on Owens's disciplinary methods – or so they said. Others in the community told him it was primarily because one trustee had a family candidate to advance for the position.[24]

Even though commonly there were many more candidates than teaching jobs, there were always schools that, for a variety of reasons, had to go recruiting. In the remote Panhandle, during World War I, Lee L. Johnson found himself much in demand. He was the only person willing to take the Dumas School, and there were so few teachers in the area that several schools could not find teachers for their regular terms. For a while Johnson went from school to school, teaching four- and five-month terms back to back. One year he taught at three different schools.[25] Bradshaw, on the other hand, was a prosperous farming community in southern Taylor County, and in the normal course of things could have waited for teachers to come to it. However, in the spring of 1924 there was a massive political blowout at the school, a new board of trustees was elected on the slogan "Clean the Slate," and all the teachers quit or were fired. Then the new board wrote to the registrar of North Texas Agriculture College, at Arlington, telling him the community's troubles and asking him to suggest four persons to take the school. This the registrar did, and as one of the four candidates told us, "The Board unanimously elected us and sent each of us a silver Eversharp pencil with our initials for a graduation gift."[26]

Most of the schools that went recruiting did so because their communities were both remote and outside the cultural mainstream of Anglo Texas. In these situations the new teachers could experience a considerable degree of culture shock. Here are three first-school stories about young schoolteachers a long way from home.

163

In 1927 when teachers were a dime a dozen, I was lured to a position in the Bean School in Hudspeth County not only by the munificent salary of $100 a month, but also by an urge for adventure.

When I excitedly descended from the Pullman at dawn, the postmistress of Fort Hancock directed me to Hare's Hotel-Cafe-Dancehall-Mercantile Company across the tracks. There I was given a room and told that Bud Bean, one of the trustees, would be in for his mail in a day or two; he would take me to Esperanza, ten miles down the Rio Grande where the school was located.

That night I was invited to the regular Saturday night dance in Hare's Hall. I danced a few times with burly cowboys in boiled white shirts and shined boots, but I was too tired from excitement to enjoy the shindig. As soon as I fell into bed, I was out like a light, only to be rudely awakened at 2 a.m. by a drunken man shaking me and demanding a dance with the new schoolmarm. Laughing uproariously, two other men evicted him, leaving me trembling and determined to return to Austin by the next train.

I pushed the dresser against the lockless door and piled every other available piece of furniture to make a mountain. The rest of the night I sat bolt upright with the covers pulled up to my chin, my heart pounding like the clapper of a trail bell at a crossing.

Trustee Bud Bean arrived early the next morning, and in his persuasive manner, talked me into staying. In fact, I stayed and experienced many more events new to an incredibly naive 18-year-old.[27]

That story came from the Trans-Pecos. The second comes from a young East Texas girl bound for the environs of Zapata, Texas, which was steeped in ancient Hispanic culture. The teacher was nineteen, and the year was 1924.

I boarded the train in Arp and traveled to Laredo, Texas, which was 467 miles. Then in Laredo I boarded the U.S. Mail car and went to Zapata, the county seat, which was 80 miles. There my credentials were recorded at the courthouse. The next lap of my journey was by U.S. Mail cart drawn by a donkey. The driver and I rode 20 miles in silence, as he did not speak a word of English. On my arrival in La Peña I was taken to my boardinghouse. The house was one room made of mesquite logs for walls, a dirt floor, and a thatched roof. That room was shared by the owner and myself. Her kitchen was a smaller house of the same description, separated from the larger house by a walkway. . . .

Come Monday morning I went to school to meet my students and to see the school building. The building was a former mission with twelve-inch-thick walls and cobblestone floor. The key to the door was about eight inches long and solid brass. There were two doors to the building but no windows at all. My students were all Mexican. They spoke no English unless they had to. I had instructions to never use Spanish, in order to force them to use English. There were eight grades in the school and about twenty students. There was a nice teacher's desk and chair and conventional desks for the students and a supply of books. Also a blackboard behind the teacher's desk and a box of crayon. There was an eighth-grade girl who spoke English very well, and she became my interpreter.[28]

A final first-school account shows that a young teacher could find herself in a situation of culture shock right in her home county.

Graduating from Bryan High School in May of 1922, I knew that I must become a teacher. . . . By the time I had qualified, there remained only one school without a teacher [in the county]. It was a one-room, one-teacher school, having five grades and forty pupils. I learned that two teachers had accepted the Goodson School before I [but had] later resigned because there was no place to room and board. There were a few other obstacles of which I learned later.

This small community was made up of Polish and Italian families. After I accepted the job, my superintendent told me to "put my spurs on." He offered to help me find a place to stay. The idea of teaching scared me a bit, since I was only five feet tall and weighed about 105 pounds. My father accompanied us to this community, and after much persuading and talking with a board member, we learned of a family that might let me stay with them. A Polish family with two grown girls, two grown boys, and two small boys offered me a room to be shared with their two grown daughters. This made seven grown people and two children living in a four-room house, with no running water and no indoor bath. The windows had no screens, and the only beds and covers were "feather beds." You slept on one and covered with another. I did sleep warm! The mother, father, and three grown children had been born in Poland.[29]

All this, of course, was only the beginning. The eighteen-year-old teacher from Bryan learned to pronounce such names as Shikorski, Zulkorski, and Glowski when she called her school roll each morning. Though she had been raised "a proud Baptist," she visited her community's Catholic church on Sunday and was "invited (and expected) to attend Italian wedding feasts and Polish dances on Sunday nights. . . . With my father's permission, I did go, because I couldn't stay home without screens on the windows, and besides the entire family went along to enjoy the 'fiddling' and

165

dancing. Learning to do the polka and eating the good Polish and Italian food were experiences I can't or would never want to forget as a part of my first year's teaching experience."[30] Some of the cultural differences the teacher was reacting to were attributable not to her host family's Polish heritage but to the life-style of rural Texans in the 1920s and 1930s. The feather beds, the lack of running water, indoor baths, and toilets – even the lack of screens – were common to many country homes in 1920. Emma Shirley's account of her first day at the Concord community offers a detailed town-girl's-eye-view of a typical rural Texas community – and suggests some important things about the semipaternal relationships between young female teachers and their trustee employers:

We rented our house from a man who owned a big farm outside of Waco. He came to me one time and said, "I know you've always said you wanted to be a teacher. I've got a school out on my farm if you'd like to have it. If you'll get a certificate, I'll let you have it." I was 15. The next Saturday afternoon I took off from work and took the exam. I couldn't teach until I was 16 but I had a birthday in November and I started teaching 7 days after that. The name of the school was Concord. I taught 53 years.

On Saturday morning, December 1, 1912, I rode the I. G. and N. train for fourteen miles north of Waco to its first stop, a road crossing. I stepped out into a world of picked-over cotton fields and was met by two trustees. They hurried me into a surrey pulled by two grey horses and we began the four mile drive to the little settlement of Concord.

I was wearing an ankle-length black skirt, white blouse, high-heeled black shoes, and a knee-length tan coat which had cost eleven dollars, almost the last dollar I had. My long hair was in a knot on top of my head, and I was wearing pinch-nose glasses on a silver chain, the style of that day. I hoped I looked like a school teacher.

Concord consisted of a large cotton gin, Burke's General Store, a snow-white Baptist Church with a graveyard adjoining, and a one-room schoolhouse, once painted red, but fading now. We stopped and met Mr. and Mrs. Burke and Mary, who would be in the first grade. We all went to the schoolhouse which Mrs. Burke and Mary had scrubbed clean. I assured the group that I could make a fire in the big wood stove when Monday morning came. The trustees showed me the pile of wood and the kindling they had cut and stacked near the wall. The two men and I then drove for a mile and a half to the Parrish home where I was to board for twelve dollars a month. Mrs. Parrish showed me my room, which was cold as ice with no stove nor fireplace. "You can sit with us or in the kitchen," she said.

On Sunday morning, the Parrishes took me to church. I was surprised to see all the men sat on the left-hand side and the women and children on the right. Of course, the women had all the care of the children who squirmed and cried and sometimes had to be taken outside. Between the church and Burke's Store were two Ford cars, several wagons, and one or two buggies. After church, I shook hands with everybody there.

That evening, Mr. Parrish regaled me with stories of "bad kids" he had known during his brief years of schooling. He related how he, himself, had carved his name in a desktop, and how he had dipped the pigtails of the girls who sat in front of him in the inkwell. In addition, he warned me about many other devious practices the children might try out on me, and offered to intercede any time he was needed. That night I learned I could undress in the cold and go to bed cold, but get warm snuggled in a feather mattress under a homemade wool quilt.[31]

The story of Emma Shirley's initiation to the Concord community just prior to beginning her career as a teacher brings out several pertinent points. First, the job was arranged by means of a family contact, in this case the trustee-landlord, whose recommendation admitted Emma Shirley into the Concord community. Second, the youthfulness of the teacher made the community role rather complex; to begin with, it must provide the teacher physical and emotional support much like that provided for the community's own youth. Living accommodations were arranged, transportation provided, a guided tour of the facilities given, and an introduction to the community performed much as for a visiting relative. In addition, while protecting Emma Shirley as a young teenager, the community of Concord was obligated to present her in an adult role with the aura of authority and respectability. Hence, the formal introductions to everyone at the church. Finally, Mr. Parrish's offer of more forceful support points up the familial responsibility often felt by the keepers of young schoolteachers in the rural community.[32]

The next account of the initiation of new rural teachers into the occupation shows the more usual phenomenon of teachers employed near the family home and receiving support from both the employing community and their own family in the transition from pupil to teacher. This pair of young teachers had the mixed blessing of a landlord full of both fatherly and teacherly advice:

My first job was in the rural school called Valley View. It was a two-teacher school, and my sister and I were teachers together. I was eighteen years old. At Valley View I lived with an old couple, Mr. and Mrs. Carter. Mr. Carter was a pioneer teacher and never lacked for advice. Papa and Mr. Carter were very close friends. They were early pioneers together, and Papa went over there and told him his daughters needed a place to stay. There's something to be said about the keeping, too.

Mr. Carter knew a lot of the problems that rural teachers were facing because he had worked in the rural schools. For example, one thing he said was that if you had trouble bringing the children in when the bell rang in the morning, it was normal because children were socially minded and didn't want to give up their contact in playing. "If you'll just read a segment of *Peck's Bad Boy* when school starts [he said], you'll get every kid in there because they like to hear the story." It was just one escapade after the other, and the youngsters were at an age when they enjoyed it and didn't want to miss hearing the next episode. It solved a big problem.

Another thing that Mr. Carter got on to me about was keeping my shoes neat. "You walk a mile to school and you'll get some pretty rough-looking shoes." By the time I directed school yard play for part of the day and walked to and from school over those rocky hills my shoes were always in need. And he censured me quite severely from time to time for my becomingness and dress.

Another time, his cow got out in the Arledge pasture, so I took his horse and rounded up old Daisy. He censured me because I wore my gym bloomers to ride the horse [laughs]. Wasn't becoming to a schoolteacher to ride astride. He was more than a father away from home. I was never disciplined quite so much by my father.

I seldom spent a weekend at the Carters'. My father's ranch was over on the north side of the river. It was twenty-four miles by car or carriage. If you went straight across the river and rode through the Arledge Ranch then went off the cliff it was a little more than five miles. Quite often Dad would come over and bring horses and we would just ride back home on Friday. We seldom spent a weekend at the Carters' if we could swim the river. It wasn't a choice place to stay. You had him for a companion, and he was long on advice.[33]

One gets the impression that the river had to be very high indeed before Mrs. Johnson failed to make it home for the weekend. This going home for the weekend, however, was not always permitted; many communities expected the teacher to stay around and become involved in weekend social life in a useful and highly visible way. Parents were well aware of the great impact the rural schoolteacher had on their children, so they demanded high standards of moral and social behavior, and part of this involved direct participation in the affairs of the community. The teacher's job, as defined by the school patrons, did not stop when school was dismissed on Friday afternoon.

This had not always been the case. As we have seen, most of the pioneer teachers were males, and rather rough cut at that. As W. W. Campbell described in a speech at the annual homecoming of the Tip Top community, in Parker County, communities at first had to take what they could get: "I will mention only two of the minor things that stayed the progress and development of the old settlers: very limited finances and illiteracy. If anyone came into the community who could read *McGuffey's Fourth Reader* and could cipher a little and pronounce words in the *Blue Speller,* he was a SCHOOLMASTER!"[34] Emma Shirley, writing as Clara Weems, described one version of the schoolteacher style of an earlier day:

An old-fashioned "professor" at the Walhalla School, Fayette County, ca. 1893–96. Milton L. Speckels, copy courtesy University of Texas Institute of Texan Cultures.

169

The pupils and their male teacher at Converse School, Bexar County, 1900. Courtesy East Central Historical Group, East Central ISD, Bexar County.

Old Mr. Grigsby, who taught school over the county for sixty years or more, bragged that he never went to college. He declared that college teachers were so smart-ikey that he couldn't teach with them. "Why they say two times two feet make four square feet," he used to say. "Now if that is true then two ducks times two ducks makes four square ducks. Now that's just the kind of foolishness they get in college."

Mr. Grigsby was very proud of his calling, and he wore a long-tailed coat at least twenty years after they went out of style. He became fat in his old age and he had to fasten his coat with a string tied through the buttonhole and looped over the button. The boys were always happy at the school where Mr. Grigsby taught, because they could chew tobacco all they desired because Mr. Grigsby chewed, too, and was not always talking about the evil effects of narcotics like the

170

lady teachers did. The fortunate boys under his tutelage did not have to bother to spit their tobacco in the ink bottles, but could spit out the windows or aim at the stove as the occasion demanded.[35]

Some of the old-style male schoolteachers were still around in the 1920s, but they were no longer generally accepted. The teacher who preceded the paragon Miss Grace at the Peach School chewed tobacco, spat out the open windows, rang the school bell from inside, and let his students "just rush through the door." Wanda DuBose was shocked because she "had always had this conception that a teacher was supposed to be almost like a holy person!" Parents evidently felt the same way; this teacher was fired in mid-term.[36]

By 1920, however, the cloth for the role of rural schoolteacher had been cut for a young, usually unmarried woman in her teens or twenties. The community expectations of the teacher at Maxwell School, in Bell County, were entirely typical. Teachers there had to be unmarried and could leave the community on only one weekend a month. They couldn't smoke, drink, dance, or have dates on school nights. They were expected to attend local church services regularly, teach Sunday school classes, and sing in the choir or play the organ or piano for church services regardless of their personal convictions. "They were required to be models of virtue and examples for all youth to see and follow."[37]

Sometimes the "moral exemplar" aspect of the schoolteacher's role was written into her contract, which often specified such things as the teaching of Sunday school, the number of weekends allowed away from the community, and the policy about dating on weeknights:

In 1927, my wife and I applied for a school in the Panhandle of Texas. After asking us many questions, the trustees said we were just what they were looking for.
Then they gave us the terms of the contract. Both of us would teach Sunday school and be there each Sunday. We belonged to different churches, but my wife would have to play the piano for church. (She didn't know how to play the piano.) We would not be permitted to leave on any weekend, smoke, dance, or attend picture shows. We asked if they would sign the same kind of contract with us. They said, "Certainly not." We did not get the school.[38]

171

Bessie Arnold Dodson, Hill County schoolteacher, 1906. Courtesy Ione Young.

The trustees in this case were making unusually stringent demands, but some kinds of informal restriction and requirements were usually in place. Perhaps most common of the formal agreements teachers would be asked to make was the agreement not to marry during the school term upon pain of losing the school. Here is one teacher's summary of the rural schoolteachers' "Thou shalts" and "Thou shalt nots" in the 1920s.

No female teacher in the Texas rural schools could be on her own. Teachers were elected with severe, strange, and sometimes ridiculous guidelines and restrictions. For example, no Catholic teacher need apply in many Texas schools. No dancing, no smoking, no dates with pupils, no dates on weeknights (only on weekends), no staying out after 10 p.m., no leaving community every weekend (only once per month), no playing bridge, no sick leaves, no substitute pay. What a negative life!

However, on the affirmative side, she could (and was expected to) attend church, teach Sunday school class, sing in the choir, attend prayer meeting, attend church suppers and festivals, plan entertainment for school and community, direct programs for school, church, and community. She must live in the community. Her life (personal, social, and religious) had been cut out for her long before she ever applied for a teaching position.[39]

These informal requirements grated on many, as apparently on this teacher. Others found community expectations entirely in line with their personal inclinations and so experienced no problems with their role as exemplar to the young and servant to the community. Some, like Lula Byars, took charge to clean up the community graveyard and make other contributions to the community. Other teachers, at various places and times, conducted the county school census,[40] set up special programs of adult education,[41] helped with the laying out of the dead and their transportation to the cemetery,[42] and even started a broom factory in the school to help defray its expenses.[43] Some very much enjoyed fulfilling community social expectations, including "Sunday afternoon singings at the church, community-wide mulligan stews, Saturday-night candy makings at various homes, trips to ribbon cane mills where fresh juice was served while the syrup was being cooked, all ball games and also all funerals.[44] Sometimes the teacher could not dance, and sometimes she had to. At Meeks School, in Bell County, a Czech community required the school's two teachers to attend all community dances and to "show no partiality." They were to dance with all who tapped them on the shoulder, with no rights of refusal.[45] Somewhere else a teacher played the organ for all-day singings in a brush arbor near the school, while young boys from the community pumped away. "Such famous quartets were there as the Stamp's Quartet and the Rippeytoe Brothers."[46] Many a teacher went "possum hunting" with his big boys, as did William Owens at Pin Hook School, or went on "bird thrashings," one of the lost entertainments of the rural world. As one teacher summed it up, "Never again will the teacher go robin and possum hunting with the students and their hounds; attend 'play parties' complete with square dancing and callers; walk to school with the students sharing a bucket of coals to keep their hands warm; be courted in the parlors and on the porches by proper young men with more than adequate chaperones; and play dominoes, and dominoes, and dominoes."[47]

When teachers violated (or even seemed to violate) the moral code, community response could be swift and drastic. At the Bradshaw School, in Taylor County, in 1924, three young women teachers made plans to put aside the frustrations of weeks of "pan" baths in the home of their trustee and landlord and go down to the barbershop for a real tub bath on Friday night. They made special arrangements with the barber to open his shop to do this, and accompanied by the trustee and his wife, they proceeded to the barber shop. The barber shop was normally a male stronghold in this community, and while they bathed innocently therein, the word went out, "The teachers are down at the barbershop! . . . When we came out, we were surprised to see what looked like half the community outside the door. I don't know what they were expecting to see, but they saw three clean girls, fully clothed, and chaperoned by Mr. and Mrs. Saunders. We never heard any criticism for our actions, but we did not go again."[48]

Things had become much more serious at one black school in Caldwell County in the 1930s. At this school the teacher had been leaving her classes unattended while she sat with her boyfriend in his car outside the school. The children, of course, watched all that went on with great interest from the windows. This violation of teacherly behavior so outraged the Anglo trustees' wives of the district that, "these ladies gave this girl word to get out of town and not be seen in that area any more. [If they] did, they were going to kill her." Appalled at these developments, the county superintendent called upon his star black teacher, Lula Byars, to go into the tense situation at the school to bring things under control and back to the proper moral plane. She described what happened as follows:

> So, when I went out there, my husband went with me that morning. They's all sitting there. The trustees came in and quite a few of the parents, you know, and the children, was sitting there. I told 'em, "I'm coming out here to work. When I go on a job, regardless of what kind of job it is, I try to give my very best in whatever I'm doing. And when I work, Lula's looking for her pay, and I'm not giving a nickel to let me work!" I said, "I'm going to let you know that now." I said, "If that's the type of person you're looking for, you don't want me!" The trustees were white, and the meeting was mixed, and the others was just prospectors, because there was a lot of 'em there [who] were not wives. And they never said a word – they never said a mumbling word![49]

The "nickel to let me work" Byars referred to probably had reference to the occasional practice reported from various places across Texas of Anglo trustees making black teachers pay to get a teaching position, and suggests that this had been the custom in the past at this unidentified school. Byars was letting them know in no uncertain terms that she would have none of it.

Lula Byars was one of a small group of rural teachers who commuted to their country schools on a daily basis from a nearby town. (Byars's town was Lockhart, the county seat.) As we have seen, the general expectation was that the teacher would reside in the community if at all possible. The 1924 survey found 73 percent of rural teachers reporting that they lived in their communities, 19 percent who resided there Monday through Friday, and only 8 percent who came and went on a daily basis.[50]

Many teachers roomed with trustees or other school patrons who lived in the general vicinity of the school. Sometimes, however, distances from the school to nearby homes were judged too great, or else no one was willing to board the teacher. For these

175

teachers the district built a home, or teacherage, right on the school grounds. This practice was reported from all across the state but seemed most common in the more remote parts of West and Central Texas. Teacherages tended to provide Spartan accommodations, even by the rough-and-ready standards of the time. Thelma Easterling stayed with three other teachers in a three-room teacherage at Ingleside School, near Olney, in 1929. As she said, "It was only three small rooms, and the roof leaked – we set a dishpan on the foot of the bed when it rained. We carried water from a pump. One double bed and a single bed furnished our bedroom. Our clothes hung on the wall."[51] Another teacher took up housekeeping with her co-teacher husband at Rabbit Creek School in a two-room teacherage her new husband had built himself right on the school grounds. The building cost $102.[52] Three young teachers in a school in Young County shared a teacherage with the principal teacher and his wife. The principal took the only room with a fireplace, while the unmarried women shivered in the cold northeast bedroom. One teacher said, "I learned then that I could freeze on the back part of me and burn on the front. We had a chance to be in [the room with the fireplace] some during the daylight hours."[53] Perhaps the housing problems had something to do with the fact that one of the three young teachers was secretly married at Thanksgiving, in violation of the district rules, and was taken away by her new husband at Christmas recess. Pauline Underwood gave us an excellent description of two of the teacherages in which she and her husband lived in West Texas. These were do-it-yourself affairs!

> After I married and was teaching in the little Silver Peak School, in Coke County, we had a four-room teacherage. 'Course the house was unpainted and completely unfurnished inside – just raw lumber with wind whistling through, or sand, or snow, or rain, or whatever. So every time we went to the grocery store we saved and flattened all the cardboard boxes in which our groceries were packed. My husband then covered walls and ceilings with this cardboard to insulate and keep out the cold. Later we tacked building paper on top of the cardboard. It wasn't very much to look at, just coarse gray paper with a little blue design and all those ugly black tacks showing, but it gave a certain finished appearance to our first home. No gas, no electricity, no water, no bathroom. We had one good Coleman lantern that gave a softer,

prettier light. There was a water well and windmill and tank down at the school. And, oh yes, I had the convenience of an ugly home-made tin sink in the kitchen. It was built onto a raw wooden frame and it drained through a pipe in the wall right out onto the ground outside. There were no kitchen cabinets, no closets in the bedroom either. But my husband put a rod across one corner of the bedroom to hang our clothes on, and I hung a sheet to cover and hide and pro-tect them. I told you my husband was handy with his hands. He even put a windcharger on our roof there. It looked something like a small windmill. It could generate just enough electricity to light one bare 60-watt bulb handing from electric wire that he put up in the center of each room. The first time we turned on the light I thought it was the most beautiful sight since Christmas! And our West Texas wind blew enough to keep us well lighted most of the time.

When we moved to the six-teacher Buford School, in Mitchell County, there were two teacherages. They were painted inside and out, and they were more modern-looking than others I had seen. I remem-ber wondering why that principal and his family of four people chose to live in the small teacherage and to give us and our family a big five-room house. I soon learned the unpleasant truth. The people of the community intended to get as much mileage as possible out of their teacherages. That's why they built them only for the married couples, and that is why they intended for our family of five to share our larger house with another couple. I well remember that that sec-ond couple did not get moved in until about midnight one night, after we were already in bed. I remember it so well because they had to drag their mattress and furniture through our bedroom, because their part of the house, which they had chosen themselves, had no outside door! After several months of this, my husband built them an out-side door.[54]

By and large, rural teachers reported that their trustees were helpful and supportive, both for the young teacher just getting started, and when conflicts occasionally arose with parents. In ad-dition to hiring the teacher, the trustees were committed to the management of school tax monies allocated through the county school fund and other monies received from the state in the form of rural aid. Few trustees concerned themselves with the day-to-day instructional program of the school, except to monitor com-munity complaints. The bulk of trustee duties were more manual than administrative in nature. As State Superintendent R. B. Cousins wrote in 1909, "It is the duty of the trustees to see that the schoolhouse is kept in repair, including the windows, doors,

177

chimneys, papering and painting inside and outside . . . fences mended, etc. He should see that the toilets are cleaned and fumigated once a week."[55] In the country schools the trustees performed these maintenance chores themselves, if the work was done at all.[56]

Rural teachers functioned in an atmosphere of nearly complete freedom during the school day, and trustees rarely came around.[57] As Velma Adams told us, "The trustees only came if I needed them to move any books or move some wood, but they never did come in and sit and watch the work."[58] Teachers approved of trustees who would drop by occasionally to see that everything was all right and that the teacher had all the things she needed. One teacher contrasted the quality of trustee maintenance at two of the schools where she taught:

> Out at McMahan, the trustees would occasionally come by and ask if there was anything I needed, that I didn't have, or if there was anything to do to help. I never did have anybody come by from Lytton. You'd never see them until you go to them for something. Vernon Woods I shall never forget, 'cause he would always come by and say, "Mrs. Byars, anything you need and don't have, don't stay here and do without and make out." He said, "Come by the store and let us know what you need." He ran the store in McMahan at that time.[59]

The careers of G. C. Gregory and of other male teachers suggest that they had more conflicts with their trustees than did the women. Gregory, who clearly resented being bossed around by undereducated farmers and ranchers with cow manure on their boots, got into political trouble with trustees wherever he went. Once he was asked to leave a board meeting to which he thought he had been properly invited. Later, he believed, he found out why: "I learned that the board members would occasionally let out the auditorium to traveling shows and charge 25 percent of the gate receipts. What became of the receipts I never found out. A Negro janitor at the bank building owned by the president of the school board told me, 'I hears 'um talking about what's my share of the money?' I found out one of the conditions for leasing the building in addition to the 25 percent rental, was a free pass to the show for every member of the trustees' families."[60]

For both men and women teachers the business of disciplining a trustee's child was always a delicate matter. Many trustees went out of their way to tell the teacher they wanted their sons and daughters treated like all the rest, but for others the teacher expected a different reaction. One rural teacher told how she had to punish a trustee's boy, sensed trouble for her reelection to the school, and then moved to tactfully defuse the conflict:

> Usually it was about March every year that they elected teachers. I always wanted to know. I didn't want to be hanging on, not knowing what was going to happen. . . . I'll tell you what happened just about a week before a new teacher election was coming up. One of the little boys [who] belonged to one of the trustees, he was a fighter, and one Friday afternoon he walked down the road with a little Darrow boy that he didn't get along with too well, and he hit this little boy with his dinner bucket and cut a great place on his head.
>
> Well, I gave the boy a whipping for it, and this boy's daddy was very angry about it for a little while. One of the other trustees told me, he said, "I think you may have some trouble with Mr. So-and-So." I said, "I didn't think whether that was the trustee's boy or anybody else's boy. I did what I thought was right, and if it had been your child, or anybody else's child, he would have been punished one way or another for that."
>
> So, late one evening I went to this fellow's house and talked to him about it. I said, "Now, Mr. So-and-So, I understand that you are very displeased that I punished your boy for this fight he had on the road home last Friday evening, and I want you to know that I'm just democratic enough that I'm not going to show any partiality to your child or anybody else's child, because he happens to be the trustee's. I know that you are a good Christian man, and you have democratic views, too, and I hope that you don't hold that against me. You know me well enough to know that I don't punish children very often." And I said, "Now, you think that over, and if you think that's enough to disqualify me, OK."[61]

Sometimes the problem bothering a trustee was somewhat obscure. One trustee went to the father of his young teacher and said with some considerable embarrassment, "We think your daughter is a fine young teacher, but she simply must wear a petticoat." Once the trustee's delicate message was conveyed to the teacher, she was quite nonplussed. She always wore a petticoat when she taught, sometimes two of them![62]

On those rare occasions when a trustee did feel it necessary to reprimand the teacher, the encounter was most often a friendly one. Given the large number of young female teachers, and the familial atmosphere of the rural school within the small community, these infrequent engagements between a trustee and a young teacher resembled an affectionate exchange between a father and a grown daughter:

> Mary Span, my sister and fellow teacher in the two-teacher Paint Creek School, had a little conflict in point of view about the children breaking windows with the balls when they played ball games. One father said to her — I remember quite well — he said, "Now, Miss Smith, we're just gonna have to stop the ball games if you can't keep them from breaking the windows." Mary Span replied, "Mr. Caudill, they're your children, and if you don't want them to play baseball, that's all right with me. You might clean off that corner of the yard where we can move the baseball field a little farther from the school building. But if you don't want your kids to play baseball, that's all right with me, Mr. Caudill. He's your kid for life, and he's mine for just this year."
>
> Yes, Mr. Caudill was a trustee. And I didn't know Mary Span would ever say anything like that to Mr. Caudill. He rubbed that red, bristly chin, and he looked at her and kind of squinted his eyes as he said to her, "Miss Smith, you know I think you've got an idea there. We might just clear off that corner of the school grounds, and if they knock the balls out there into somebody's pasture, and the children trespass hunting the ball out there, that's gonna be your problem." He laughed. So, they cleared it off and we moved the baseball playing a little farther from the building. Mr. Caudill had a good sense of humor. He thought there was just too much window repairing, and I expect he was right.[63]

If the trustees had little day-to-day impact on the teacher's life in the rural school, the county superintendent had even less. Though the superintendent was ostensibly in charge of the "county school system," bad roads and the fact that there were scores of separate school sites usually kept him or her from anything but the most token of school inspections. In the 1924 survey, 42 percent of Texas rural schools reported they had received no visit from the county superintendent the preceding year, 30 percent reported one visit, 21 percent had been visited two times, and 7 percent three times or more.[64] An occasional county superintendent might have something to say to the teacher to help her improve her instruction, but he was more likely to comment on matters relating to school administration, records, or facilities. One teacher told us,

"Yes, there was a county superintendent, but he never came by. I don't remember seeing him. I don't know what he did."[65] Another said, "There was a county superintendent, and he was my boss, but I never did see him. Never did see him at all. Never came to visit. I didn't have any idea what he did."[66] A third teacher commented about a typical visit of her county superintendent, "I guess he stayed for two hours in my room. I asked him if he had anything to say, and he told the story of Little Black Sambo."[67]

Ties were far closer with the rural parents. They often came to school for programs and entertainments, and the teacher was constantly interacting with parents at the many social occasions she participated in within the community. She saw them at church, at picnics, and on many other occasions. The teacher regarded it as part of her job to get to know all her students' parents as well as possible. With its several constraints – multiple grades, different levels of understanding among children, and restriction on the length of term – the rural school afforded mostly an introduction to learning and a place to demonstrate competency. Because students acquired their proficiency outside the school, the role of parents was critical in the instruction of children.[68]

Recognizing the importance of all the parents' role in the education of their children, teachers often made a special effort to visit in the children's homes. The 1924 survey showed that almost 90 percent of the teachers in common school districts visited in some of the homes, and 10 percent made visits to all of them.[69] Visiting was a touchy issue for teachers, because if they accepted one invitation – any invitation – how could they refuse others without giving offense?

> I had the cutest little boy in first grade. His name was Edwards. He wanted me to go home with him. Well, I knew that if I went home with him I left myself open to go home with every child in my room. So, when I made up my mind I could go home with every child, [I accepted his invitation.] This little Dan that I went home with had a sister and a brother going to school there, and the sweetest mother and daddy. We left school at four, and we got home just before the sun went down – it was about five to six miles away from school. He walked, and I rode a horse two or three miles. I spent the night there, ate supper, had the best meal and loving fellowship. We left for school the next morning just as the sun came up. You know what I promised

myself? I would see that that little boy learned something every day he came to school. If he put out that much effort, I was going to see that he learned all he possibly could.[70]

Another teacher told a similar story:

> We visited in the homes a lot, stayed all night in different homes with people in the community. . . . Visiting parents was the only real socializing we had out there. We enjoyed being in the homes of children we loved. It really did give us a deep insight. I remember one place we stayed all night, and they had a little closet added onto the house at the front. And we had to sleep in that little tiny room that night. We just barely could get in there, but that was the best they had for us. That was all right. I knew the parents at Opelila and Shady Grove better than when I taught in consolidated schools.[71]

Finally, William Owens's eloquent description of his visits to children's homes in the Pin Hook community includes an account of one memorable incident involving a bowl of squirrel stew: "In a few homes I had pie or cake for supper and a bed to myself to sleep in. More often I had cornbread and side meat and beans or greens and slept in a double bed with one of the boys. I learned to know them as teeth gritters, teeth chompers, snorers, and bed wetters, but once I had gone to one place I had to go to others. I could not afford to make anyone feel slighted."[72] One day Owens was invited to the home of a poor widower who was able to make this social gesture because of a successful squirrel hunt that day. Owens and the parent went into the kitchen to eat the supper prepared by the man's oldest daughter, and —

> In the middle of the table there was a bowl of squirrel and flour dumplings, with the squirrel head in the middle, the eyes glazed and staring. We took our chairs, and the man returned thanks. When I looked up again I was looking straight at the squirrel eyes. The oldest girl must have seen the look on my face. Before the bowl was passed to me, she turned the head over. I dipped, but the head turned back. The bowl went around and the others dipped, but the head stayed in the middle, the eyes up. The older girl grew red from embarrassment, the younger from trying to keep from giggling. Without saying we should, we hurried through supper and went to the fireplace room.[73]

There was reciprocity in the home visit. Just as the teacher got a chance to view her student's home environment and to get to know the parents, the parents had an opportunity to assess the teacher as a suitable moral exemplar for their children. As we have seen, the moral exemplar aspect of the teacher's role placed a great many restraints upon her behavior. The "shalts" and "shalt nots" were numerous and constraining. For this reason, and doubtless because of low salaries as well, the careers of many teachers in the rural schools spanned only a very few years. Fewer than 70 percent of the teachers in Texas rural schools in 1935 had more than three years of teaching experience.[74] In the 1890s, when teaching had been for the most part the profession of young men, many of these men used their teaching careers as stepping-stones to careers as doctors, lawyers, or businessmen. In the 1920s and 1930s, the majority of young women teachers went on to marriage and a family, sometimes coming back to teaching, but often not. The job of rural schoolteacher was an interim status for many young females. As one man from Deaf Smith County put it regarding a certain country school, "The single teachers lost an excellent husband-finding location when it consolidated with Hereford. It used to be said that if a school teacher wanted to get married she should move to Dawn."[75] The writer should know; he married a Dawn school-teacher himself.

Marriage was one of the reasons for the rapid turnover of schoolteachers in many rural schools. Another reason was the constant search for a better salary. School district records show a very high rate of teacher turnover, particularly in the smaller schools. The one-room Balch School in Parker County had no fewer than thirteen teachers between 1905 and 1920. Then it became a two-room school and had twenty-four teachers from 1921 to 1944.[76] Salaries, calibrated at levels suitable for the subsistence of a young, unmarried female, stood at an average of $663 a year for rural elementary teachers in 1935. This was only $55 a month for the year.[77] If a school in a nearby district offered $10 more per month, that was reason enough to move, because the job was likely to be very much the same.

Men in particular had great difficulty staying in the teaching profession, though their salaries usually were larger and they tended to move into positions in the town schools. G. C. Gregory's story is typical of what many family men faced:

183

Along in 1915 I made application for a teaching job in a small town near Waco. I had been attending the University of Texas, and ran out of funds. The 1915–16 term closed. I was out of money and desperate for a job. Teaching jobs were scarce and the pay was small. I had a wife and two children who had to be fed.

I met with the school board, and was elected for an eight months term at a salary of $100 per month. I sold my milk cow for $50 which gave me enough money to move.

By staying at our people's homes until the school began I survived a financial crisis. During the summer I worked some at the thresher in the harvest fields picking up enough change to buy a few clothes. I and my wife were star boarders at my wife's and my families during the summer.[78]

Despite his hardships, Gregory spent long years in public school teaching. Despite the social constraints of the rural teacher's role, and despite the low salaries, many responded as did Ella Bozarth to the description of the "dedicated teacher's pay" in that long-ago teachers' institute at Goliad: "First of all, the salary, and it's small. Then you get paid by the love of the children. Then, I hope there'll be a star in your crown for being faithful."[79]

It is not surprising that Bozarth responded so strongly to this statement. For the "born" country teacher, teaching was more than a job; it was described in the language of a spiritual calling and was perceived as a mission with implications beyond the immediate present, beyond the teacher's own lifetime.[80] Teaching was a cause, an endeavor larger than the individual, one requiring special attitudes and special perceptions of one's fellow human beings. Florence Jones told us, "You've got to love humanity if you teach school! If you don't love humanity, get out of it!"[81] And Mrs. W. R. Barron said, "Teaching was not just a job. There was service connected with it — the service of helping others. And teaching was not just for my benefit. I felt obligated to influence the mind and body and the morals of children."[82] According to Velma Adams, "My beliefs about teaching came out of my family background. Teaching was helping people. I enjoyed it, and it gave me satisfaction. There was a social obligation to teaching that was an advantage over other jobs. There was a certain Christian element in the job of teaching."[83]

The model that many teachers had in mind as they ran their

rural classrooms was the Christian family. Many students were treated in parental fashion by their early teachers – teachers they never forgot: "When I first went to school, I was just six years old. That would be sixty-eight years ago. We moved about four miles west of Emery in a little country school. I don't remember what this little country school was called, but I can recall that the teacher was a very large fat man and his name was Mr. Vineyard. And he picked me up and set me in his lap. He petted me I guess because I was unusually small."[84] Another person remembered the actions of teacher J. H. Doss, at China Grove School, in King County, who was solicitous of the welfare of the children who walked to school barefooted in the ice and snow, and who would daily examine the children's feet, rub their frostbitten heels, and apply soothing medication.[85]

The teachers who felt the spiritual calling of schoolteaching treated their pupils in the manner of a caring Christian parent:

> The second one-room school I taught in was Utah, in Limestone County. This was a very poor little community. The attendance was small. . . . Two little boys rode a donkey to school all the time, sweet little old fellas. They gave the least trouble of any children in the world. I had one little girl that came, and she wasn't really old enough to go to school, but I'd let her stay because her parents wanted her to. She used to sit in my lap while she did her reading [laughs]. . . . Some of those little old things would be so ragged it was pitiful. It would get so muddy, and their little old feet would be caked with mud. We had a great big old jacket stove, so, when they got there, I just slipped those wet stockings off them and rinsed them out and hung them on the jacket of the stove. They would just sit there by the fire and warm their toes, and we'd have our reading lesson while they were warming.[86]

The rural schoolteachers' sense of calling sometimes took them on missions into the larger community outside the rural schools. The following stories represent many from Texas country schools:

> There were two adults, parents, who had grown up in cotton country and couldn't read or write. Their little daughter was underage, and they didn't have any place to leave her, so I told them to send her on to school.
>
> She was worrying me to death wanting copies of this and that to take home. I said to her one day, "Ruby, what in the world are you

185

doing with all those papers I make for you?" She answered, "Oh, I'm teaching Mother and Daddy. They don't read nor write." So the mother came up in a few days and told me what they were doing with those papers — said Ruby had told her I had gotten after her for asking for so many. She said, "I wonder if you would teach Dunk and I to read and write. It's an awful handicap. He doesn't always have work right here, and he goes off and finds work someplace else, and we can't correspond to each other. If we write, we have to have somebody do the writing for us. If we get a letter, we have to have someone read that letter." So I taught them, and when I left Snowden Lake and moved to Laketon, they left that community and moved over to Laketon with me and continued to school. I taught them five years. Yes, they learned to read and write. They sure did.[87]

One of the little girls in my room had a baby sister eighteen months old who caught pneumonia. I took a turn sitting up with the baby at night. After nine days the baby died. Nobody had enough money for a mortician. Just digging the grave cost ten dollars. So the men in the community dug the grave and made a wooden box for a coffin. I bought the shroud, a baby gown, and a baby bonnet. The funeral was held in the home. There was no preacher in town, and since my father was a Baptist preacher, and I knew the service, I read the scripture and said the words for the service. There wasn't any hearse. I transported the box to the cemetery in the backseat of my car.[88]

The second year I taught at Stampede the children told me one day there was a little boy living three or four miles away, that he'd moved in but wasn't able to go to school. . . . I asked why he couldn't come to school. They said he'd had an operation. So I went over to see him. The little boy had had his appendix out, [but] they thought he was dying on the table, so they stopped the operation. And he lived. Therefore, he had a place where his bowels moved right here on his side, and he had to stay wrapped up, don't you see. So he wouldn't go to school. He was about seven or eight. I said to his mother, "My lands, let him come to school! If you'll send me the clothes, I'll be happy to take care of him." Of course, she was happy, and the little boy was happy as he could be that he could come to school. I could tell by the odor when he needed to have his bandage changed, and I'd ask the children to go outside for a while. He'd get up on the desk, and I'd change it and then ring a little bell. The kids were so nice; they never did say anything about it.[89]

I had a little boy that was a spastic. He walked on his tiptoes, and he drooled from his mouth all the time. He was in my first grade. He was overage because no other teacher would fool with him. I told 'em to send him, and I'd do the best I could. Now there's where I used some of my older students to help a lot. He stood around with me just like I was his mother. I taught him numbers. He'd go up to the board and go around with his little old spastic arm, and he'd make a two that big! His mother and daddy were so grateful; you can't believe how happy they were. I taught that child to read. [My husband] taught him to play baseball and hit a ball. He'd fall down trying to get to first base, but Marlon wouldn't let 'em put him out. It just delighted them the things we taught that little child.[90]

10. A Pretty Nasty Fight

🆃

ᴇARLY AND LATE in the history of the Texas country schools, consolidation of one district with another was a political issue capable of raising strong emotions. Around 1919 there was a move afoot in Bell County to persuade Reed Lake School to merge with the nearby Academy School, forming a bigger and better Academy Independent School District. The chief impetus for this came from Academy, and one evening in 1919 an Academy patron, V. C. Marshall, visited in the home of Reed Lake trustee Fritz Wohleb to argue the case for the merger with Academy. Wohleb listened soberly to Marshall's arguments for some time, then reluctantly agreed that probably it would be for the best if Reed Lake consolidated. Meanwhile, in the kitchen, Mrs. Ella Wohleb had been following the parlor conversation with great interest, and when she heard her husband say this, "she became so frustrated she accidentally poured a gallon of buttermilk into the flour bin."[1]

Doubtless others at Reed Lake shared Mrs. Wohleb's frustration. The issue of consolidation was simply a modern version of the controversy over where the school should be located, an issue as old as rural education itself. School location had always mattered a great deal to rural parents and had been a subject of contention since the establishment of the first-generation schools in the 1880s and 1890s. In its earliest days the issue had focused upon placement of the school within the district, because its location always benefited some children and put others at a disadvantage. In districts where children had to be kept out of school for a year or more beyond the norm, until they were judged ready to "pull the mud," school location was no small matter.

There were two distinct eras of rural-school consolidation in Texas. In the first three decades of this century the consolidation of country schools was characterized by local control and was closely related to the earlier issue of location or relocation of the school building. A second phase of school consolidation was less personal and more permanent. By the late 1940s the School Reform Movement had accumulated a legal force that appeared to threaten termination of the rural schools by fiat. However, a closer examination of the situation reveals that the real pressures for school consolidation came not from the school reformers but from changing social and economic conditions within the state.

In the primary accounts of Texas rural education there are many stories about schools being moved and a few about them being "stolen." Rather often when new trustees were elected in the Texas country districts, the school would be moved, sometimes miles, to a new location. Occasionally the move came as a surprise for the losers, but more often the question about moving the school had been the chief debate of the election campaign, with those who wished to see it remain where it was set against those who wished to move it.[2] In some districts the school was moved several times over the years, often with the full consent of all concerned.[3] All parents were in agreement about the basic right of every rural child to have a public school within reasonable traveling distance from his home. The problems surfaced when it came to deciding what distance was "reasonable," and from whose home!

Rural school buildings were simple frame structures, quite movable by means of the animal-powered technology of the day, but the roads were bad, and anything could happen. Theo School, a one-room frame structure, originally was located in Falls County, but when the county line was changed in 1912, Theo was in Bell County and needed to be moved to a site more centrally located in its new district. A man was hired to move the school with the help of local parents. Unfortunately, because the school moving did not begin until September, the enterprise was caught by the fall rains and, eventually, by the prodigious Bell County mud. Theo School stuck fast out in the middle of a farmer's field, and nothing more could be done until things thoroughly dried out the following summer.[4]

In 1923 the Tierra Blanca School, in Deaf Smith County, went traveling to West Way. "Arthur Brooks, a road contractor, put the little building up on rollers but two teams couldn't move it. Mr. Woods, a house mover, used block and tackles and moved it with a team of bay ponies. Judge Slaton named the school 'West Way,' the purpose being to show the direction from town. The two south rooms were added to the building shortly after it was moved, and in four or five years the north part was added."[5]

In 1929 four rural districts consolidated to form the new Gruver Consolidated High School District, and we are told, "The districts were Grand Plains, Lakeside, Woodrow, and Maupin. The term of 1929–30 was taught in small frame buildings scattered over the townsite. Two of them were the Maupin and Grand Plains school houses that had been moved in."[6]

Early and late the peripatetic Texas rural school traveled about in just this manner. When districts agreed upon a compromise location for a new consolidated district at some central location, the old school buildings were often moved in, sometimes forming a two-room school from two one-room structures. Conversely a two- or three-room schoolhouse might be broken up and moved off in two or more directions to serve as one-room schools.[7] As happened at Gruver, many rural schools followed their students "in to town" as the day of consolidation dawned.[8]

On rare occasions when the issue of moving the school could not be resolved by the usual course of discussion and compromise, some rural school patrons took things into their own hands and "stole" the school, moving it to another location without permission. One night cowboys moved the Bronco School, in Wheeler County, to a new location.[9] For a similar case in Ochiltree County there is a detailed account:

> During the three years that were spent in the Wamble house, the most momentous event was when the school house was moved. . . . There were the two Norris boys, the two Wooten girls, five Goods and five

190

Gerharts who would benefit by the school house being moved a couple of miles east. The heads of those four households decided to move it, not without the knowledge of Mr. Taylor, but certainly without his consent. A young lawyer advised the would-be movers to get all of their equipment together, ready for an early Sunday morning start. The move should be completed upon a legal holiday and, relocated, it would require an extended effort to have it returned. All went according to plan. The building was jacked up, placed upon huge wooden rollers, which had been hitched to at least a dozen horses. At a given signal, each man shouted to his horses to giddy-up. When the horses lunged in several different directions the brick chimney fell off. About half-way down the first slope one wheel broke and the holiday move was over. Mr. Taylor rode old Topsy across the Canadian River Sunday night to the district court at Miami. On Monday morning, he obtained an injunction against the movers. The remainder of that school term was taught in the combination living room, bedroom of the Good home.[10]

Stealing the school was an extreme case, however. Normally, the earlier political issue about school location within the rural district was handled by the same process of compromise and mutual agreement that characterized the first-stage consolidation of one rural district with another. Rural school patrons usually worked these matters to suit themselves, only then going to the county superintendent for formal approval. This kind of school consolidation was very different from that at the end of the rural schools. As Weldon Hutcheson described this earlier kind of grassroots consolidation, "You would have a consolidation every now and then in order to have a better system, in order to build a better building, and so on like that. A lot of those schools back then, I don't even remember their names; they were gone before my time."[11]

In the earlier pattern of consolidation, schools and school districts merged and separated as the rural population shifted about. A school needed to have at least fifteen pupils to be viable; thus, the migration of one large family out of the district could cause a school consolidation. Likewise, a couple of new families moving in might necessitate the conversion of a one-room school to a two-room school, or even require the formation of a new common school district. The processes of district consolidation and district fracture went on all the time, but the process of consolidation gradu-

191

ally predominated. In the 1920s the Schrader School that Nora Gambrell attended in Caldwell County merged with Black Ankle School, which then merged with High Point School—all within the space of five years. All these schools were within three or four miles of each other. When Susie Bell Anderson left Hall School in the middle 1920s to take a job at the two-room Walters-Nixon School, she found that a similar process had been going on there: "There had been three little one-teacher schools. They had gotten down until there weren't more than ten pupils in each school, I think. And they consolidated—put that Walters-Nixon [School] kind of in the middle of the school district. The other schools had gotten so small, they just had to come together."[12] Legally this early form of school consolidation was very simple. In 1919 in Bell County, the parents in the Sparta and Cedar Grove school districts signed petitions to consolidate their two schools, the petition was sent to the Bell County School Board, and this body routinely consolidated the schools into a new Sparta-Grove Common School District.[13] Virtually all districts with hyphenated names arose from just this process. Likewise, in Bell County in 1916 Center Lake School No. 10 had merged with Post Oak School No. 55 to form Center Oak No. 10.[14] Why the new school took the district number of Center Lake and not that of Post Oak is unclear. As county historians know, the school district number systems are a nightmare of confusion. At any point in time there seem to have been many gaps in district numbers, perhaps because of districts consolidating with each other, going "dormant," or simply dropping out of existence. Later, lost numbers in the sequence might be utilized again to designate a newly formed (or hybrid) district.

Many of these early school consolidations came about because, as in the case of Schrader with Black Ankle and Walters with Nixon, "They had gotten down until there weren't more than ten pupils in each school." Another common reason was the desire to pool students, school supporters, and tax monies to have a better rural school. These motives seem to have predominated in the formation of a new Union Hill School from the districts of Word, New Home, and Union Hill, in Swisher County in 1923: "A large new building was built another mile north of the old location and became a five-teacher school with Vocational Home Economics and

Agriculture and private piano lessons in addition to the regular curriculum. The school house was still used as the center of all community activities, such as: Saturday night baseball games, singing conventions, Friday night literary society programs put on by both school students, and, also, outsiders and any other get-togethers that made for a very tight community spirit."[15] This approving account by a resident of Union Hill points up the fact that the attitudes of rural school patrons often depended on which side of the school merger they were on. In this case, the other schools came in to an augmented Union Hill; some school support-ers in the other two districts may have felt that they had "lost their school."

A common practice when rural districts consolidated was to establish the new school at some compromise location equidistant from the previous school sites, and to give the new school a "com-promise name." This might be a simple hyphenated form of the merging schools (e.g., Walters-Nixon), or it might be a new name emphasizing the compromise nature of the site, such as Midway, Three-Way, Two-Point, and Halfway. Midway School, in Parker County, for example, was formed by a merger of the Old County Line and Bedford school districts and, as the name suggests, was midway between the two.[16] Virtually all the stories of the complex negotiations between school patrons in these early rural consoli-dations have been lost, but there is one magnificent exception, the story of the origins of Center Point School, Mills County, as told by a former student and teacher in the school:

> My father, Jim Fallon, Ed Davis and a few other interested citi-zens saw the need for a better school and met with a group of men from Rock Springs community to consider consolidation, but noth-ing materialized. Later Joe Spinks and Jodie Williams, both promi-nent men in the area, expressed their desire to help consolidate the schools of Picking Springs, Williams Ranch and Miller Grove. In 1920 consolidation of the three schools was completed and a three-teacher school was built at a central location between the communities and the school was thusly named "Center Point."
> First the men looked into the county records, found the exact bound-aries of the three communities and discovered that the centermost land belonged to Mr. and Mrs. J. T. Jones. A dim county road led through the Jones place going north to the Brownwood Highway and

193

Mr. Jones gave consent to let this access be used for Williams Ranch until a country road could be constructed. It took several meetings at night for my father and other interested parties to work out the details and for plans to be made. Specifications from the State Board of Education as to how a three-teacher school should be built were acquired.

Trustees of Miller Grove School sold their schoolhouse to Parks McWhorter and he moved the building to be used as a residence.

Trustees at Williams Ranch agreed to sell their schoolhouse to Frank Huggett, and he gave consent to let the old school bell from Williams Ranch School be used in the new Center Point Building. That old bell had seen more history than any other single object in the county, and had it been able to speak it could have told stories of Indian fights, the silent movements of mobs by night, the struggles of people along Herd Pen Branch to establish a community against odds so great – of barefoot children sitting on split-log benches in a schoolhouse with a dirt floor. It could have told of the great herds of cattle milling around Williams Ranch – the cowboys – and livestock driven to the springs by their owners for water when severe droughts struck the area. The old bell witnessed hundreds of wagons loaded with corn to be ground at the old mill in Williams Ranch; and pioneers by the hundreds as they moved westward and stopped at the Hutch Hotel to spend the night along their way. It could have told of good men and bad men – desperadoes – of marching soldiers, famous lawmen and Generals. Every person in Center Point community was proud of the old school bell.

Lumber from the Picking Springs School was used to build the Center Point School, along with new lumber. All our fathers were good with their hammers and saws, but a foreman was needed for the job and a Mr. Williams from Mullin was hired. Some of the men and boys that helped build the school were the Spinks, Williams, Meyers, Davis, Newmans, Caulder, Pearson, Cleve and Garl Perry, Sheltons, Teffentelers, French, Mahan, Edlin, the Hutchins, Davees, Taylors, Fallons, Uncle Bud Smith and others.

As usually happens when there is unity and a joint effort, there was soon a three-teacher school building ready for the old school bell to ring the opening of the first school at Center Point in 1920. Teachers were Willie Wasserman, Irene French and Sybil Guthrie the first year and the term lasted six months.

When students arrived the first morning there were folding doors between rooms to enlarge the space for programs, new blackboards and erasers, new desks that were the latest thing in school desks – with storage for books underneath the top – a library, the smell of new lumber and paint, and atop it all hung the old Williams Ranch bell

194

in a new tower. We had a basketball court and a brush arbor—both enjoyed by the whole community.[17]

Very often these compromise schools gave rise to a new community that took the school name, and this seems to be true of Center Point. Such early school mergers arose directly from the wishes of the rural people themselves and owed little to the activities of the county school superintendents or the would-be school reformers at the State Board of Education in Austin. The trend was toward larger and larger rural schools, but the trend was gradual and was based on local initiative. In 1924, the year of the school survey, 6,888 rural common schools operated in Texas (as compared with 868 independent nonrural districts). At the time of the school adequacy survey in 1935 there were still 5,984 rural schools and 1,015 independent districts. In other words, 84 percent of the state public school system was still rural.

Despite the lack of any dramatic success, school reformers continued the pressure for rural-school consolidation, and as the century progressed, the number of laws passed by the legislature gradually threatened the existence of the rural schools: teacher-certification requirements were consistently increased, the legal school term was lengthened, school building construction was standardized, the taxing authority of the rural school was curtailed while that of the consolidated districts was enlarged, and a limit was established on how much of the rural teacher's salary could be paid from state monies. The Compulsory School Attendance Law was aimed directly at parental control of the rural schools. As L. D. Haskew told us, "They coerced—made it costly to remain a common school, and they bribed—contributed extra monies to schools that did consolidate."[18]

There were both "carrots" and "sticks" in the reform plan to force consolidation, and one of the carrots was the Rural High School District. Bertha M. Stephens referred to this law as "the Grouping Plan, Article 2806, 1927 of the Texas School Law," as she described the formation of a typical rural high school district.[19] In the spring of 1935 the citizens of several districts in the western part of Collingsworth County voted to consolidate. These districts voted "by a big majority" to form a new Quail Rural Consolidated District. Before the merger Quail had just been one of the common school districts in the area, but it was centrally located. In 1948 four more Collingsworth County schools and two Donley County schools joined the Quail District, making Quail RCD one of the largest rural consolidated high schools in the United States. The informal motto of the district was "If a child anywhere in the district wants to come to Quail School, we will take a bus to get him." Up to seven hundred students were enrolled in what was by all accounts an excellent high school facility.[20] Under the Rural Consolidated School Plan, participating communities were allowed to keep their local elementary schools, sending their students in to the central high school facility for advanced grades.

If the rural consolidated high school was a "carrot" of the new school laws, the 1930 Dormant School Law was one of the "sticks." County Superintendent I. W. Popham of Travis County told us how the dormant school law worked:

> I took office in 1935. We got a law passed in 1930 that districts could go dormant. If they didn't have enough children out there to operate a school – I believe they had to have fifteen children – and [if] they didn't operate a school for one year, it was the duty of the county school board to annex that school to one or more districts. I would take a copy of the law [regarding dormant schools] and call a meeting of the school board at the schoolhouse at night in the dormant district, and invite the public in that community that wanted to come. I'd go at night and meet with 'em and preside over the meeting and read the law to them. I'd say, "Now, the county board wants to know where do you want to go? Where would you like to be annexed?" I'd say, "You don't have a choice in the matter, because you're dormant." They accepted it. We had several districts went to Round Rock, that many more went to Elgin, one or two went to Buda, and a great many went to Austin.[21]

Some county superintendents may not have been as zealous as Popham in enforcing the dormancy law, but where it was enforced, the law had large effects in compelling rural districts to consolidate. Sometimes, as in this instance reported by Popham, the results were painful to all concerned:

> People didn't want to give up their . . . little mountain school up here that was annexed to Eanes. That man just loved that school and community, and he and some neighbors built the schoolhouse themselves

196

out of their own money, put up a little old frame school building. When I told him he was gonna have to close up that school, [that] he didn't have enough children in it to legally maintain its upkeep, he sat in my office and he cried. That was because of a selfish pride he had in that community.[22]

Pride in community made rural school consolidation a harsh pill to swallow for many Texans in the 1940s and 1950s, as each locality's instinctive urge to somehow hang on to its school was pitted against unified professional opinion and, increasingly, state school laws. More often than not, however, the factor that swayed these rural communities and paved the way for large-scale consolidation after the passage of the Gilmer-Akin Act was the need to send rural children into town for high school. Clementine Johnson has given us an excellent description of her father's dilemma regarding this matter:

My father was the schoolman in the area. He used to say that there wasn't a school building within a radius of so many miles but what he didn't have a few boards in the building. That was the way he would put it. He had helped get schools organized and started, and when Bronte was taking in the little schools all around, Papa fought for the rural schools. He said if the school could not provide the transportation, it was not right to put those first graders in the schools ten or twelve miles from there. . . . In the meantime Mineral Springs, where I went to school, started deteriorating. . . . So my father bought a house in town [Bronte]. Well, for a time he sent us to school in a Ford, then he sent us on horseback. During that time they elected him a school trustee [in Bronte]. They said anybody that would work so hard to keep the school in Mineral Springs, they needed him to transfer his efforts to Bronte, and Bronte would really get going.[23]

During the 1930s and 1940s many rural schools established cordial relationships with nearby independent school districts to provide for the high school education of district schoolchildren and paid a certain amount of tuition for each child to defray the high schools' increased costs. Later, after the passage of Gilmer-Akin made maintenance of the rural schools all but impossible, they tended to consolidate with the ISDs with which they had this arrangement.[24]

Clementine Johnson did not explain what she meant when she said that her father's beloved Mineral Springs School was "deteriorating," but she probably meant that enrollment was declining. Rural Texas society was changing rapidly in the decade after World War II. The war had drastically disrupted rural populations. Many young people had gone away to war plants and into the service and many of these did not come back. Cotton agriculture and the closely related tenant system were on the decline, sending a shock wave throughout rural Texas. Once again, Weldon Hutcheson went right to the point when he observed, "The trouble was, they was running out of kids. That's all there were; that's the whole thing boiled down to it."[25] Before Gilmer-Akin, before the mass consolidations of the early 1950s, the rural schools were undermined by a wholesale loss of scholastics. This trend is clear in the overall population statistics for rural counties all across the state. Caldwell County's population declined from 31,397 in 1930 to 19,350 in 1950, and Hopkins County from 29,410 to 23,400 over those two decades.[26] Throughout Texas there was a general shift of population to the towns and cities even in those counties that remained constant or increased in population. As their population declined the communities of rural Texas evolved into societies of a very different order. Rural districts were "running out of kids" and Gilmer-Akin only provided the coup de grace to a system of education that was already doomed.

Few rural school communities could find the money to attain the Minimum Foundation Program required of all districts under Gilmer-Akin. These were uniform standards of curriculum, minimum class size, minimum teachers' salaries, and length of school year – stringent standards that literally put the rural schools out of business. Gilmer-Akin was passed in 1949, at which time there were approximately four thousand school districts in Texas; one year later almost two thousand of those school districts had consolidated. The law now provided that as many as ten rural districts could consolidate with an independent school district at one time. Trustees could act for each district to vote for an election, then a general election would be called for all the rural districts and the voters in the ISD. Almost always the large number of votes from the ISD, in conjunction with the consolidationist votes from the country districts, swamped the votes of opponents – even if the opponents were numerically dominant in a single rural district.[27]

Caldwell County was typical in that nine rural schools went in at once to Lockhart.

In this last phase of the country schools, county superintendents such as R. E. Harris in Caldwell County and I. W. Popham in Travis County, played important roles as mediators and negotiators of these inevitable consolidations. Popham described his role: "Practically every consolidation that was made was a different problem from the others. It'd be little problems that would come up to make it different. You couldn't say, 'We're gonna take districts seven, eight and nine and put 'em some place' like you would your herd of cattle in the lots. It didn't work that way. I didn't want it to work that way. [I wanted them] to be satisfied with where they're going—to try to work that out."[28] Such diplomacy was needed. McMahan School, in Caldwell County, was representative of many rural districts that were bitterly divided over the issue of school consolidation, and certain parents and school patrons were unreconciled right to the end. Well before Gilmer-Akin at McMahan the consolidation issue surfaced when the question of sending the school's eighth and ninth grades into Lockhart arose. Lonie Brite reported a particularly divisive community meeting regarding this question:

> It was heated! I shook within myself that morning. I can remember two ladies who got up, that were in favor of sending their children in to Lockhart, where they could get more. . . . It was a very tense time. One man, and he was a trustee, got on his feet and said he had a boy in high school. He said, "My boy can learn right enough in the McMahan School, where he can go out and be a good farmer, and that's what he's going to be, anyway!" But it carried, the motion carried to move the eighth and ninth to Lockhart. But this man was the very one to come back, and I was in his presence when he said, "I was wrong." When his boy came up here and headed the grades in Lockhart and stood at the top of his class, Mr. White was the first to say, "I was wrong." But it had to be proved to him.[29]

For McMahan, that did not settle the consolidation issue, and Weldon Hutcheson described the community reaction after the final election following Gilmer-Akin:

> You had a pretty nasty fight, and a lot of those people was sincere about it because they felt like that when they lost their school their

community spirit was gone. It wasn't that they didn't want their kids to have a better education. You take right here at McMahan, for example, a real good friend of mine, he and his daddy worked all their lives to build that good school system there. They were leaders in their community, and I'm telling you, they fought that consolidation teeth and toenail. And if you wanted to make him fuss, you'd still bring it up to him before he died. He wouldn't argue with you that the kids was probably getting better opportunities in school, but he had put so much in it, you see? And a lot of people was like that. By golly, they'd put their whole life in it. They wanted to save their community, and they wanted to keep that feeling of desire to get together, and they knew that when they lost that school they lost a big part of it right there, because they was nothing to hold them together.[30]

Communities' internal conflicts over consolidation were sometimes exacerbated by the political maneuverings of the independent school districts, which were very eager to bring the nearby rural districts into their respective systems in order to increase their tax bases. With indignation undiminished by the passage of almost forty years, Susie Bell Anderson told how the citizens of Kingsbury Common School District woke up one morning to discover that they had become part of Seguin ISD:

I had been at Kingsbury for three years, and it was in the spring, and everything was going so good there, and everybody was so happy, and we just had things so nice! Seguin had already gotten Dowdy [School District], and they just kept trying to get Kingsbury. And every time there would be an election, Kingsbury would vote against it. So, they had another election and Kingsbury voted against it. Well, we got up one morning and listened to the Seguin radio and heard Kingsbury had been consolidated with Seguin! Well, everybody just went to pieces, and everybody got together and was standing on the street corners in groups and talking about it. I said, "I don't know a thing about it. I thought the election was the end of it." Then the Seguin superintendent notified me later in the day that they had taken over Kingsbury School. And I said, "How in the world can you do that?" And he said, "Well, the county school board voted for us to do it." He said, "You're no longer teaching in Kingsbury District; you're now a member of Seguin District." I thought the law read that both districts had to vote for consolidation! There's not so much freedom in America after all![31]

In Caldwell County, as in most of Texas, the process of consolidation has been completed since the 1950s. A few diehards hung on against long odds until the 1970s – for example, Moffit School, in Bell County – and a handful of atypical common school districts persist in remote areas up to the present day, but the curtain fell on the country school more than thirty years ago. Although most residents of rural areas seem well enough satisfied with the present system, satisfaction is not total. Lula Byars taught in the black one-room schools of Lytton Springs and McMahan before going in to serve as the first black teacher in the Lockhart elementary school, and Byars still had her doubts:

> They seemed to think it would be better for the schools, better for the teachers, and better equipment and everything. But you know, I don't think it benefited too much. I really don't, even though these here in the larger schools had more equipment ('cause in the one-teacher schools you had nothing; you had to make all the equipment you needed). I've brought kids in from the country to school here, [and] those children was just as far over these children here in town as day is over night! That's true, and we had to deal with everything, all kinds of students, every kind. And above that, we had to be our janitor, we had to sweep the floor, we were everything! We had to be mama, papa, teacher, nurse, janitor, everything. And we actually did it, and the children seemed to have learned. I just don't understand it, I'm going to be honest. With all of the things they have, and all of the new advancements, so they call 'em, children are not learning a darned thing![32]

Other former rural school teachers have expressed similar sentiments. Lula Byars certainly had a right to her opinions about the relative effectiveness of the rural and town schools, since she spent many years of her teaching career in both. When her McMahan students went in to Lockhart as part of the general consolidation of the day, Byars was told by the county superintendent that they consistently tested out at almost two grades above chronological age on the standardized achievement tests.

Often the close of the country schools brought other losses. At the end of a long account of the history of the Toto community in Parker County, Toto's historians, Clarence Other and Annie Josephine Stephens Durham, wrote, "The school closed in 1943 and that was the end of the community of Toto."[33] The writers did not say that the Toto community died soon after the school closing, but that the school closing *was* the end of the community. They believed, as did many rural Texans, "When the school dies, the community dies." The common school had been an integral part of the rural community — both a symbol of the community's identity and an organizational center for holding it together. In the 1980s many older Texans whose lives coincided with the era of the country school still felt a certain sense of loss, a vacancy in their communities where the common schools had been. Sometimes, as for Frankie Franks, the community loss merged with the personal losses of retirement, symbolized for her by the sound of children's voices:

> The absence of the school would let down their community, all communities, black or white. It's quiet, all the children in town school, and you couldn't hear the voices of the children from the schoolhouse hollering at noontime. Well, you missed all of that. After I retired to Lockhart I could hear those children over there on the school campus hollering. I'd be hanging clothes out sometimes and say, "Well, it's recess; I hear the kids." You know, we rang a bell, stood in the door and rang a bell. And every year, after teaching so long, look like I could just hear that bell, about the middle of the day, ringing, ringing, ringing the children in.[34]

11. Epilogue

W HEN FALL CAME to Texas in 1950, hundreds of rural schools did not reopen. Unlike a score of autumns before, this autumn found the buildings undisturbed in the summer's growth of grass, sunflowers, and bitterweed, the empires of red wasps still clinging to the eaves.

In many of our interviews with rural students and schoolteachers, they seemed to grope for some way to communicate the inexpressible – the enormous gap they felt between the educational experience of the present day and the world they had known. Most of the teachers began in one world and ended in another, and some felt, as one teacher told us, "a thousand years old." They tried to convey to us some sense of the great depth of social change they felt separating us from the country schools. They spoke of the strangeness of returning to their one-room schools at the end of summer and finding them almost lost in tall grass growing to the eaves. They made us see the files of schoolchildren plodding down the fencerows in Bell County mud time, the older breaking trail for the younger, and another file of children in Shelby County following a pine-knot torch through dark winter woods.

As American social historians move further into an exploration of the evolution of the patterns of everyday life in the twentieth century – into what C. L. Sonnichsen called "grassroots history" – they further substantiate the teachers' view. The world has

203

been transformed over the last seventy-five years, and this social transformation has been greatest, not in the urban areas, but in the small towns and the countryside. In many ways the rural Texas of 1920 had more in common with the medieval world than with the last two decades of the twentieth century. It was an animal-powered, agrarian society based on close family ties and face-to-face communities, which were stable across time. Like agricultural societies all across the world, it valued continuity more than change, and the rural school was seen as primary agent of that continuity. The man who rose to defend McMahan School at the meeting over consolidation expressed the feelings of many: "My boy can learn right enough in the McMahan School, where he can go out and be a good farmer, and that's what he's going to be, anyway."

But even as he spoke, the rural world he valued was being over-whelmed by a wave of economic, social, and political change that would sweep away the country school as it did many elements of the rural way of life. "The school reflects society," and rural society was rapidly evolving into something very different from before. Like all the rest, McMahan School had to make way for a newer, bigger, and, presumably, better version of public education.

However, the question beginning to be asked in the 1970s, and perhaps more loudly in the 1980s, was, "Have we gone too far?" Have we followed the doctrine that "bigger is always better" and the strategy of school consolidation past the point of diminishing returns? The keynote speaker at the 1974 conference of the National Federation for the Improvement of Rural Education (a mainstream professional organization) roused little disagreement by stating, "At one time the consolidation of school districts was seen as the way to [secure needed services] for large numbers of students at one time. Not any more, after the sobering experiences of trial leading to the conclusion that *big* is not always *better.* ... The symbol of consolidation—impressive looking glass, steel, and concrete structures—came to mean little to the student who spent hours getting to one of these superconglomerates and home again, often to receive less than a 'quality' education."[1]

In a pioneering field study published in 1964, Roger B. Barker and P. V. Gump of the University of Kansas looked closely at the

204

relative advantages and disadvantages of size in a study of thirteen Kansas high schools, and found that the small schools had significant virtues in the areas of student participation, assumption of responsibility by students, and community participation in the school.[2] Also in the 1960s, various researchers studying the relationship between school size and student achievement began controlling for the extraneous factors of IQ and socioeconomic class and concluded that "the effect of this development has been nothing less than a complete reversal of the traditional conclusions about the correlation between size and achievement. In fact, of the recent, controlled studies, there is not *one* which records a consistent, positive correlation between size and achievement, independent of IQ and social class."[3] Some studies, like that of Summers and Wolfe, even indicated that "higher achievement correlated with smaller schools at both the elementary and senior high school levels."[4]

In two lengthy articles in *Educational Forum* in 1976 and 1977, Jonathan P. Sher and Rachel B. Tompkins offered a comprehensive review of the whole issue of school consolidation and concluded that the consolidationists' own research failed to support their claims of greater cost-effectiveness and improved quality of education. This research, it was found, consistently overestimated the economies of scale deriving from consolidation, and underestimated (or ignored) the accompanying diseconomies. As Sher and Tompkins summed up their review of past and present research, they concluded, "No compelling evidence exists which proves that the consolidation of rural schools and school districts produced any net economic advantages. Thus, any effort to legitimize the massive rural consolidation programs implemented since 1930 must find its rationale somewhere other than [in] the economics of the situation."[5]

As we have seen, neither did the evidence about student academic achievement and participation in school life support the consolidationists' arguments: "Despite the massive human and financial investments made on its behalf, consolidation has not dramatically alleviated the educational problems endemic to rural areas. And, perhaps most damning of all, consolidated units have not even proved to be more successful than existing small districts

—ones which had to make do with relatively meager resources and only the scantiest professional attention. By consolidating, rural communities relinquished the advantages of smallness and received pitifully little in return."[6]

But what are the "advantages of smallness"? This is only a modern version of the question posed long ago by the pioneer researchers of the Texas School Survey of 1924, who, by using a more sophisticated research design than was customary in their day, found that Texas rural schools were doing their job very well. That pioneering rural school study was buried for more than half a century, but the question the researchers posed has risen to haunt this book: "The findings that rural schools are not inefficient leaves open the possibility that the small school has compensating advantages which enable it, with the very obvious handicap of poorly trained teachers and less adequate facilities, to compete with the larger schools in the final product."[7] In other words, what are "the advantages of smallness," the "compensating advantages" of the rural school? Drawing upon all the primary sources used for our social history of Texas country schools, and summarizing conclusions that are both explicit and implicit in the chapters above, we can suggest answers to the question.

Rural schools had low teacher-student ratios. No aspect of the negative myth of the country schools is less true than the notion of the average rural teacher swamped with an unteachable number of pupils. In 1935, Anglo teachers in Texas common schools had an average of twenty-four pupils, while Anglo teachers in independent school districts had thirty-six. Black rural schools had average classes of thirty-four; black urban schools had forty-five.[8] Many research studies have shown the direct relationship between size of class and student achievement; as teacher-student ratio goes down, learning as expressed in student achievement increases. Doubtless there were some disadvantages to dealing with classes of several grades, unlike the single-graded classes of most of the teachers in the town schools, but in peer teaching and other aspects of the internal dynamics of the rural school, we have advantages as well. In any case, part of the explanation is simple; rural teachers had 20–25 percent fewer pupils.

Teachers felt increased responsibility for children's learning. Teachers had the same children in their classes over and over and were well aware that things unlearned one year would haunt them the next. They were, consequently, more determined and careful to see that children did learn. Single-grade teachers sometimes have attitudes analogous to "piece workers" in large-scale industry, doing a part of the total job and passing the student "product" along to someone else to complete. Multigrade teachers were more like "craftsmen" in a cottage industry, taking responsibility for every stage in the student's learning. Many rural teachers had the experience of bringing a student from first grade to graduation in the seventh or eighth grade, all under their tutelage.

Teachers' in-depth knowledge of the children facilitated individualized instruction. Many of the elements inherent in the rural school encouraged or even required individualization of instruction. Classes were small, students in each grade level within the class were few, older students were ready to give younger ones personal attention in peer teaching, and (at least in the early days) textbooks were not standardized. Hence, instruction in the rural school was often highly personalized – adjusted to the individual requirements of each student. Much learning went on as each student assumed the initiative during seatwork and home study. At times the system resembled the British "tutorial" approach. As in the tutorial system, recitation periods in the country school were not primarily for learning but for displays of learning already mastered. The most important requirement for any effective system of individualized instruction is the teacher's detailed understanding of the personality of the individual learner and his or her degree of mastery of the subject. As we have seen, rural teachers in small country schools had the opportunity to get to know their students extremely well.

Rural classrooms generally lacked discipline problems. There were always some disciplinary incidents requiring the teacher's attention, but former rural teachers who also had experience in the town schools spoke with one voice on the matter of discipline: Country schools had fewer problems than town schools, and when there were problems, parental support was usually close and sure. Once again, the general rule all across Texas was, "A licking at school means a licking at home." This teacher-parent solidarity served to minimize serious discipline problems, as did the teacher's detailed knowledge of each child and his or her family. There is also considerable evidence that older students helped to keep the younger ones in line, just as they helped with their instruction.

There was an effective use of peer teaching in a familial classroom atmosphere. No doubt, the practice of having older pupils help younger ones was an instructional secret weapon of the country school. Some teachers formalized this with rules and procedures; some just winked at it and allowed it to happen; but former teachers and students alike report that it went on in almost every classroom. Many teachers say explicitly that they absolutely depended on their young peer teachers to get through the day. The younger children got help in their learning, and the older ones got reinforcement for their own knowledge of the subject and the chance to play an active, teacherlike role in the classroom. Peer teaching went on all the time in the country school and needed little or no assistance from the teacher.

There was "instructional spillover" from higher grades to younger, creating an enriched learning environment. A second secret weapon of instruction in the rural classroom was, like peer instruction, a natural consequence of the teaching of several grades in a single classroom. Students engaged in seatwork regularly listened in on other classes. Upperclassmen could listen to lower-level classes in a subject to get a review, and younger students could listen to more advanced classes to leap ahead in subjects that drew their interest. Many teachers encouraged this, and all were aware that it went on in their classrooms. Unlike single-grade classrooms, multigrade classrooms were seldom boring to bright pupils, since they had opportunities to play the teacher role in peer instruction and to advance at their own speed by listening in on upper-level classes.

The rural classroom tended to act as an ungraded system, with each student advancing at his or her own speed. Implicit in several of the characteristics described above is the idea of the classroom as an ungraded system. Students learned at their own speed, and there was a strong tendency for the teacher to group them by level of learning rather than by chronological age. In addition, a student might be at one level in reading and another in math, all without strong praise or blame attached. Failure, or being behind in a subject, did not mean the same thing in such a classroom; one was "held back" only in the sense of remaining in a certain reading or spelling text to begin the next year. This was just another way in which instruction in the rural classroom was adjusted to the individual.

The school and the community were one. This is one of the more intangible advantages of the rural school, but it may have been one of the most important. The country school was, first and foremost, a community institution. As Weldon Hutcheson said, "It comes back again to your community participation in the school. In other words, this is our school. This is *ours.*" From the student's perspective, the rural school was a friendly, homelike environment which belonged to the community and whose policies and procedures were under community control. The feelings of confidence and environmental control that this engendered were a significant factor. As Kirkpatrick Sale summed up some important findings of the Coleman report of 1966 (perhaps the most extensive educational survey ever conducted):

> They concluded that the major determinants of classroom success had very little to do with the actual content of courses or teachers, but rather with "the attitudes of student interest in school, self-concept, and sense of environmental control"–in other words, with the student's sense of being at one with the school. Moreover, the factor "which appears to have a stronger relationship to achievement than do all the school factors together is the extent to which an individual feels that he has some control over his own destiny." It is exactly that control, that sense of oneness, which the small school has always been able to foster, simply by virtue of its size in relationship to the individual student; it is exactly that which has been lost in the urban blackboard jungle.[9]

There is good evidence that children felt comfortable and in control in the country school. Schools were simple frame structures

209

similar to the average rural home and were run by most teachers very much in the manner of the rural family. There was little "shock of institutionalization" when a child first came to attend such a school. When there was a significant difference between the child's "house culture" and the culture of mainstream Texas as practiced in the classroom, the cultural clash was muted in the country school, and the culturally different child could be taught mainstream culture and language in an informal and nonthreatening setting. Finally, there were all the ways that the community and the school intertwined – school programs and entertainments presented for the parents, social events involving teachers and students outside the school, and all the "community center" uses of the school building. In the scheduling of the school year and the school day, as in the methods of discipline the teacher was expected to use, there were many adjustments of school curriculum and instructional practice to the wishes and expectations of the community. Rural schools were responsive to community needs, and the political lines of authority that ran from rural parents to trustees to teachers, were very short. Most rural parents and students felt, "This is our school. This is *ours*," and that made a great deal of difference in many things.

If these are at least some of the "compensating advantages" thought by the researchers of the 1924 school survey to be at work in the rural schools, what, if anything, do they suggest to us as we confront the educational problems of the present? The anticonsolidation findings of Barker and Gump and of Sher and Tompkins are only a small part of the growing body of evidence and speculation questioning the doctrine that "bigger is always better" in many areas of American society. Kirkpatrick Sale's nonfiction best-seller of 1980, *Human Scale,* drew together rapidly accumulating evidence that we have pursued this shibboleth into the realms of dysfunction in several aspects of our political, economic, and social life – matters involving how we deal with problems of energy, food, health care, and waste disposal as well as the education of the young.[10]

We will never go back to the one-room school, but it is possible that the educational planners of the future will reverse the trend toward bigger public schools and return to a more decentralized, community- and neighborhood-based system. We seem to have gone almost as far as we can in enlarging educational units, and the results have not been altogether good. Between 1966 and 1977 the number of people scoring about 600 (out of a possible 800) on the verbal part of the Scholastic Aptitude Test declined by 36 percent, and on the math part, by 11 percent.

If the pendulum ever does begin to swing back, we will have much to learn from the teachers and students of the old country schools, who taught and learned in a decentralized, community-based, highly economical system that conveyed basic skills in reading, writing, and math very well indeed. Already the professionals of rural education are listening. In Colorado the Rocky Mountain Area Project for Small High Schools (RMAP) has "attempted to capitalize on the strengths of smallness to overcome the limited and often weak programs found in such schools. RMAP explored the use of multiple-class teaching and small-group techniques."[11] In an economically depressed rural community in Minnesota, school administrators and parents launched a model elementary school that was "an attempt to preserve some of the traditional features of the one-room schools in its incorporating of nongraded informal, individualized instruction, while at the same time offering the advantages of a larger school in its instructional resources and specialized staff. It would be, Hegre said, 'a school for kids, with true individualization and personalization.' The rural tradition would be further upheld by frequent parent-teacher meetings and the use of community resource persons in teaching."[12] By the middle 1970s the Staples School project was so well known that a half-dozen major grants kept Staples teachers constantly on the go, telling other rural schools how they might adapt the Staples program to their circumstances. Student achievement scores reached impressive levels at Staples Elementary School. In a rural county where only 51 percent of adults over age twenty-five had gone past the eighth grade, Staples students consistently scored at or above the Minnesota norm (which itself was above the national norm) on achievement tests.[13] Clearly, in Staples School some of the common elements of the ungraded rural schools were working very well.

Sher and Tompkins's ground-breaking study of the cost-effectiveness and instructional efficiency of school consolidation ended with several recommendations. First was that there should be additional studies of small schools and decentralized systems of education, past and present. Another recommendation was that "alternatives to consolidation and reorganization should be seriously considered." It may be that the schools of the future may return to something more familiar to the former inhabitants of the Texas common schools. Perhaps, as Sher and Tompkins argue, we can retain the advantages of smallness while transcending most of the disadvantages, linking small local schools into larger instructional units by a variety of telephone, radio, television, microwave, and tape systems. By 1985 there were many indications that this was already happening.[14] As Sher and Tompkins observed, "The underlying premise here is that resources can be brought to children, rather than forcing children to go to the resources. The benefits of smallness *can* be coupled with the benefits of specialization."[15] The small-scale, localized system of ungraded schools may turn out to have been not so much obsolete, as simply out of educational fashion. And in modern Texas, as elsewhere, fashions can change.

Notes

𝕳

Chapter 1. Introduction

1. David Tyack, *The One Best System* (Cambridge, Mass.: Harvard University Press, 1974).

2. Frederick Eby, *The Development of Education in Texas* (New York: Macmillan, 1923), p. 93.

3. Ibid., p. 170.

4. Ibid., p. 173.

5. *House Journal,* January 29, 1883, pp. 87–89.

6. Frederick Eby, "Education in Texas: Source Materials," *University of Texas Bulletin* no. 1824 (April, 1918), p. 794.

7. R. B. Cousins, *Fifteenth Biennial Report of the State Superintendent for Public Instruction* (Austin, Tex.: von Boeckmann-Jones, 1900).

8. F. M. Bralley, *Seventeenth Biennial Report of the State Superintendent for Public Instruction* (Austin, Tex.: von Boeckmann-Jones, 1910).

9. Eby, "Education in Texas," p. 794.

10. Eby, *Development of Education in Texas,* p. 198.

11. Tyack, *One Best System,* p. 5.

12. R. E. Callahan, *Education and the Cult of Efficiency* (Chicago: University of Chicago Press, 1962).

13. E. P. Cubberly, *Rural Life and Education: A Study of the Rural School Problem as a Phase of the Rural-Life Problem* (Boston: Houghton Mifflin, 1914), pp. 105–106.

14. F. M. Bralley, "Consolidation of Rural Schools," *Texas State Department Bulletin* no. 15, (May, 1912), p. 5.

15. S. M. N. Marrs, *Proceedings of the First Annual Conference for Education in Texas* (Austin: Texas Conference for Education, 1907), p. 121.

16. Milam C. Rowold, "The Texas Rural Schools Revisited" (Ph.D. diss., University of Texas at Austin, 1984), pp. 83–92.

17. Eby, *Development of Education in Texas,* p. 227.

18. W. S. Sutton, "Some Wholesome Educational Statistics," *University of Texas Bulletin* no. 28 (March, 1904), pp. 10–11.

19. E. V. White and E. E. Davis, "A Study of Rural Schools in Texas," *University of Texas Bulletin* no. 364 (October, 1914).

20. W. S. Sutton, "Problems in Educational Administration," *University of Texas Bulletin* no. 2345 (December, 1923), pp. 10–11.

21. Pat M. Neff, "People Perish for Lack of Knowledge," in *Speeches Delivered by Pat M. Neff* (Austin, Tex.: von Boeckmann-Jones, 1923), p. 14.

22. *General Laws of the State of Texas,* Thirty-eighth Legislature at the Regular Session, Library of the House of Representatives (Austin, Tex.: A. C. Baldwin and Sons, 1924), pp. 258–60.

23. *Courses of Study and Instruction,* vol. 5 of *Texas Educational Survey Report* (Austin, Tex.: Education Survey Commission, 1924), pp. 342–43.

24. *Organization and Administration,* vol. 1 of *Texas Educational Survey Report* (Austin, Tex.: Education Survey Commission, 1924), p. 222.

25. *Courses of Study and Instruction,* vol. 5, *Texas Educational Survey Report,* p. 354.

26. *Courses of Study and Instruction,* vol. 4 of *Texas Educational Survey Report* (Austin, Tex.: Education Survey Commission, 1924), p. 15.

27. Callahan, *Education and the Cult of Efficiency.*

28. *Courses of Study and Instruction,* vol. 4 of *Texas Educational Survey Report,* p. 119.

29. Ibid., pp. 119–20.

30. Ibid., p. 120.

31. Ibid., p. 135.

32. Ibid., p. 127.

33. S. M. N. Marrs, *Twenty-third Biennial Report of the State Superintendent for Public Instruction* (Austin, Tex.: von Boeckmann-Jones, 1924).

34. *Courses of Study and Instruction,* vol. 4, *Texas Educational Survey Report,* p. 121.

35. L. D. Haskew, taped interview with Milam C. Rowold, December 14, 1982, Austin, Tex.

36. *A Report of the Adequacy of Texas Schools,* Works Progress Administration, State Board of Education, Project No. 65-66-7752. October, 1937.

37. J. W. Edgar, taped interview with Milam C. Rowold, December 14, 1982, Austin, Tex.

38. "Texas Population by Counties," *Texas Almanac and State Industrial Guide* (Dallas, Tex.: A. H. Belo, 1970–71), pp. 167–70.

39. Ibid.

40. Edgar interview.

41. Ibid.

42. *Courses of Study and Instruction,* vol. 4, *Texas Educational Survey Report,* p. 21.

43. Jonathan P. Sher and Rachel B. Tompkins, "The Myths of Rural School Consolidation, Part I," *Educational Forum* 40, no. 1 (November, 1976): 96–107.

44. C. L. Sonnichsen, *The Grave of John Wesley Hardin: Three Essays on Grassroots History* (College Station, Tex.: Texas A&M University Press, 1979), p. 26.

Chapter 2. Riding Shank's Mare

1. Byrdie Leigh Bounds Sistrunk, interview with Tina Davis, 1984, Panola Junior College Oral History Project, Carthage, Tex. (hereafter cited as PJCOHP).

2. Frankie Franks, taped interview with Thad Sitton, July 16, 1979, Texas Common Schools Collection, Barker Texas History Center, University of Texas at Austin (hereafter cited as TCSC).

3. Mrs. Wanda DuBose, taped interview with Thad Sitton, June 28, 1980, TCSC.

4. M. M. Kennedy, "From Old Time Schools in Texas," in Mrs. A. J. H. Pennybacker, *A History of Texas for Schools* (Austin, Tex.: privately printed, 1908), p. 220.

5. Texas Retired Teachers Association, *As We Remember.*

6. Josephine Ballard, letter to O. L. Davis, Jr., December 8, 1980.

7. Temple-Belton Retired Teachers Association, *History of Bell County Public Schools,* p. 196.

8. William Owens, *This Stubborn Soil,* p. 11.

9. Bill O'Neal, "The Country School in East Texas: One Room + 3 R's" (Paper delivered at 1985 meeting of East Texas Historical Association, Nacogdoches, Tex.).

10. Bessie Sanders, interview with Tangela Howard, 1984, PJCOHP.

11. Katy Rayson, interview with Carolyn Moore, 1984, PJCOHP.

12. Nell Buchanan, interview with Greg Weesner, 1984, PJCOHP.

13. O'Neal, "Country School in East Texas," p. 15.

14. Ochiltree County Historical Survey Committee, *Wheatheart of the Plains: Early History of Ochiltree County,* p. 488.

15. Mattie Gray, interview with Debra Greenleaf, September 11, 1985, PJCOHP.

16. Rosie Lee Moody, interview with Kellie Lavern Mattox, 1984, PJCOHP.

17. Sistrunk interview.

18. *History of Bell County Public Schools,* p. 191.

19. Ibid., p. 218.

20. Ibid., p. 265.

21. Ibid., p. 174.

22. Interview with grandmother, by B. Byassee, March 14, 1984, PJCOHP.

23. Emma Ohlendorf, taped interview with Thad Sitton, July 2, 1979, TCSC.

24. Eleanor M. Traweek, *Of Such as These: A History of Motley County*, p. 81.

25. Deaf Smith County Historical Society, *The Land and Its People, 1876–1981: Deaf Smith County, Texas*, p. 75.

26. Traweek, *Of Such as These*, p. 81.

27. *Wheatheart of the Plains*, p. 208.

28. Donald Windell Shires, taped interview with Laneta Fay Shires Holland, 1984, PJCOHP.

29. *History of Bell County Public Schools*, p. 201.

30. Ibid., p. 332; interview with aunt, by Gay Nell Goodson, April 3, 1984, PJCOHP.

31. Bertha M. Stephens, letter to O. L. Davis, Jr., October 24, 1980, TCSC.

32. *As We Remember*, p. 112.

33. King County Historical Society, *King County: Windmills and Barbed Wire*, p. 117.

34. Essie Adele Haynes, taped memoir, 1984, TCSC.

35. Fred I. Soape, interview with Bryan Stacy, 1984, PJCOHP.

36. *Wheatheart of the Plains*, p. 444.

37. Elva Oliver, interview with Tony Baldwin, 1984, PJCOHP.

38. Swisher County Historical Commission, *Windmilling: 101 Years of Swisher County, Texas, 1876–1977*, p. 122.

39. Ibid.

40. *King County*, p. 103.

41. *Windmilling*, p. 235.

42. *The Land and Its People*, p. 75.

43. *Windmilling*, p. 122.

44. Fred Arrington, ed., *A History of Dickens County*, p. 175.

45. Stephens letter.

46. Menard County Historical Society, *Menard County History: An Anthology*, p. 80.

47. *As We Remember*, p. 156.

48. Annie McElroy, in *Those Comforting Hills* (Comfort Middle School: Comfort, Tex., 1977), p. 12.

Chapter 3. Shiloh to Shake Rag

1. *Menard County History*, p. 79.

2. *Wheatheart of the Plains*, p. 43.

3. Rosalie Gregg, ed., *History of Wise County*, vol. 1, p. 73.

4. *Wheatheart of the Plains,* p. 43.

5. Hansford County Historical Commission, *Hansford County Texas,* p. 45.

6. Ibid.

7. Parker County Historical Commission, *History of Parker County,* p. 57.

8. Ibid., p. 18.

9. *As We Remember,* p. 59.

10. *History of Bell County Public Schools,* p. 253.

11. *King County,* p. 107.

12. *Windmilling,* p. 67.

13. Houston County Historical Commission, *History of Houston County, Texas,* p. 115.

14. *King County,* p. 106.

15. *History of Bell County Public Schools,* p. 185.

16. *Wheatheart of the Plains,* p. 496.

17. *History of Houston County,* p. 97.

18. *History of Parker County,* p. 157.

19. *King County,* p. 105.

20. *History of Parker County,* p. 56.

21. *History of Wise County,* p. 70.

22. *History of Bell County Public Schools,* p. 211.

23. Ibid., p. 188.

24. Ibid., p. 248.

25. Bryant Jernigan, interview with Cindy Moon, September 8, 1984, PJCOHP.

26. *Land and Its People,* p. 77.

27. J. Stewart Randel, ed., *A Time to Purpose: A Chronicle of Carson County and Area,* vol. 3, p. 232.

28. Ibid., pp. 233-34.

29. Ibid., p. 236.

Chapter 4. *Little Buildings in the Tall Grass*

1. *As We Remember,* p. 103.

2. Haynes memoir.

3. William A. Owens, *A Season of Weathering,* p. 183.

4. Lula Byars, taped interview with Thad Sitton, June 27, 1979, TCSC.

5. D. C. McSwain, interview with Thomas Henry, February 4, 1985, PJCOHP.

6. Sistrunk interview with Tina Davis, 1984, PJCOHP.

7. Ballard, letter.

8. *As We Remember,* p. 118.

9. Mildred Abshier, "Country Schools" (Manuscript, 1983), TCSC.

10. *Report of the Adequacy of Texas Schools.* The social historian of Texas schools is fortunate to have this statistical cross-section of the whole of Texas education for the school year 1934–35. This 1,813-page, five-pound document was sponsored by the new Texas State Board of Education (founded in 1929) and funded by the Works Progress Administration. Hundreds of professionals in the field of education, most of them out of work during the Great Depression, visited every county seat and local school district to compile statistics for most of the state's common and independent school districts. The data gathered included school names, numbers of teachers, scholastics enrolled and average daily attendance, and valuation of school property, even the structural material of each school building – its heating, toilet, and water facilities and the presence or absence of such instructional accoutrements as globes, maps, libraries, pianos, and electric clocks. A county map showing all common and independent districts accompanies most sections.

11. Ibid., pp. 19–23.

12. Mrs. Wright, interview with Sonya Hicks, 1984, PJCOHP.

13. Rev. Charles White and Ada M. Holland, *No Quittin Sense,* p. 28.

14. *Report of the Adequacy of Texas Schools,* pp. 1742–45.

15. Ibid., p. 78.

16. Owens, *Season of Weathering,* p. 204.

17. *Windmilling,* p. 174.

18. *Report of the Adequacy of Texas Schools,* p. 87.

19. Ohlendorf interview.

20. *Report of the Adequacy of Texas Schools,* p. 89.

21. Ibid., p. 88.

22. Ibid., p. 90.

23. O. T. Baker, taped interview with Thad Sitton, August 26, 1985, TCSC.

24. Allen Langford, interview with Joe Armstrong, 1984, PJCOHP.

25. *Wheatheart of the Plains,* p. 42.

26. *History of Bell County Public Schools,* p. 168.

27. Ballard letter.

28. Ohlendorf interview.

29. Onita King, taped interview with Thad Sitton, June 25, 1979, TCSC.

30. Abshier, "Country Schools."

31. *History of Bell County Public Schools,* p. 360.

32. Ibid., p. 398.

33. DuBose interview.

34. Abshier, "Country Schools."

35. *Report of the Adequacy of Texas Schools,* p. 89.

36. *As We Remember,* p. 44.

37. Hartal Langford Blackwell, *Mills County: The Way It Was,* p. 232.

38. *History of Bell County Public Schools,* p. 355.

39. *As We Remember,* p. 79.
40. *History of Parker County,* p. 26.
41. *As We Remember,* p. 118.
42. *Mills County,* p. 232.
43. *History of Bell County Public Schools,* p. 269; interview with grandmother, by David Griffin, 1984, PJCOHP.
44. *Windmilling,* p. 351.
45. *History of Bell County Public Schools,* p. 337.
46. Mrs. Roy Powell, taped interview with Milam C. Rowold, January 29, 1982, TCSC.
47. *Report of the Adequacy of Texas Schools,* p. 91.
48. *History of Parker County,* p. 26.
49. *Mills County,* p. 130.
50. Ballard letter.
51. Jernigan interview.
52. O'Neal, "The Country School in East Texas."
53. Baker interview.
54. Sistrunk interview.
55. *As We Remember,* p. 79.
56. *King County,* p. 233.
57. *As We Remember,* pp. 1–2.

Chapter 5. Reading, Spelling, Ciphering

1. *Season of Weathering,* p. 178.
2. Bessie Brown, interview with Delbert Walker, January 31, 1984, PJCOHP.
3. Abshier, "Country Schools."
4. *History of Bell County Public Schools,* p. 167.
5. Randel, ed., *A Time to Purpose,* p. 237.
6. Mrs. W. R. Barron, taped interview with Milam C. Rowold, January 4, 1982, TCSC.
7. Velma Adams, taped interview with Milam C. Rowold, January 28, 1982, TCSC.
8. Ibid.
9. Emma Shirley, "Riding Herd in a Country Schoolhouse," *Dallas Morning News,* October 21, 1928.
10. Myra Blount, taped interview with Milam C. Rowold, December 28, 1981, TCSC.
11. Abshier, "Country Schools."
12. Clementine Johnson, taped interview with Milam C. Rowold, February 4, 1982, TCSC.
13. Randel, ed., *A Time to Purpose,* p. 236.
14. DuBose interview.
15. Franks interview.

16. Weldon Hutcheson, taped interview with Gordon H. Grubbs, July 3, 1979, TCSC.

17. Franks interview.

18. Stephens letter.

19. *As We Remember,* p. 153.

20. *King County,* p. 102.

21. Pauline Walker Underwood, taped memoir, August 30, 1984, TCSC.

22. R. E. Harris, taped interview with Thad Sitton, June 12, 1979.

23. Susie Bell Anderson, taped interview with Thad Sitton, July 19, 1979, TCSC.

24. Marie Burton, taped interview with Thad Sitton, July 10, 1979, TCSC.

25. Mrs. Joe B. Coopwood, taped interview with Mary E. Keeble, July 26, 1979, TCSC.

26. James Conrad, letter to Thad Sitton, July 18, 1985, TCSC.

27. Owens, *Season of Weathering,* p. 186.

28. Franks interview.

29. Lonie Brite, taped interview with Thad Sitton, July 18, 1979, TCSC.

30. *Report of the Adequacy of Texas Schools.*

31. Franks interview.

32. King interview.

33. Franks interview.

34. Anonymous, interview with David Sweet, November 1, 1984, PJCOHP.

35. Interview with Byassee grandmother.

36. *As We Remember,* p. 153.

37. Rowold, "Texas Rural Schools Revisited," p. 119.

38. Alma McBride, taped interview with Milam C. Rowold, January 7, 1982, TCSC.

39. Doris Green, taped interview with Milam C. Rowold, January 14, 1982, TCSC.

40. Clementine Johnson interview.

41. Emma Shirley, taped interview with Milam C. Rowold, February 11, 1982, TCSC.

42. Anderson interview.

43. Brite interview.

44. Franks interview.

45. *Menard County History,* p. 80.

46. Stella Murphree, taped interview with Thad Sitton, June 21, 1979, TCSC.

47. Ohlendorf interview.

48. Franks interview.

49. Marguerite Page, interview with Michelle Page, 1984, PJCOHP.

50. *History of Bell County Public Schools,* p. 180.

51. James C. Dailey, interview with Becky Parker, 1984, PJCOHP.

52. Annie Jay Cane, interview with Delbert Walker, April 2, 1984, PJCOHP.

53. Bessie Sanders, interview with Tangela Howard, 1984, PJCOHP.

54. Elsie Hamill, taped interview with Milam C. Rowold, January 29, 1982, TCSC.

55. Ballard, letter.

56. Clementine Johnson interview.

57. Walter Neuenberg, in *Those Comforting Hills.*

58. Anderson interview.

59. Hutcheson interview.

60. White and Holland, *No Quittin Sense,* p. 34.

61. Owens, *This Stubborn Soil,* p. 110.

62. Ibid., p. 142.

63. *Compulsory School Attendance,* Department of Education Bulletin, no. 53 (July 1916), p. 5.

64. *Organization and Administration,* vol. 1 of *Texas Educational Survey Report,* (Austin, Tex.: Education Survey Commission, 1924), p. 222.

65. *As We Remember,* p. 102.

66. *Menard County History,* p. 80.

67. White and Holland, *No Quittin Sense,* p. 25.

68. Rayson interview.

69. Ardessa Cloudy, interview with Imogene Cloudy, April 2, 1984, PJCOHP.

70. *History of the Bell County Public Schools,* p. 363.

71. Hinkle Schillengs, interview with Jim Fenton, 1984, PJCOHP.

72. White and Holland, *No Quittin Sense,* pp. 46–48.

73. Baylor County Historical Society, *Salt Pork to Sirloin: The History of Baylor County Texas from 1879 to 1930,* p. 189.

Chapter 6. Syrup Buckets and Flying Jennies

1. *History of Parker County,* p. 26.

2. Schillengs interview.

3. Stephens letter.

4. O'Neal, "Country School in East Texas."

5. Katie Adams, interview with Cheyenne Adams, February 18, 1985, PJCOHP.

6. Emma Grant, interview with Kathy Cockrell, November 31, 1984, PJCOHP.

7. Interview with Byassee grandmother.

8. Merrill D. Doyle, *Reminiscences of My Youth and Other Catastrophes,* p. 20.

9. Prince Etta Thompson, interview with Delbert Walker, May 1, 1984, PJCOHP.

10. Underwood, memoir.

11. Randel, ed., *A Time to Purpose*, p. 236.

12. Lucille Sonmor, interview with Janet Belrose, February 4, 1985, PJCOHP.

13. *The Land and Its People*, p. 71.

14. *History of the Bell County Public Schools*, p. 238.

15. Anonymous, interview with Charles Barr, February 3, 1984, PJCOHP.

16. *History of the Bell County Public Schools*, p. 288.

17. *As We Remember,* p. 156.

18. Diane Sistrunk Cole, interview with Tina Davis, 1984, PJCOHP.

19. Hamill, interview.

20. Owens, *This Stubborn Soil,* pp. 204–205.

21. O'Neal, "Country School in East Texas."

22. Baker, interview.

23. *History of the Bell County Public Schools*, p. 242.

24. Lucille Sonmor, interview with Janet Belrose, February 4, 1985, PJCOHP.

25. Gilbert J. Jordan, *Yesterday in the Texas Hill Country,* p. 112.

26. *A Time to Purpose*, p. 186.

27. *Menard County History,* p. 79.

28. Clovis Baker, in handwritten manuscript to Bill O'Neal, February 9, 1984, PJCOHP.

29. *History of the Bell County Public Schools*, p. 269.

30. Thelma Reid, interview with Kim Still, January 4, 1984, PJCOHP.

31. *History of the Bell County Public Schools*, p. 178; anonymous, interview with Gay Nell Goodson, April 3, 1984, PJCOHP.

32. Anonymous, interview with Michelle Welch, April 2, 1984, PJCOHP.

33. Baker interview.

34. Jordan, *Yesterday in the Texas Hill Country,* p. 112.

35. Ballard letter.

36. Lily Waskom, interview with Daren Jeans, February 4, 1985, PJCOHP.

37. W. Silas Vance, "Life and Leisure at Lucky Ridge," in F. E. Abernethy, ed., *The Folklore of Texas Cultures*, pp. 94–95.

38. *Windmilling*, p. 245.

39. *History of Bell County Public Schools*, p. 198.

40. Baker interview.

41. *As We Remember,* p. 13.

Chapter 7. Heaven's First Law

1. *History of Bell County Public Schools*, p. 343.

2. Lonie Brite interview.

3. Byars interview.

4. Franks interview.

5. Hutcheson interview.

6. Mrs. Ochee Holt, taped interview with Milam C. Rowold, January 28, 1982, TCSC.

7. Shirley, "Riding Herd."

8. Shirley interview.

9. Ibid.

10. Shirley, "Riding Herd."

11. Randel, ed., *A Time to Purpose,* p. 185.

12. *History of Bell County Public Schools,* p. 313.

13. *History of Parker County,* p. 46.

14. *As We Remember,* p. 96.

15. Deborah Brown and Katharine Gust, *Between the Creeks: Recollections of Northeast Texas,* p. 23.

16. *History of Bell County Public Schools,* p. 311.

17. *King County,* p. 115.

18. Herman Allen, taped interview with Vernon C. Lochausen, August 6, 1979, TCSC.

19. *History of Bell County Public Schools,* p. 269.

20. Owens, *Season of Weathering,* p. 256.

21. *As We Remember,* p. 40.

22. DuBose interview.

23. Mrs. Elmarie Miles Harris, interview with Delbert Walker, February 14, 1984, PJCOHP.

24. Velma Adams interview.

25. Mrs. Robert Page, taped interview with Milam C. Rowold, November 13, 1982, TCSC.

26. Charles Gregg, taped interview with Milam C. Rowold, November 6, 1982, TCSC.

27. Hamill interview.

28. Blount interview.

29. *As We Remember,* p. 98.

30. Blount interview.

31. Arba Sewell, taped interview with Thad Sitton, September 20, 1980, TCSC.

32. Anderson interview.

33. Hutcheson interview.

34. Anderson interview.

35. King interview.

36. Lee L. Johnson, taped interview with Milam C. Rowold, February 11, 1982, TCSC.

37. Mrs. F. B. McDonald, taped interview with Milam C. Rowold, February 4, 1982, TCSC.

38. Sewell interview.

39. DuBose interview.

40. Anonymous, interview with Alan Scarborough, February 7, 1985, PJCOHP.

41. O'Neal, "Country School in East Texas."

42. Hinkle Schillengs, interview with Jim Fenton, 1984, PJCOHP.

43. *Wheatheart of the Plains*, p. 340.

44. Anderson interview.

45. J. T. Holt, interview, 1984, PJCOHP.

46. Ronnie Tyler and Laurence R. Murphy, eds., *The Slave Narratives of Texas* (Austin, Tex.: Encino Press, 1974), p. 23.

47. *A Time to Purpose*, p. 186.

48. *Salt Pork to Sirloin*, p. 82.

49. Ibid., p. 83.

50. *History of Bell County Public Schools*, p. 171.

51. Ibid., p. 218.

52. *Windmilling*, p. 122.

53. *History of Bell County Public Schools*, p. 305.

54. *Salt Pork to Sirloin*, p. 85.

55. Blackwell, *Mills County*, p. 130.

56. White and Holland, *No Quittin Sense*, p. 34.

57. *History of Bell County Public Schools*, p. 296.

58. Burton interview.

59. Jernigan interview.

60. Baker interview.

61. King interview.

Chapter 8. Spelling Bees and School Closings

1. Byars interview.

2. Mrs. H. M. Gunn, taped interview with Thad Sitton, August 2, 1980, TCSC.

3. Hutcheson interview.

4. Blackwell, *Mills County*, p. 227.

5. *History of Parker County*, p. 43.

6. *Hansford County Texas*, p. 22.

7. *History of Wise County*, p. 74.

8. Byars interview.

9. DuBose interview.

10. Byars interview.

11. Carmen Taylor Bennett, ed., *Our Roots Grow Deep: A History of Cottle County*, p. 147.

12. *Season of Weathering*, p. 215.

13. *As We Remember*, p. 22.

14. *History of Parker County*, pp. 46–48.

15. *History of Bell County Public Schools*, p. 214.

16. Ballard letter.

17. *History of Parker County,* p. 57.
18. *History of Bell County Public Schools,* p. 168.
19. Franks interview.
20. *History of Bell County Public Schools,* p. 283.
21. Interview with Byassee grandmother.
22. Anderson interview.
23. Ibid.
24. Franks interview.
25. Ibid.
26. Byars interview.
27. Brite interview.
28. Rev. S. L. Davis, taped interview with Caldwell County Oral History Project, (Lockhart Public Library, 1976).
29. Franks interview.
30. *History of Wise County,* p. 77.
31. Ballard letter.
32. Mrs. Roy Powell, taped interview with Milam C. Rowold, January 29, 1982, TCSC.
33. DuBose interview.
34. Byars interview.
35. Randel, ed., *A Time to Purpose,* p. 239.
36. Anonymous, interview with Michelle Welch.
37. Jordan, *Yesterday in the Texas Hill Country,* pp. 114–15.

Chapter 9. Professors and Schoolmarms

1. Haynes memoir.
2. Holt interview.
3. Green interview.
4. Mrs. Robert Page interview.
5. Velma Adams interview.
6. Gregg interview.
7. Rowold, "Texas Rural Schools Revisited," pp. 33–34.
8. Ballard letter.
9. Josephine Ballard, letter to O. L. Davis, Jr., January 13, 1981, TCSC.
10. *As We Remember,* p. 146.
11. Ibid., p. 153.
12. Ella Bozarth, taped interview with Thad Sitton, August 16, 1979, TCSC.
13. Rowold, "Texas Rural Schools Revisited," p. 38.
14. G. C. Gregory, "Stilwell Diary" (undated manuscript in Texas Common Schools Collection, Barker Texas History Center, University of Texas at Austin).
15. Hamill interview.

16. Haynes memoir.

17. Gregory, "Stilwell Diary."

18. *As We Remember,* p. 113.

19. Blackwell, *Mills County,* p. 231.

20. Lillian Denton Milam, taped memoir, February 7, 1985, TCSC.

21. *Mills County,* p. 230.

22. "Memories of Teaching in Texas Rural Schools," unpublished manuscript by Beta Sigma chapter of Delta Kappa Gamma, 1985, TCSC.

23. Owens, *Season of Weathering,* p. 114.

24. Ibid., pp. 114–15.

25. Lee L. Johnson interview.

26. *As We Remember,* p. 32.

27. Ibid., p. 50.

28. Genia Bonner Johns, taped memoir, August 1, 1984, TCSC.

29. *As We Remember,* p. 155.

30. Ibid., p. 155.

31. Emma Shirley, "My First Day as a Teacher," *Waco Citizen,* March 15, 19, 23, 1982.

32. Rowold, "Texas Rural Schools Revisited," p. 90.

33. Clementine Johnson interview.

34. *History of Parker County,* p. 58.

35. Shirley, "Riding Herd."

36. DuBose interview.

37. *History of Bell County Public Schools,* p. 283.

38. *As We Remember,* p. 93.

39. Ibid., p. 81.

40. Ibid., p. 22.

41. *History of Bell County Public Schools,* p. 264.

42. *As We Remember,* p. 41.

43. Franks interview.

44. *As We Remember,* p. 41.

45. *History of Bell County Public Schools,* p. 288.

46. Mrs. Cecil Long, letter to O. L. Davis, Jr., November 25, 1980, TCSC.

47. *History of Bell County Public Schools,* p. 202.

48. *As We Remember,* p. 32.

49. Byars interview.

50. Rowold, "Texas Rural Schools Revisited," p. 198.

51. "Memories of Teaching in Texas Rural Schools" p. 23.

52. Ibid., p. 24.

53. Ibid., p. 47.

54. Underwood memoir.

55. R. B. Cousins, "Five Years of Progress of the Common Schools of Texas," *Department of Education Bulletin* (Austin, Tex., 1909), pp. 9–10.

56. Rowold, "Texas Rural Schools Revisited," p. 77.

57. Mrs. O. R. Smith, taped interview with Milam C. Rowold, January 15, 1982, TCSC.

58. Adams interview.

59. Byars interview.

60. Gregory, "Stilwell Diary."

61. Stella Murphree, taped interview with Thad Sitton, June 21, 1979, TCSC.

62. Underwood memoir.

63. Clementine Johnson interview.

64. Rowold, "Texas Rural Schools Revisited," p. 191.

65. McDonald interview.

66. Mrs. O. R. Smith, taped interview with Milam C. Rowold, January 15, 1982, TCSC.

67. Holt interview.

68. Rowold, "Texas Rural Schools Revisited," pp. 80–81.

69. Ibid., p. 198.

70. Holt interview.

71. Hamill interview.

72. Owens, *Season of Weathering,* p. 196.

73. Ibid., pp. 198–99.

74. *Report of the Adequacy of Texas Schools,* p. 28.

75. *The Land and Its People,* p. 71.

76. *History of Parker County,* p. 18.

77. *Report of the Adequacy of Texas Schools,* p. 30.

78. Gregory, "Stilwell Diary."

79. Bozarth interview.

80. Rowold, "Texas Rural Schools Revisited," p. 153.

81. Florence Jones, taped interview with Milam C. Rowold, February 11, 1982, TCSC.

82. Barron interview.

83. Velma Adams interview.

84. Hamill interview.

85. *King County,* p. 116.

86. Velma Adams interview.

87. Jones interview.

88. Mrs. Robert Page interview.

89. Holt interview.

90. Gunn interview.

Chapter 10. A Pretty Nasty Fight

1. *History of Bell County Public Schools,* p. 187.

2. *Menard County History,* p. 79.

3. *Wheatheart of the Plains,* p. 43.

4. *History of Bell County Public Schools,* p. 374.

5. *The Land and Its People,* p. 79.

6. *Hansford County Texas,* p. 24.

7. *Wheatheart of the Plains,* p. 340.

8. *History of Wise County,* p. 75.

9. Sallie B. Harris, ed., *Hide Town in the Texas Panhandle,* p. 209.

10. *Wheatheart of the Plains,* p. 440.

11. Hutcheson interview.

12. Anderson interview.

13. *History of Bell County Public Schools,* p. 356.

14. Ibid., p. 205.

15. *Windmilling,* p. 334.

16. *History of Parker County,* p. 42.

17. Blackwell, *Mills County,* p. 203. (The story of Center Point School was written by Ms. Fallon.)

18. Haskew interview.

19. Stephens letter.

20. Ibid.

21. I. W. Popham, taped interview with Thad Sitton, June 30, 1980, TCSC.

22. Ibid.

23. Clementine Johnson, taped interview with Milam C. Rowold, February 4, 1982, TCSC.

24. Popham interview.

25. Hutcheson interview.

26. Rowold, "Texas Schools Revisited," p. 226.

27. Harris interview.

28. Popham interview.

29. Brite interview.

30. Hutcheson interview.

31. Anderson interview.

32. Byars interview.

33. *History of Parker County,* p. 64.

34. Franks interview.

Chapter 11. Epilogue

1. Gerald J. Lluempke, "The Emerging Role of the Regional Service Center in Rural Areas," *Proceedings of the Second National Conference of NFIRE* (Las Cruces, N.Mex.: ERIC/CRESS, 1974), p. 9.

2. Roger G. Barker and Paul V. Gump, *Big School, Small School* (Stanford, Calif.: Stanford University Press, 1964).

3. Jonathan P. Sher and Rachel B. Tompkins, "The Myths of Rural School and District Consolidation, Part II," *Educational Forum* 40, no. 2 (January, 1977): 141.

4. A. Summers and B. Wolfe, "Which School Resources Help Learning?" *Business Review* 16 (February, 1975): 131–38.

5. Sher and Tompkins, "The Myths of Rural School and District Consolidation, Part I," p. 105.

6. Sher and Tompkins, "Myths of Rural School and District Consolidation, Part II," p. 149.

7. *Courses of Study and Instruction*, vol. 4 of *Texas Educational Survey Report*, p. 121.

8. *Report of the Adequacy of Texas Schools.*

9. Kirkpatrick Sale, *Human Scale* (New York: Coward, McCann, and Geoghegan, 1980), p. 283.

10. Ibid.

11. Paul Nachtigal, "Rural School Improvement Efforts: An Interpretive History," in *Rural Education: In Search of a Better Way*, ed. Paul Nachtigal, (Boulder, Colo.: Westview Press, 1982), p. 17.

12. Thomas Gjelten, "Staples, Minnesota: Improving the Schools to Save the Town," in *Rural Education*, ed. Nachtigal, p. 255.

13. Ibid., p. 259.

14. Cynthia Y. Levinson, "Tuning in Long Distance Classes," *New York Times Educational Supplement*, August 18, 1985.

15. Sher and Tompkins, "Myths of Rural School and District Consolidation, Part II," p. 150.

Selected Bibliography

✯

OUR STORY of the Texas country schools was heavily dependent upon the oral history tapes, personal memoirs, and letters accumulated over the years by the Texas Common Schools Project of the School of Education, University of Texas at Austin. These primary sources may be found in the Texas Common Schools Collection of Barker Texas History Center, University of Texas at Austin (designated in the endnotes as TCSC). The interview notes collected in 1984–85 by the students of Bill O'Neal at Panola County Junior College may be found in his care in Carthage, Texas, and are designated in the endnotes as PJCOHP. This book is based in part upon the unpublished doctoral dissertation of Milam C. Rowold, "Texas Rural Schools Revisited," University of Texas at Austin, 1984. Published sources contributing primary accounts from former teachers and students in the common schools are listed below.

Arrington, Fred, ed. *A History of Dickens County.* Wichita Falls, Tex.: Nortex Publications, 1971.

Baylor County Historical Society. *Salt Pork to Sirloin: The History of Baylor County, Texas From 1879 to 1930.* Wichita Falls, Tex.: Nortex Publications, 1972.

Bennett, Carmen Taylor, ed. *Our Roots Grow Deep: A History of Cottle County.* Floydada, Tex.: Blanco, 1970.

Blackwell, Hartal Langford. *Mills County: The Way It Was.* Goldthwaite, Tex.: Eagle Press, 1976.

Bowman, Bob, ed. *Land of the Little Angel: A History of Angelina County, Texas.* Lufkin, Tex.: Angelina County Historical Survey Committee, 1976.

Brown, Deborah, and Katharine Gust. *Between the Creeks: Recollections of Northeast Texas*. Austin, Tex.: Encino Press, 1976.

Deaf Smith County Historical Society. *The Land and Its People, 1876–1981, Deaf Smith County, Texas*. Dallas, Tex.: Taylor Publishing, 1981.

Doyle, Merrill D. *Reminiscences of My Youth and Other Catastrophes*. Kerrville, Tex.: Merrill D. Doyle, 1975.

Gregg, Rosalie, ed. *History of Wise County*. Vol. 1. Wise County Historical Survey Committee, 1975.

Hansford County Historical Commission. *Hansford County Texas*. Dallas, Tex.: Taylor Publishing, n.d.

Harris, Sallie B., ed. *Hide Town in the Texas Panhandle*. Hereford, Tex.: Pioneer Book Publishers, 1968.

Houston County Historical Commission. *History of Houston County, Texas*. Tulsa, Okla.: Heritage Publishing, 1979.

Jordan, Gilbert J. *Yesterday in the Texas Hill Country*. College Station, Tex.: Texas A&M University Press, 1979.

King County Historical Society. *King County: Windmills and Barbed Wire*. Quanah, Tex.: Nortex Press, 1976.

Killeen, Mrs. James C. *History of Lee County Texas*. Quanah, Tex.: Nortex Press, 1974.

McDaniel, Marylou, ed. *God Grass and Grit: History of the Sherman County Trade Area*. Hereford, Tex.: Pioneer Book Publishers, 1971.

Menard County Historical Society. *Menard County History: An Anthology*. San Angelo, Tex.: Anchor Publishing, 1982.

Morris, Ruth D. "Memories of Old Chita School." *East Texas Historical Journal* 16, no. 2 (1978): 46–51.

Oatman, William, ed. *Llano: Gem of the Hill Country*. Hereford, Tex.: Pioneer Book Publishers, 1970.

Ochiltree County Historical Survey Committee. *Wheatheart of the Plains: Early History of Ochiltree County*. Perryton, Tex.: Ochiltree County Historical Survey Committee, 1979.

Owens, William A. *A Season of Weathering*. New York: Scribner's, 1973.
———. *This Stubborn Soil*. New York: Scribner's, 1966.

Parker County Historical Commission. *History of Parker County*. Dallas, Tex.: Taylor Publishing, 1980.

Pruett, Jakie L., and Everett B. Cole, eds. *The History and Heritage of Goliad County*. Austin, Tex.: Eakin, 1983.

Randel, J. Stewart, ed. *A Time to Purpose: A Chronicle of Carson County and Area*. Vol. 3. Hereford, Tex.: Pioneer Book Publishers, 1972.

Spiller, Wayne, ed. *Handbook of McCulloch County History*. Vol. 1. Seagraves, Tex.: Pioneer Book Publishers, 1976.

Swisher County Historical Commission. *Windmilling: 101 Years of Swisher County Texas, 1876–1977*. Dallas, Tex.: Taylor Publishing, 1978.

Temple-Belton Retired Teachers Association. *History of Bell County Public Schools*. Temple, Tex.: 1976.

Texas Retired Teachers Association. *As We Remember.* 1976.

Traweek, Eleanor M. *Of Such as These: A History of Motley County.* Wichita Falls, Tex.: Nortex Publications, 1973.

Vance, W. Silas. "Life and Leisure at Lucky Ridge." Pp. 91–110 in F. E. Abernethy, ed., *The Folklore of Texas Cultures.* Austin, Tex.: Encino Press, 1974.

White, Rev. Charles, and Ada M. Holland. *No Quittin Sense.* Austin, Tex.: University of Texas Press, 1969.

Index

𝕬

Italicized page numbers indicate that the subject appears in a photograph.

Ringing the Children In was composed into type on a Compu-graphic digital phototypesetter in ten point Century Schoolbook with two points of spacing between the lines. Century Schoolbook Italic was selected for display. The book was designed by Larry Hirst, typeset by Metricomp, Inc., printed offset by Thomson-Shore, Inc., and bound by John H. Dekker & Sons. The paper on which the book is printed carries acid-free characteristics for an effective life of at least three hundred years.

Texas A&M University Press : College Station